BEYOND THE END TIMES

The Rest of... The Greatest Story Ever Told

by
John Noē

Author of The Apocalypse Conspiracy

"A compelling introduction to past fulfillment of Bible prophecy"

Edward E. Stevens, President
International Preterist Association

Preterist Resources
122 Seaward Avenue
Bradford, PA 16701-1515 USA

Library of Congress Cataloging-in-Publication Data

(In application)
Noē, John, 1945—
    Beyond The End Times: The Rest of the Greatest
Story Ever Told.
1st ed.

ISBN: 0-9621311-4-8

Dedication

To my preterist colleagues, past and present,
on whose shoulders I am standing.
Thank you for helping me see these truths in God's Word.

To my editor, Pat Forseth,
for her invaluable contributions.
Thank you for being frank and making less more.

To those over the years
who have listened to my teachings, and questioned
and challenged me.
Thank you for your encouragement to publish this book
and other materials.

Contents

Foreword

Tradition is hard to change simply because change of any kind is hard to accept. If we've been mistaken, we hate to admit it. When we don't want to change, any excuse is a good excuse. It is like the story of "The Emperor's New Clothes." People saw what they wanted to see. But then came the disturber-of-the-peace who suggested that the emperor was not wearing any clothes. It was "kill the messenger" time! That was easier than changing their views.

Some will call John Noē a disturber-of-the-peace, but don't take up arms until you hear him out. Christ warns us against being gullible, but He also commands us to be teachable. Those clinging to the futuristic fulfillment systems that this book challenges can be the least teachable sometimes. But John Noē is a gifted Bible teacher, and he exposes their "fatal flaw" and the reason they will always have failed predictions.

I first became aware of John Noē in 1991 when his book, *The Apocalypse Conspiracy*, was published by Wolgemuth and Hyatt/ Word. At that time, John was not aware of the already existing preterist movement and what it stood for. But he had seen enough of the excesses of the futurist date-setters to realize there was a serious problem with their interpretation of Bible prophecy. He also was convinced that the book of Revelation could be understood by all believers. In his pursuit to interpret it he noticed what seemed to be almost a conspiracy to obscure its meaning and profiteer from its fearful images. He wrote *The Apocalypse Conspiracy* for those reasons. It was a harbinger of even better things to come from his pen.

John is not a professional theologian. He has had no formal seminary training, but that may be an advantage—it might have handicapped his communication style. He writes out of a deep love for the common man and connects with a readership that theologians seldom reach. Yet he is a scholar, and he has an intense commitment to biblical truth. What he lacks in formal training he more than makes up for in his relentless pursuit of understanding eschatology.

I first met John in 1993. He attended one of our seminars. Although he did not embrace the full preterist view at that time, he was willing to discuss and study it. He made us prove everything in a true Berean spirit. We have kept in touch quite often over the last six years. He never stopped his quest for a better understanding of the last things. Once he began to grasp the full significance of A.D. 70, he put everything we preterists have said through an acid test. He didn't let us get away with anything. It took him a little while, but he has now come to a position on the fulfillment of Bible prophecy that is almost the same position that I take. Since I know how hard I studied, I appreciate how much effort he must have expended in his analysis.

John is not the kind of person to keep these things to himself, although he fully understands what a radical paradigm shift this book presents. He immediately set out to explain many confused and complex issues of end-time prophecy in simple terms that we can easily grasp.

I also believe that theologians from all traditions can benefit tremendously from reading and studying this book. It is especially important for all of us in the Reformed tradition who subscribe to Calvin's principle that "the Church is reformed and always reforming." For too long we have been stymied by eschatological views that have not been developed beyond 2nd-century concepts. The creedal councils did not devote any significant attention to

"the Church is reformed and always reforming."

eschatology, and neither did the Reformers, other than to use it as a tool to demonize the Pope and the Roman Catholic hierarchy, and fuel reformation fervor. We will greatly benefit from this book's reformational message and (full) preterist presentation. Indeed, eschatology (the study of last things) is the next frontier of the continuing reformation.

Regarding the validity and viability of preterism, Reformed theologian and partial preterist R.C. Sproul said it well in his latest book *The Last Days According to Jesus*:

> The purpose of *The Last Days According to Jesus* has been to examine and evaluate the various claims of preterism, both full and partial. The great service preterism performs is to focus attention on two major issues. The first is the time-frame references of the New Testament regarding eschatological prophecy. The preterist is a sentinel standing guard against frivolous and superficial attempts to downplay or explain away the force of these references.
>
> The second major issue is the destruction of Jerusalem. This event certainly spelled the end of a crucial redemptive-historical epoch. It must be viewed as the end of some age. It also represents a significant visitation of the Lord in judgment and a vitally important "day of the Lord." Whether this was the *only* day of the Lord about which Scripture speaks remains a major point of controversy among preterists.[1]

I highly recommend John Noē's full-preterist book for three important reasons: (1) It proves from correctly interpreted Scripture that we are living "beyond the end times," (2) it is written in common language for all people, and (3) he represents a fresh and formidable voice in the growing preterist movement. John Noē is a messenger of good news for those willing to change their thinking when convinced by biblical exegesis, like the Bereans. I commend this book to your serious attention. It's a compelling introduction to past fulfillment of Bible prophecy.

John is already working on a sequel that will explore more implications for Christians living after A.D. 70.

Edward E. Stevens, President
International Preterist Association

Introduction

The Appointed Time of the End

We are a time-oriented people. God is time-oriented, too. That's why seven centuries before Christ, the God of the Bible inspired the ancient prophet Habakkuk to write:

> For the revelation awaits an appointed time; it speaks of the end and will not prove false. Though it linger, wait for it; it will certainly come and will not delay. (Habakkuk 2:3)

One century later, God gave another Old Testament prophet, Daniel, two specific prophecies that pinpointed the exact time in human history for this "appointed time...of the end." He described its historical setting, its nature, and its defining characteristic. This end is the only end the Bible ever proclaims. What's more, its time came. It is now history. Today, we are living beyond the end times. This book presents the proof. It's the rest of...the greatest story ever told.[1]

You may be surprised, impressed, or shocked by the "rest of the story." That's to be expected. But to date, as far as this author knows, no one has more effectively challenged the current endsaying consensus with solid biblical substance and historical evidence, than the Preterists. Full Preterists believe the appointed time of the end came long ago.[2]

Yet thousands of books that focus on fatalism and feed on universal, apocalyptic fears, have sold by the millions, and more are on the way as we near the crisis point of the year 2000. Before we get swept away by termination tirades, or join the company of the alarmed, or detach ourselves from society, let us seriously consider the Bible's "appointed time...of the end."

Predictably, this book will be controversial. This cannot and should not be avoided.

Exciting discoveries await you in the chapters ahead. You'll find a positive and sound alternative to the popular views of global doom. So, take your time. Be critical. Think it through.

Predictably, this book will be controversial. This cannot and should not be avoided. Those who are comfortable with their endsaying traditions of an end yet to come—the sooner the better—may view this book as a threat. Others will find its reformational message compelling and a breath of fresh air. Either way, this book offers positive hope for our world and confidence in the future. We simply must not take the negative baggage of endsaying, with its inherent fallacies, flaws, and fatalism, into the new millennium. We are living on the other side of history from the end times, as you will see. If you're ready for an adventure, read on.

1

Is There Really No Future?

Here in the Midwest where I live, I love to drive into the country-side on a pleasant summer's day. I take the back roads, roll down the windows, and feel the summer breeze. I pass by quaint farms, fields, barns and farmhouses. I smell the gentle freshness and catch a scent of new-mown hay. Suddenly, I hit a patch of some-thing that stinks. It's the manure that farmers spread on their fields.

We live in an exciting, information-age world. But just as we begin to enjoy our TV and radio programs, books, magazines, news-papers, videos or computers, we catch a whiff of something rather odorous. What is it? It's the awful smell of our future being fried.

Down on the farm, one learns to count on the future. Every year farmers plow their ground, sow seed, and fertilize. The plants grow and are harvested. It's nature's basic pattern. Of course, some years are better than others, but there is always next year. Farmers have learned to count on the future.

Not so for masses of people in our world today. They have been programmed, by church people and nonchurch people alike, not to count on the future. Chalk it up to "millennial madness" if you will, but never before have so many prophets from so many perspec-tives bombarded humankind with so much gloom and doom.

Speculation and urgent apocalyptic warnings have convinced many people that there is no future, for the world is about to end. According to the *Chicago Tribune*, "at least 50 million Americans buy the 'end is near' forecasts."[1] That's a lot of people!

A recent *U.S. News and World Report* magazine poll discovered that nearly 60 percent of Americans think the world will end sometime in the future. A third of those think it will happen within a few years.[2] The rest are in a quandary about what to think. And who can blame them? Termination tirades and end-time belief systems are pervasive. Their influence has infected the whole world.

The Bombardment of Termination Tirades

Doomsday prophets abound, and their influence is astonishing. Below are a few examples of big-name sources and institutions who are jumping on the end-of-the-world-is-coming bandwagon[3] (all emphasis mine):

The Late Great Planet Earth. In a class by itself, with a title that speaks for itself, this book by Hal Lindsey is the number one all-time bestseller of our century (next to the Bible). In the 1970s, the *New York Times* proclaimed it "the book of the decade." It sold over 10 million copies. Today, it has sold over 40 million copies worldwide. Nothing else comes close. Without a doubt, Lindsey has exerted the greatest influence on the termination thinking of this century. He has often been dubbed "the dean of prophecy." On his opening page Lindsey writes:

> The Bible foretold modern man's countdown to extinction. *
> I believe this generation is overlooking the most authentic voice of all,
> and that's the voice of the Hebrew prophets. They predicted that as
> man neared the end for history as we know it that there would be a
> precise pattern of events....And all of this would be around the most
> important sign of all—that is the Jew returning to the land of Israel
> after thousands of years of being dispersed.

---

* *As we shall see, this statement is dead wrong.*

In another of his doomsday books, *Planet Earth - 2000 A.D.: Will Mankind Survive?* (1994) Lindsey warns, "Never before have all these signs come together like this." In a section titled *Gone by 2000?*, Lindsey advises, "I wouldn't make any long-term earthly plans... *the end times are almost here.*" His latest book is titled, *Planet Earth: The Final Chapter* (1998), and addresses "what will shortly come to pass, and how it will all turn out."

Nostradamus. The 16th-century Jewish-French physician and psychic, Nostradamus, purportedly predicted the great fire and plague of London, the execution of Charles I, the rise of Oliver Cromwell, the French Revolution, Napoleon's campaigns, both World Wars, the ravages of Hitler, and even the deposing of the Shah of Iran. Relying on this impressive track record, Nostradamians are keying in on July 1999 as the rapidly approaching end. They cite Nostradamus' Quatrain X:72 in his massive volume of verses known as the *Centuries*, which says, "The year 1999, the seventh month, from the sky will come the great King of Terror. He will bring back to life the great king of the Mongols. Before and after War reigns happily."

The opening line of a full-page ad in *Publisher's Weekly* magazine, December 9, 1996 for the book, *Nostradamus 1999* ('96) by Stefan Paulus, reads:

> On the evening of November 15, 1996, author Stefan Paulus generated such tremendous interest that 32,000 radio listeners in New Orleans jammed the phone lines-all because they wanted to know how to survive the end of the world.

The Reverend Billy Graham. Are You Ready for the Last Days? This headline appeared on the front cover of the Billy Graham Evangelical Association's Decision magazine in September 1995. In it (pages 1-3) Dr. Graham writes:

> There are 'signs of the times' given to us in Scripture, and each day, as we read our newspapers or watch the news on television, we are reminded of some of the signs Jesus told us to look for...famines...

earthquakes...weapons that can destroy the entire world with fire...'nation shall rise against nation.' We are seeing that today....When will the end be? We don't know...But every indication is that it will be sooner than we think.

As we shall see, we moderns are *not* living in the biblical "last days," and we *can* know the time for the end.

Network Television. The opening for ***NBC's*** two-hour, prime-time show, *Ancient Prophecies III, New Visions of the Future*, a third in a four-part series, which aired February 28, 1996, teased:

> The clock is ticking and time may be running out! Over the centuries prophets have seen the close of this millennium as the end of time as we know it. Some trace the warnings back to the prophets of the Bible. Others find evidence in the book of Psalms. And then there are voices alive today from mystics and visionaries, seemingly blessed with supernatural insight, to the more common seers, ordinary men and women, some of them forever changed after a brush with death. But whatever the source, the prophecy remains the same. Something cataclysmic seems headed in our direction. Is our world doomed by fate? Or is our future conditioned? The answers may come sooner than we think.

ABC's weekend show *Sightings,* which aired on April 22, 1995, included a news segment that asked, "Is the end really near?" Featured were:

- Dire predictions of a diverse group of "modern prophets" claiming that half of the world's population will soon be killed.

- Visions of an impending "end of the world" given by "ascended-master" spirit beings.

- A foreboding alignment of all nine planets due to occur on May 5, 2000.

- A segment on using the Bible's book of Revelation as "blueprint for imminent disaster."

CNN's Larry King Live, March 8, 1993, featured yours truly to refute the doomsday contentions of Harold Camping, the author of the book *1994*. Camping calculated from the Bible that the world would end in September 1994.

The world did not end in 1994, just as I said it wouldn't. For the reasons you'll find in this book, it will *never* end. You can count on it.

Religious Television.   Televangelist Pat Robertson, during a week-long fundraiser on CBN's *The 700 Club*, with the theme "Signs of the Times 1995," pleaded with viewers, "All is being set up for us just like the book of Revelation said...All signs point to the end of the world and the end of life as we have known it...Nobody knows the day or the hour...What all this means is we're coming up on the time of the end...Now the time is urgent to bolster the resources of CBN...This world is not going to get any better...The worst is yet to come...Now is the lull before the storm...Your dollars may not do any good in five years or so."

During the previous year's fundraiser Robertson told viewers (May 12, 1994), "We are possibly talking about the final age of humankind, right now. Let's work together while we have a chance. Please call and make a pledge."

Jack Van Impe, popular television Bible prophecy teacher, spreads the "good news" of Armageddon. On his nationally televised program of June 22, 1994, he prognosticated "everything is winding up within the next ten years." On his February 5, 1997 show he changed his timetable to between "2001 and 2012."

Televangelist *Paul Crouch* of *TBN* declared during his internationally televised "Spring '94 Praise-A-Thon" fundraiser on February

22, 1994, "we are in the last moments of grace before the wrath of God is revealed. This is the windup. The curtain is about to come down. We don't have much time left.... If Jesus hasn't come back by the year 2000 A.D., then we [he and his guest preachers] have misread the Scriptures." Crouch and Hal Lindsey, a frequent guest, discussed how they don't see "it [this world] can go beyond 2005 or 2010" at the most.

As we shall see, Crouch and his guests have indeed misread the Scriptures.

Rod Parsley, another televanglist, August 13, 1995 confirmed, "We are in the final moments of the End Times!" Ad copy for his latest book, *The Day Before Eternity* ('99 Creation House), counsels, "History's final hour ticks away minute by minute..."

News Magazines. US News & World Report's December 19, 1994 cover story reported, "The approach of a new millennium in the year 2000 is unleashing a flood of doomsday prophecies, not only from zealous Christians who are convinced that Christ's return is imminent and will end history and inaugurate a divine kingdom...but also from those...far removed from Christian belief."

Newsweek magazine's cover of November 23, 1992, portrays a bright, menacing comet speeding toward Earth under the headline, "Doomsday Science: New Theories About Comets, Asteroids and How the World Might End."

Time magazine, in the fall of 1992, published a special issue devoted entirely to the mystical year 2000 and the new millennium. It stated that "no symbol of the future has sparked more anticipation and mystery than the year 2000.... It promises a new age, or an apocalypse."

The June 24, 1997 issue of this supermarket tabloid **Weekly World News**, citing Dr. Robert Calke, a doomsday expert, reported that the Battle of Armageddon will start when China and Iraq attack

Israel on May 3, 2000, and that the world will come to an end on or before May 13, 2000. The issue also reported that the U.S. Government is hiding the information and suppressing the Bible prophecies that prove it.

Nationally Syndicated Cartoon Strips. ***Beetle Bailey***, cartoon strip, in the Indianapolis Star, June 12, 1995 echoes this popular sense of foreboding.

Frank & Earnest, June 30, 1995, captured a crucial question of the endsaying tradition. Two angels ask God:

Recent Apocalyptic Books. *The Celestine Prophecy* ('95 Warner Books), playing off of apocalyptic themes, shoots to the top of the *New York Times* best-seller list and stays there for an astonishing 152 weeks, selling 8 million copies worldwide, once again proving the power and appeal of the apocalyptic and huge public interest.

The Bible Code ('97 Simon & Schuster) jumps onto the *New York Times* best- seller list with a controversial claim, a secret code hidden in the Hebrew text of the Bible's first five books. The code has just now been unlocked by computers, and supposedly reveals future world events. It warns that the Bible foretold disasters set to come upon the world. Among the cataclysms, both past and future, are the rise of Hilter, the Holocaust, the atomic bomb, President Kennedy's assassination, the Gulf War, and Yitzhak Rabin's assassination. According to author Michael Drosnin, this hidden code also reveals the time predicted for the biblical "time of the end" should have begun in September, 1996, with Armageddon to follow in 2000.[4]

The Beginning of the End ('96 ThomasNelson). Not to be out-done, TV preacher John Hagee connects the November 4, 1995 assassination of Israel's Yitzhak Rabin with "the beginning of the end and the coming Antichrist." His end-times book marches to the top of the Christian bestseller list. Hagee contends that the end-time countdown to the Rapture, Tribulation and Armageddon has already begun. In 1997, his publisher (the largest Christian publisher) releases its new Bible, called the *Prophecy Study Bible*, edited by Hagee. In it, he identifies ten prophetic signs indicating that our generation today is the "terminal generation"—a phrase borrowed from Hal Lindsey.

Left Behind: A Novel of the Earth's Last Days (Tyndale House Publishers '95) sparks a series of four "fictional" books, with more forthcoming. These books reflect the popular end-time view of most evangelical Christians. Focus on the Family's *Citizen* magazine called this series "the hottest trend in apocalyptic literature since author Hal Lindsey's million-selling *The Late Great Planet Earth*."[5] The *New York Times* ran a front page feature story about it on October 4, 1998 and reported, "In an instant, millions of people [will] disappear from the face of the earth, shedding their clothing, shoes, eyeglasses and jewelry."

CBA Marketplace, the Christian Bookseller Association's trade journal, headlined feature article titles in its November, 1998, issue: "No End to Success for End-Time Videos," "End-Times Books: Fact and Fiction," and "Book momentum builds as the year 2000 approaches."

A Few Other Notable Endsayers. *Pyramidians*, claiming one inch equals 1 year from measurements taken within the chambers of the mystical Great Pyramid of Giza in Egypt, have predicted cataclysms for our century. Some hit right on target, such as World War I and II. Some didn't, such as the Second Coming of Christ in 1934. But they warn that there are virtually no measurement prophecies for anything beyond the year 2000.

The House of Yahweh, a Jewish-oriented newsletter, in their February 1998 headlined, "World Destruction in Only Three Years." Previously, front-page headlines in the November 1997 issue proclaimed, "Nuclear War Through The Hebrew Year 5760" (which corresponds with the Roman year 2000). Inside they write, "All nations will be affected...the time of destruction is here." They believe the Arab-Israeli peace treaty signed by Prime Minister Yitzhak Rabin on September 13, 1993, was the "confirmation of the covenant" prophesied by the Old Testament prophet Daniel. This supposedly started God's prophetic time clock ticking again and gives humankind just seven years preceding the world's last war—the infamous Battle of Armageddon. This seven-year period "will end in destruction for all nations."

Jerry Falwell, in a mass mailer in late 1989, wrote, "With all of my heart—I believe—in just a few days we will enter what may very well be...THE FINAL DECADE!...Jesus is coming soon. And I want you to be ready."

In 1990, *Elizabeth Clare Prophet*, a New Age guru who claims she communicates with Jesus and Buddha, moved her followers onto a thirty-three-thousand-acre range in Montana to prepare for the coming Armageddon and imminent end. They are still there and waiting.

The militia group the *Patriots* held their 1995 *"End of the World" Expo* in Dallas, exhibiting anti-government and conspiracy literature, and the latest in survivalist gear. At "Preparedness Expo '96" in Indianapolis, Bo Gritz, former Green Beret turned negotiator in the Montana Freeman standoff, conducted the featured seminar, titled, "Are We in the Biblical End Times?" His answer? "Yes." A common thread in the patriot and militia movements is an apocalyptic vision from the Bible that they view as an imminent and threatening scenario.

In Cheiry, Switzerland, 48 members of *The Order of the Solar Temple*, a bizarre doomsday cult, are found dead in October of 1994 in the burning rubble of two Swiss villages. Their leader, Luc Jouret, had urged his members to stockpile an arsenal and prepare for the end of the world. Oddly, the apocalyptic beliefs of this religious fanatic group were quite similar to those of Waco's David Koresh (1993) and the popular evangelical Christian view.

New Agers point to the year 2012 as the time of great cataclysm, based upon their interpretation of ancient Mayan and Aztec calendars. Some astrologers point to *5/5/2000*, the title of a recent book from Crown (1997), and the date on which Mercury, Venus, Mars, Jupiter, and Saturn will align with Earth for the first time in 6,000 years.

Six-day Theorists, using "the six-day, world-age theory" from the Genesis creation account, are predicting that all sorts of things are about to happen in or around the year 2000. They assume that God created the universe in 4004 B.C.[6] and within six literal days. Then they add the theory that God's plan for ending the world is similar, but equated by the time scale of "one day is as a thousand years" (Ps. 90:4 and 2 Pe. 3:8). Therefore, their 6-day, 6,000-year time line is up, and something big is about to happen. It's another reason many Christians warn that we are living in the apocalyptic "end times," in the biblical "last days." As we shall see, in spite of the notion that the world may have been created in six 24-hour days, there is no reason to misrepresent this verse as a "day *equals* one thousand years" or misapply it as a time scale to argue for a so-called end of the world.

The *Mount of Olives Hotel* in Jerusalem advertises itself as "the best place to be for the anticipated second coming." Nearly a hundred Americans now live on this hill, located just across a small valley from the old city. They've destroyed their American passports and sold their earthly possessions, and are watching and praying for history's climactic event from this ringside seat. In the meantime, Israel is girding itself for a deluge of Christian pilgrims as the year 2000 approaches.[7] $12 million has been budgeted by the Israeli government to upgrade security, especially around the Temple Mount, "fearing extremists might undertake suicidal attacks in Jerusalem as a way to bring about the fulfillment of end-times prophecy."[8]

Should We Heed the Words of the Prophets?

With so many voices coming from so many sources with so much uniformity and all pinpointing the same time frame, let's face it, we are being bombarded as never before. And we humans are fascinated by these prophetic visions and claims. But are they true? Is "the end of the world" near? Are we now living in the apocalyptic "end times," the biblical "last days"? Is history drawing to a close? Or, is this a fantasy perpetuated by profit-hungry media and self-serving ministries cashing in on the public's almost insatiable appetite for doomsday scenarios? These questions are being asked by more and more people, more and more often, and with a greater sense of urgency as we near the turn of millennium.

Perhaps you too have wondered what's in store for us. Could this actually be it? Should we be heeding the words of these "prophets"? Worldwide, people want to know what's going to happen. Are things going to get worse? Is there hope for the future? If there is, what is the basis for that hope? Two things are certain: uncertainty about the future is running at an all-time high and apocalypticism is burgeoning.

As the 20th Century draws to a close the conviction grows, more than ever before, that the end is surely coming, and coming very soon. Others try to avoid thinking about it, and only pay a degree of uneasy attention to the doomsday pundits in times of global crisis. After the heat's off they forget about it until the next time. Some spend a lifetime harboring secret doubts and worries. A few simply dismiss the whole thing as ignorance gone to seed, but lack an authoritative reason for doing so. Whatever we try to do with it, it's always there, waiting to rear its ugly head and spread its stench.

If the "end of the world" was an established fact, it would be tragic for most if not all people alive at the time. But, as we shall see in this book, it's not the truth. Still, we must recognize that endsaying will not go away easily. The idea that the end is coming soon is not only a deeply embedded religious concept and dominant ideology, it's also an effective marketing and fund-raising tool. Those who profit by it will not want to let it go. Sensationalism, fear-mongering, scare tactics and crisis-oriented pleas are the names of the endsaying game:

- *Environmentalists* sound alarmist trumpets of impending ecological disasters which threaten our lives and life on earth itself. The culprits are global warming, ozone depletion, deforestation, acid rain, toxic waste, and shifting weather patterns. We are headed for disaster, they tell us.

- *Economists* preach global economic apocalypse, worldwide famine, overpopulation and plagues (AIDS). The earth cannot support indefinite expansion, they plead. The stage is set. This is how the world ends.

- *Computer experts* conjure images of a secular Armageddon and predict January 1, 2000, as "The Day the World Shuts Down" and "The end of the world as we 00 it" (that's "oh-it"). Some Christians have recast this "Y2K" problem in religious terms. They see it paving the way for an end-time Antichrist and portending the return of Christ and the so-called end of the world.

- *Astronomers* project how all life could end by an asteroid or comet colliding with earth. After all, this is how the dinosaurs became extinct, they reason. It could happen to us, too.

As the 20th Century draws to a close the conviction grows, more than ever before, that the end is surely coming, and coming very soon.

- *Scientists* measure the motion of a million galaxies. Some say that the cosmos is expanding in different directions and that the whole thing could snap like a rubber band. Others warn that the universe is winding down or decaying via the Second Law of Thermodynamics (entropy). Everything could implode. Which is it? Either way spells doom.

- *Psychics* and *astrologers* galore "see" unimaginably horrific cataclysms coming our way very soon.

- *Best-selling authors* cash in on our fear of and fascination with apocalypse. They look for any excuse to bring out another doomsday book and find more reasons to be pessimistic about the future.

- *Nuclear scientists* grip us in an extended anxiety attack. They warn of the growing threats of a nuclear Holocaust—everything from global war, mad dictators, power plant accidents, and disarmament fiascos, to nuclear proliferation, accidental launches, mishandling of nuclear waste, and loose nuclear material in the hands of terrorists. The hands on the Dooms-day Clock at the *Bulletin of the Atomic Scientists* Building in Chicago are now at 11:51 P.M. When they strike midnight, it's all over.

- *Religious extremists*, like David Koresh in Waco, Texas, gar-ner major headlines and tragically lead gullible followers astray with end-of-the-world views and bunker-mentality lifestyles.

- *Self-proclaimed prophecy experts* assure us that "history's hourglass is almost empty" and that "it will all be over soon." Many base their predictions on personal calculations from the Bible. Others base them on the frequency of natural calamities like earthquakes, floods, plagues, and famines, which are supposedly occurring more than ever before. Almost every major, global crisis is regarded as a sign of the end. In the popular style, they assure us that "it's all happening just like the Good Book says it would."

- Saddest of all are the *devout, well-known, respected, and gifted church leaders* who are now, more than ever, echoing the termination refrains they have been taught in their particular tradition. They were taught that God determined a specific plan for history's last days and the earth's demise, a plan now coming to fruition. For many, it's a driving force behind their ministries.

Meanwhile we, as a society, pay an enormous price. The termi-nation tirade is far more damaging than most people think. In this author's opinion, it's a crime against humanity and one of the greatest psychological and theological travesties of our century. In actuality, it's the awful smell of our future being fried. And it's spreading more rapidly than ever nowadays. But growing numbers of people are sensing that there might be something wrong with this message. Unfortunately, they don't really know what it is or how to refute it. Something is indeed wrong with the endsaying message. This book will show you where the error lies and why we can count on the future.

2

The Disastrous Power of Cataclysmic Imagery

Educators, psychologists, and communication experts tell us the world runs on ideas. They are crucial to all life, and the foundation upon which our lives are shaped, our dreams are generated and our nations are built. Conversely, ideas can ruin lives and crumble kingdoms.

Perceptions shape our ideas. Our perceptions are quite fragile; they are formed by the words we hear and the pictures we see. It's how we humans process information. Of course, words are important. But if a picture is worth a thousand words, then pictures have a much greater effect on us than words. The advertising industry is built on this principle.

Let's face it, we are susceptible to what we hear and see. But more and more we have become a people governed by pictures. The experts tell us that we think in terms of pictures, so our ideas are most often shaped by the pictures we see. If you were asked to name one picture that has had the most influence on humanity in

this century, what picture would you pick? In this author's opinion,
the picture with the greatest impact is this one:

This picture of an atomic fireball and its mushroom cloud first
flashed around the globe just fifty-some years ago. Since then, we
have had to live with the possibility of an impending apocalyptic
disaster of global proportions. This picture, along with its associated images of mass destruction and nuclear winter, has been deeply
and repeatedly etched inside our minds.

The psychological power of cataclysmic imagery should not be
underestimated by anyone seeking to understand 20th-century
American culture. A whole generation of "nuclear kids" has been
raised under the haunting reality of nuclear confrontation. We live
with its prospect of annihilation. "Picturing" this destruction casts a
numbing spell upon us. By our nature, we tend to dwell on nega-
tives and not positives. The news media latched onto this fact long
ago. Bad news sells and good news doesn't, so they bombard us
with bad news. The entertainment industry capitalizes on the
addictive power of doom as well.

The fact is, for the first time in human history, a man-made "end of the world" seems like a real, technical possibility. And once that idea is accepted, our minds are prepared for other apocalyptic scenarios. These images of the world getting worse and worse imprint our minds, feed our insecurities, and muddle our emotions. Many of us find ourselves imagining the end much too often. The cumulative effect is, we become casualties of a fatalistic mood.

Why is this impending sense of an end so harmful? It's because our concept of the future determines our philosophy of life. It affects how we live now. And unlike anything ever before, the advent of the nuclear age drastically changed humanity's vision of its earthly future. The threat of nuclear cataclysm symbolizes our era.

...our concept of the future determines our philosophy of life.

End-time Bible prophecy experts jumped on the atomic theme. Before 1945, they interpreted the Bible's use of "burning, melting and shaking" language in terms of earthquakes, comets, or volcanoes. But Hiroshima and Nagasaki changed that. Now, nuclear disasters are incorporated into prophetic passages. A torrent of prophecy writers and preachers insist that the Scriptures not only foretold atomic and nuclear weapons, but also their ultimate "end-time" use. In their opinion, the reality of nuclear war confirms the inerrancy and divine inspiration of the Bible. The earth is doomed, and the only way out is the salvation claims of the Bible and a possible mass escape.

As a result, modern-day Christianity and all of civilization are under the siege of an Armageddon mentality. We have a new language of doom and gloom. Even Dr. Billy Graham, the highly respected evangelist, uses the language warning that "there will be nuclear conflagrations, biological holocausts and chemical apocalypses rolling over earth, bringing man to the edge of the precipice."[1]

In 1950, *U.S. News & World Report* magazine commented on Dr. Graham's "youthful exuberance" at a rally in Los Angeles and quoted him as saying, "'Two years and it's all going to be over.' Since then, Graham has become more cautious regarding apocalyptic time-tables."[2] But the ominous image he depicted still hangs heavy. His unsurpassed credibility only gives this popular scenario more credence in the eyes of millions. With all due respect and appreciation for Dr. Graham, we shall see in subsequent chapters that he has subscribed to a flawed interpretation of end-time Bible prophecy. The consequences of this popular belief system are disastrous.

Pessimism for the Future

"For many Americans, the future seems about as secure as a dandelion puff," reported The *Wall Street Journal* in a recent front page story.[3]

An entire generation has grown up in despair of the future. Underlying this fear is our concept of the end, not so much the end of our lives, which is certain, but the so-called end of the world.

Make no mistake; the incessant pounding of doom and gloom scenarios and the cumulative effects of urgent warnings and apocalyptic crises take their toll and leave their mark on the human psyche. Many have "seen" the future and believe that its name is "doom." When a fatalistic perception internalizes itself, it colors one's thinking and infects all we feel and do. Call it a bunker mentality, a future funk, a global gloom, or a hanging on the edge, the bottom line is defeat.

Let's not be naïve. Like a madness, end-of-the-world rumblings impact our daily existence, affecting our behavior and undermining our goals. Like a flood, termination tirades drown our willingness to make commitments and get involved. Like a cancer, apocalyptic rumors spread and kill the fabric of a progressive society. Like a guillotine's blade, endsaying hangs poised to drop and chop off the future. For too many young people, despair for the future has wiped their great plans of life right off the drawing board.

Endsaying, in all its various forms, plays a prominent role. Even when it's viewed as nonsense, it takes a toll. And none of us is immune. Its proliferation in American life is a most significant reason why the optimism and activism of the past century have changed to pessimism and withdrawal.

Is it any wonder that millions of young people today are burdened with cynicism, loss of direction, dashed hopes and a sense of futility. They see themselves as disenfranchised, with the future drawn up before them like a gangplank. Many are angry. Some are rebellious. Others seek solace in an unproductive otherworldliness, passively waiting for the end to come. Some drop out, get hooked on drugs, or hide out in isolation. All have a fatalistic rationale for their lack of interest and neglect of responsibility. Thankfully, a fraction have refused to succumb to the notion that their lives will likely be cut short by an apocalyptic disaster. Yet the message that there really is no future, at least here on *this* earth, is the one being presented by many influential groups and people.

What's needed is sound reason and solid substance to stem the tide of world-terminating messages and scenarios. Endsaying is an age-old crime against humanity. It must be refuted, reformed, and replaced with positive hope and confidence in the future. This is exactly what you'll find in this book. We begin by learning from the past.

Failed Prophets of a False Premise

Remember the last round of apocalyptic ravings which accompanied the Persian Gulf War? Major news magazines featured headlines like: "Is This the Battle of Armageddon?" "Is The End Near?" "Apocalypse Now?" "Revelations in the Middle East." Another spate of doomsday books came out from respected church leaders touting, once again, end-of-the-world proclamations. The national television networks gave them prime-time exposure. And what happened? Nothing!

The following satirical cartoon appeared in the *Wall Street Journal*[4] shortly after the Persian Gulf War ended and the failed apocalyptic outbursts and doomsday predictions subsided without explanation:

Used by permission.

What impression does it give you? "There go those religious nuts again." Rarely if ever do endsayers explain or apologize when they're proven wrong. They back off, wait a while, update their predictions, adjust their scenarios, and start all over again. Some followers become confused, some frustrated, and some disillusioned. Surprisingly, many others don't seem to mind and rarely hold their leaders accountable.

The end-of-the-world scenario is nothing new. History is littered with good and godly people who've claimed certain knowledge of the end and tried to fit the events of their day into the fulfillment of end-time prophecy.

The following is only a partial list of past mistakes. We give these examples, as well as others used in this book, not to impugn anyone's character or demean the faith they represent, but rather to illustrate the problem. Many of them we know as people of sincerity and integrity. We report only what they have said or written publicly. Keep these two questions in mind as you read this historic list: 1) What do all these people have in common? 2) Is there a lesson to be learned here?

A.D. 500. Church father Hippolytus (A.D. 170 - 236) predicted the world would end in A.D. 500, based on his analysis of the dimensions of Noah's Ark.

A.D. 999. When the last change of millennium drew near, hardly anyone knew it, since most of the world of that day did not use the Christian-based calendar, and could not read. Europe was the exception, and Christian expectations of an imminent end of the world flooded the continent. Accounts vary, but terrified masses feared the 1,000 years spoken of in the biblical book of Revelation would be up and Christ would reappear to end it all. Signs and warnings were eagerly sought in the final months leading up to A.D. 1000. It is said that activity in European monasteries nearly ground to a halt as A.D. 999 wound down.

A.D. 1033. When Christ didn't make an appearance in A.D. 1000, quick recalculations were made on the premise that Revelation's 1,000 years should be figured from his ascension and not from his birth. But A.D. 1033 was also a bust.

A.D. 1100s. Joachim of Fiore, an Italian monk and leading biblical prophecy scholar of his day, challenged the allegorical interpretations of Augustinian origin and brought back a literal perspective. According to his date-setting technique, the end was to come between A.D. 1200 and 1260.

A.D. 1501. Christopher Columbus allowed 155 years for all mankind to be converted to Christianity, after which the world would end.[5]

A.D. 1546. Before he died, Martin Luther stated many times that "verily the day of judgment [or end of the world] is not far off; yea, will not be absent three hundred years longer." He also believed that "all the signs which are to precede the last days had already appeared."

A.D. 1835. Joseph Smith, father of Mormonism (The Church of Jesus Christ of the Latter Day Saints), prophesied that the coming of the Lord was near and that "56 years should wind up the scene."[6]

A.D. 1835. "Our lot has fallen under the solemn period emphatically designated in Daniel as the time of the end!" declared

Archdeacon Browne, of England, as quoted in *The Last Times*, by Joseph A. Seiss, D.D.

A.D. 1818. William Miller, founder of the Millerite movement in America, predicted that Christ would come and the world would end sometime between March 21, 1843, and March 21, 1844. Stressing the systematic nature of his methodology and rationality of his conclusions, Miller's end-times mass movement swept through the United States and generated much excitement. The date was later revised to October 22, 1844.

A.D. 1848. "Had the present state of Europe been prophesied fifty years ago, would any have credited the prophecy? We believe that in this year we have seen the beginning of the end." The New York Evangelist, as quoted in *The Last Times*.

A.D. 1852. "No well-informed man can look upon the world as it is, without coming to the conclusion that some great consummation is about to take place." Dr. Baird, in Rochester, as quoted in *The Last Times*.

A.D. 1856. "It is agreed, by all believers in the Bible, that mysterious scenes await our world...God's purposes are fixed, and the wheel of his wonderful providence is rolling us on to the funeral of the world that now is." *The Last Times*.

A.D. 1874. Claiming to be the sole possessors of God's revealed truth, the Jehovah's Witnesses began a string of prophecies for the end of the world which continued through the years 1874, 1878, 1881, 1910, 1914, 1918, 1925, 1975, and 1984.

A.D. 1917. Three dramatic visitations of the Virgin Mary occurred in Fatima, Portugal. The first unveiled a terrifying vision of hell and prophesied the end of World War I. The second visitation warned of another major conflict (WWII), the rise of communist Russia, and its collapse and conversion to Christianity if enough people prayed and consecrated it to Mary. The content of the third visitation, whose outward visual manifestations in the sky were witnessed by 50,000 - 70,000 people, has been kept secret by the Catholic Church. Some speculate that it predicted a fiery end to the world and is being kept secret for fear of setting off worldwide panic.

A.D. 1926. Oswald J. Smith, one of the leading missionary statesmen of his day, wrote in his book, *Is The Antichrist At Hand?* that "the Great Tribulation, the arrival of the Roman Empire, the reign of the Antichrist and the Battle of Armageddon must take place before the year 1933."

A.D. 1970s. Hal Lindsey's *The Late Great Planet Earth*, again a title that speaks for itself, outsells everything. Lindsey cites the rebirth of Israel in 1948 as *the* prophetic sign. Within one generation (forty years, by 1988) we would witness the end of the present world and the return of Christ. He envisioned the new interpretative idea of a nuclear war starting in Israel, resulting in radioactive fallout and a melted earth. The dust jacket of the book's 1977 edition warned readers not to make plans beyond 1985.

A.D. 1978. "The world must end within one generation from the birth of the State of Israel. Any opinion of world affairs that does not dovetail with this prophecy is dismissed." Gary Wilburn, "The Doomsday Chic," *Christianity Today*.[7]

A.D. 1978. "We are already living in the *age of Antichrist*! The world is on the threshold of catastrophe." Salem Kirban, *The Rise of Antichrist.*

A.D. 1978. West Coast pastor Chuck Smith writes in his book *Future Survival* that he is "convinced that the Lord is coming for his church before the end of 1981."

A.D. 1980. "Many people will be shocked by what will happen in the very near future. The decade of the 1980s could very well be the last decade of history as we know it...We are the generation that will see the end times...and the return of Christ." Hal Lindsey, *The 1980s: Countdown to Armageddon.*

A.D. 1988. Edgar C.Whisenant, a retired NASA rocket engineer and prophecy teacher, sends shock waves through fundamentalist circles with his 4.5 million copies of *88 Reasons Why the Rapture Will Be in 1988.* A revised sequel came out the next year: *89 Reasons Why the Rapture Will Be in 1989.* His first book was front-page news around the U.S. His second one wasn't.

A.D. 1990. Dallas Seminary President John F. Walvoord rereleases his 1974 book, *Armageddon, Oil and the Middle East Crisis.* It sold over one and a half million copies playing off the apocalyptic fears of an American war with Iraq leading into the final Battle of Armageddon. When the war was over, so were its sales.

A.D. 1991. The ultra-orthodox Jewish Lubavitch movement announced the imminent arrival of the Messiah. Their candidate died in 1994.

A.D. 1991. Dallas Seminary professor Charles Dyer released his book *The Rise of Babylon: Sign of the End Time,* in which he argued that Iraq's Saddam Hussein was rebuilding the ancient city of Babylon, whose end-time destruction is prophesied in the book of Revelation. His thesis was blown apart by the United States' defeat of Iraq in the Gulf War, but may soon resurface.

A.D. 1992...   "Rapture Oct 28 '92.
                    Jesus Is Coming.
             Don't Receive The 666 Mark!"

Front-page pictures of this sign were splashed around the world by the news media. The source was a Seoul, South Korean church with 20,000 members. Shortly thereafter, its pastor, Lee Jang Rim, was sentenced to a two-year jail term for defrauding members of over $4 million.

A.D. 1993. Harold Camping, the man I debated on CNN's *Larry King Live* mentioned in the last chapter, predicted the return of Christ and the end of the world for September 1994 in his book, appropriately titled *1994*.

The examples could go on and on. As times for the end have come and gone, and predicted events have failed to materialize, embarrassments are quickly forgotten. New endsayers come on the scene, adjust their scenarios to adapt to changing world conditions, and recalculate their figures. Soon a new wave of endsaying speculations and warnings washes ashore, proclaiming humankind's bleak and frightening future. It's the highly adaptive mechanism by which the endsaying trade survives. The next wave of "prophets" proves just as effective at stirring up its brand of sensationalism and fanning it from an ember into a flame. The unsuspecting hearer, encountering endsaying for the first time, may easily be sucked in by its use of current events. And on it goes.

Can there be anything more foolish than this stream of endsaying prophets whose announced times, dates, and urgent warnings have passed away without incident? Examine their track record. Laugh if you must. Better yet, ask yourself how so many of these respected leaders and their followers could be so mistaken? Surely something is wrong. Yet this is exactly how many of us are being programmed today. If there is a lesson to be learned here, why not learn it now?

What, then, do all these endsayers have in common? Obviously, they all have been proven wrong—100 percent dead wrong. Their names were added to a long and growing list of failed prophets. Their error, however, was not one of timing, as is normally assumed. Rather:

All endsayers will be proven wrong within their due time, the same as their predecessors. Why? Because it's not their timing that was or is wrong. It's their concept that's wrong. They are simply failed prophets of a false premise. If we are slow to learn from them, we are only doomed to repeat their folly and fall for their schemes.

It's a wonder the age-old endsaying tradition and doomsday-peddling trade has any credibility left. But if there is one thing we learn from the past, it's that we too seldom learn from the past. "Hitler always said, 'the bigger the lie, the more people who will believe it."[8]

Incredibly, we keep falling for it. Urgent warnings, prophetic certainties, date setting, termination tirades, the latest doomsday ideas—we're addicted. The specter of apocalypse fascinates us. Like waves beating on the shore, old, discredited prophets wash out to sea—dead in their error, and new ones, heavy on assertion and light on proof, roll in to take their place. But only for a short stay. Rarely, if ever, do they explain why past predictions failed, except, of course, when they claim that past prophets didn't have the advantage of knowing what we now know. So here we go again. Don't be surprised, for example, if Hal Lindsey's "terminal generation," the *one generation* following Israel's rebirth as a nation in 1948, is refigured to be seventy years instead of forty. That recalculation would place his predicted end date any time between now and 2018.

Why do we keep getting sucked in by the end-times peddlers? Perhaps we don't like to admit that we were duped by the last one. Besides, endsaying has been a sucker's game for centuries, and we like apocalyptic thrills and chills. We are charmed by the secret insights these prophets so attractively package and sell. Finding hidden meanings in a world of uncertainty soothes us with a sense of power and elitism. It has insider appeal. It's addictive. But this pastime has consequences—undesirable consequences. It would be to our advantage to speed up our progress along this learning curve.

Our brief review of endsaying through history should be a sobering exercise. If we find ourselves wondering, is it possible these new predictions are finally right, the answer is no, they are not. They are not bad guesses either, they are just another repetition of the same fundamental mistake. They have completely missed the biblical meaning of "the end."

The Consequences of Untruth

Midwestern farmers love to tell the story about the man who bought a long-abandoned farm. For years, he worked hard putting the farm back in shape and making it productive. It became a showplace. Then one day the preacher stopped by, looked around and said, "My hasn't the Lord blessed you with a beautiful farm."

To which the hard-working farmer replied, "Oh yeah, you should have seen it when the Lord had it by Himself."

Farming is a demanding way of life. Try slacking off on your duties and see what happens. Soon your fields will be overrun with weeds, your equipment rusted and broken down, and if you don't sow in the spring, you won't reap in the fall. Traditionally, farm families feel a sense of responsibility to pass the farm along to other family members in better shape than they received it.

The cumulative effect of end-of-the-world beliefs has the opposite effect; it creates an "abandon-the-farm" attitude and takes the significance out of human action. If the future is fixed and terminal, why bother?

Beliefs do have consequences. That's why endsaying is far more than an attempt to foresee the future; it actually conditions it. Many who otherwise would be diligent stewards and productive workers tend to sink into helplessness. They may resort to piety and isolation, or shirk away entirely. If there is no future for the future, and our planet is soon going to be destroyed, why bother? Why work to "save the Earth" if its end is just around the corner?

Environmentalists face an uphill struggle. They warn us that if our environment doesn't receive a top priority, dire consequences will result. Such a warning falls on deaf ears among "end-of-the-worlders." They have little interest in environmental concerns. In their view, the world is supposed to get worse and worse before the

Beliefs do have consequences. That's why endsaying is far more than an attempt to foresee the future; it actually conditions it.

end comes. "It's inevitable, it's desirable, it hastens the day. Anyway, we're getting out of here. So why bother? This world is a miserable place. It's not worth fighting for. And God is going to destroy it all very soon."

Someone has said, "If there's no faith in the future, there is no power in the present." Consequently, there is little desire to pass our planet along to future generations in a better condition than we found it. Endsaying negatively influences and conditions our attitudes toward ecological responsibility. The earth is doomed, and the sooner it goes, the better.

Our concept of the future is also a powerful influence in shaping our attitude toward people. If the world is soon coming to an end, what is the point in solving social injustice and human need issues, or transforming organizational structures? This short-sighted mentality impairs individuals, institutions, and nations. The major culprit in this schema is a portion of Christendom involving millions of Americans. For this group, the appeal of a great escape from the difficulties and responsibilities of this world is very attractive. They would rather ponder the end than pitch in with the job at hand. Typically, they don't care much about the welfare of the next generation, since they aren't going to be here anyhow. Add to this the negative mindset that nothing we can do will put this world on a positive course, that all our reform efforts are a waste of time, that earthly enthusiasm is pointless and in vain, and even that there's nothing we should do to stop the inevitable downfall. Their only job is to get ready for the next world, not to fix up this one.

The result is masses of sanitized souls sitting paralyzed in their pews, consoled by the preaching of demise, and increasingly isolated from society. More and more, as the end looms, they see themselves as cultural outsiders reluctant to plunge into social, moral, or political activism. Their plans for this life have a short horizon. In the armed services, they call it a "short-timer's attitude." It's too late to patch up this old troubled world, so they long for the end to come. The only hope is for Christ to come back and get them out of here. Let Him take care of the mess. Basically, this group has abandoned this world for the next.

A radio talk show host, interviewing me a few years ago, hit the nail on the head. He said, "This 'end-of-the-world' stuff just creates 'Chicken Little' people—people hiding under rocks waiting for the sky to fall, unwilling to come out and help the rest of us clean up the mess."

He's right. Endsaying is the ultimate social downer for those called to be the salt and light of the earth. Searching the headlines for more signs of the end, they shrink away from social evils and contemporary issues. Their withdrawal plays right into the hands of those hostile to the Christian faith, who are more than willing to rush in and fill the vacuum. All of which is interpreted as just another sign that the end is near. Beliefs do have consequences, affecting our personal life, community life, national life and even our international life.

Why were we glued to our television sets during the recent Persian Gulf War? One compelling reason is the effect it could have on the entire world. When you add destruction technology to a belief system that everything will get worse and worse just before the world comes to an end, what do you get? You get the possibility that personal views of Bible prophecy might influence the policy decisions of a President of the United States. And the problems of the Middle East (where "the end" always begins) always end up on the American President's desk. How far-fetched is this? As an article in the Nov. 19, 1990 issue of *U.S. News and World Report* stated, "The idea that foreign policy can sometimes be influenced by interpretations of Biblical prophecy is not as far-fetched as it may seem."

In April of 1984, a story in the *Washington Post* stated that President Reagan had a long-standing interest in Bible prophecy.

He appeared to accept the premillennial view of inevitable nuclear war and the imminence of the Battle of Armageddon. Citing various kinds of evidence, the *Post* story concluded that the President's policies toward Israel, the Soviet Union, and nuclear arms were closely tied to his understanding of Bible prophecy. Shortly thereafter, a documentary on "Ronald Reagan and the Prophecy of Armageddon" was aired on 175 public radio stations nationwide.

During the Persian Gulf War the media reported that the White House ordered nine copies of the endsaying book *Armageddon, Oil, and the Middle East Crisis* by John Walvoord. The night before the American led an air-strike against Iraq, it is reported, President Bush requested the presence of evangelist and "Armageddon theology" author, Dr. Billy Graham. Privately-held, end-of-the-world beliefs can lead to possible foreign policy follies; according to David Neff, managing editor of *Christianity Today* magazine:

> First, it may tempt us to help bring on Armageddon (by arming one side in the conflict). Second, it may offer the opposite temptation, to think that foreign policy doesn't matter since the Earth will be destroyed (leading us to ignore issues of justice and human rights).[9]

What do modern-day wars in the Mideast, the present nation of Israel, famines, and earthquakes mean for the fulfillment of end-time biblical prophecy? As we shall see, *nothing! Absolutely nothing*!

But wait a minute, the pro-Israel, endsaying contingent protests. Isn't end-time prophecy happening right before our eyes? Aren't the pieces of prophecy falling into place in Israel, fulfilling God's plan as revealed in the Bible? Won't Russia, or somebody from the 'north' (Ezekiel 38 and 39) invade Israel and begin the final Battle of Armageddon? The answer is no! In later chapters, we'll see who this "invader from the north" actually was.

Is it not strange that not one "prophet" forecast the fall of the Berlin Wall, the demise of communism, the breaking apart of the

Soviet Union, or the speedy victory of American forces against Iraq? Perhaps, as Hal Lindsey later admitted, "modern-day prophecy teachers have been a little too quick on the Armageddon trigger." Foolish predictions have been an embarrassment for the Church, and have brought both the Bible and the Church into disrepute.

Moreover, have you ever wondered about how "pro-Israel" some Christians are, when according to their Israel-focused, end-time scenario, two-thirds of the Jews will be killed during a seven-year tribulation period and final Battle of Armageddon? This mass slaughter more than rivals the Nazi Holocaust and places Israel's most tragic days still ahead. Ironically, this view is rooted in the idea that God still "loves" the Jews and has a special future for them. Some of my Jewish friends don't think this view is so "pro-Israel." But this prevalent belief system (which originated in the 19th century) has major foreign policy and political implications.

In this book, we will challenge many of the popular endsaying notions upon which this Armageddon theology is based. We'll see that our situation is not hopeless and we can indeed help shape the course of history. It is not in vain that we confront troubling world trends and strive to avoid wars. In contrast to the views of historic fatalism, we'll offer a positive worldview that can motivate us to make a viable and significant difference in our world. Remember, Jesus said, "blessed are the peacemakers..." (Mt. 5:9). And our world is a dangerous place. But peace, not destruction, is God's modern-day program. Our world leaders need to know that there are solid biblical reasons to strive for peace, and not be misguided by any view that says that it is not attainable and that their efforts are in vain.

The next question we must ask is, what has endsaying done to the Church?

Impact on the Church

By and large, secular media regard most Christians as prophecy junkies. They see most of the Church as psychologically addicted to endsaying, much as the millions of supermarket tabloid readers are attracted to astrology. This cartoon in a recent issue of *Christianity Today* says it well.[10]

Used by permission.

The reestablishment of modern Israel in 1948 was a catalyst for endsayers. For them, it was the beginning of the biblical last days, and the first step in the final countdown to the end of the world. Hal Lindsey's bestseller, *The Late Great Planet Earth*, burst on the scene in 1970 and confirmed this event as the authentication of their end-time view. Lindsey then claimed that we are living in the last generation, the terminal generation. He assured his readers that the next event on God's prophetic timetable would be their "blessed-hope" (i.e., their removal from planet Earth just before horrible, too frightening-to-imagine, final events took place).

Although this view is advocated by only a minority in Christendom, they are the most vocal, most televised, most broadcast, and most published and are therefore the most often heard. They dominate Christian media, publishing, and marketing today for a good reason—millions of Christians love sensationalism. Lindsey is sensational. But he has one severe drawback; his prophecies do not come true. So he keeps revising them. We scarcely know what to expect next. But failed prophecies have a backlash— they can trigger laughter, scorn, and disbelief.

A cartoon in the *Wall Street Journal* [11] shortly after the Persian Gulf War illustrates the sad truth; the Christian Church has become a joke.

"Hey—you win some—you lose some. . ."

Used by permission.

In the eyes of the world, the whole Church is commonly lumped together with its failed prophets of doom. What's worse, the assumption is made that if the Church isn't right on its facts, it probably isn't right on its faith, either. Therefore, why take it seriously about anything? This is a major reason the Church has difficulty being a relevant player and effective communicator in modern society.

What's even more troubling, Christianity, as one of the three major religions in the world, is in danger of being labeled a false religion. Repeated failures to predict the end, and incessant endsaying by some of its high-profile spokespersons are perceived as false promises, and false promises are perceived as lies. A growing number of non-Christians have relegated the whole of Christianity to a failed cause. They remember that its founder "failed" to return as and when He said He would, and as and when He was expected to by his supposedly Spirit-guided followers (Jn. 16:13). This leads to the belief that Christianity is an illusion.

If you're a Christian, as I am, these accusations hurt. But let's face it; they are valid. Few Christians have any idea how to refute these criticisms. So before we get caught up in the cosmic curtain coming down in the Holy Land, or turning to another endsayer for terminational insight, we'd be well advised to take another look at what the Bible really says or doesn't say about the end time.

Christianity... is in danger of being labeled a false religion.

Of course, Christian endsayers always claim the Bible as their authority. And many are reputable church leaders. End-time urgency underscores their final-push pitches. Some think this approach will spur missionary efforts and cause people to run after God and eternal values as never before. In reality, this fear approach has had more of an opposite effect, fostering complacency, ineptness, and laziness. Most people unconsciously react to a message of doom with a feeling that nothing earthly really matters. It can no longer be claimed that endsaying inspires faith and hope. Rather, it inspires anxiety, paranoia, and surrender.

With its failed predictions and wolf-cries of imminency, the whole endsaying message does great harm and little good. What's more, the all-too-silent majority in the Church are offended by it. They consider end-time claims outlandish and their scare tactics as cheap theatrics. "It's a 'sky is falling,' 'last days' religion," complained one pastor. "Its focus is on frantic appeals and quick fixes. Scare people into salvation, into giving money, into staying in church. It's one of the most cruel con games ever perpetrated on a lost world and in the Church itself."

Another pastor commented, "Any religion that uses fear is questionable. Fear is the devil's tool. Too many of our brethren have tried to turn the 'good news' that Christ came to bring salvation to the world into the 'bad news' that He's poised ready at any moment to return and destroy it all."[12]

Prior to the 20th century, the Church was culturally relevant, involved, and positive. Not so anymore. After the turn of the century, Hal Lindsey's brand of premillennialism and its doomsday mentality spread like a wildfire through Christianity's evangelical ranks and devastated postmillennial gains.

In this book, we are going to look at what God had in mind when He gave the prophetic scriptures to humankind. We'll see how end-time Bible prophecy has been mishandled and misunderstood. We'll expose the basic flaw in the popular interpretive methods that have led to false conclusions, as well as other flaws that have attempted to cover-up for the basic one.

If the Church is to regain its prominent role in modern society, two things must change. First, we in the Church must get our faith right, especially if we are going to profess the Bible as inerrant. Second, we need to craft a credible and effective apologetic (defense) in response to our endsaying brethren. In spite of its current popularity, a crisis of faith is approaching. Soon the failed predictions of many church spokespersons (surrounding the year 2000) will be apparent to all, and disillusion will set in. We need to replace the negative and unscriptural message of futuristic endsaying with a positive and scripturally-honoring one. That's what this book is about. Once it's heard and tested (1 Th. 5:21), the face of Christianity could drastically change in the coming millennium.

But isn't the world really going to end someday? In our next chapter, we'll sift the wheat from the chaff, cut right to the chase, and debunk this myth as we uncover the long-lost truth about the proverbial end of the world.

3

Why the World Will Never Ever End

Endsaying is nothing new. Ever since the first caveman looked skyward and was frightened by a comet flashing across the sky or an eclipse darkening the forest, we humans have been mystified by the specter of an ultimate demise. And never has there been a time when intelligent men didn't look around and become convinced that the world was going to end in their lifetime. We've heard for so long and from so many different sources that the world is going to end, we assume it must be true. But is it?

Where can we turn for the truth about the end of the world? To a scientific theory? To another endsaying prophet? To a psychic's latest revelation? At best, human opinions come and go like waves lapping on the shore. Some might suggest that we turn to the historic creeds of the Church. But no creed mentions an end of the world, an end to human history, an end of time, or a demise of the planet. So where can we turn?

Since the end of the world concerns the creation made by God, we should go to the one book that tells about his creation, the Bible. Down through the ages the majority of people have always wanted to know what the Bible has to say about the important issues of life.

Modern-day polls indicate the same desire. Christians turn to the Bible because they believe that "all Scripture is God-breathed" (2 Ti. 3:16). Scholars turn to the Bible because of its literary prominence. For these reasons alone, the Bible should be our first source of information in this matter.

But the Bible is by far the single most popular source of end-of-the-world speculations. From within its pages come a wide variety of cosmic-cataclysm and earth-catastrophe language. Nevertheless, only the Bible can provide solid answers to our questions. Yet we must let the Bible speak for itself. And as we shall see, *it's not the timing of the Bible-reading endsayers that has been wrong, it's the concept itself.*

What the Bible Actually Says

What the Bible says about the end of the world is *nothing*! That's right—just like the historic creeds. *Nothing*! Many Bible teachers qualify the end by telling us that the world and human history will certainly end in its present form or as we know it. What do these qualifying phrases mean? They don't know. Nobody knows. Yet they keep saying them. The fact is, the world is always changing or coming to an end in its present form or as we know it, and a new one is continually coming in. Ask your parents or grandparents if the world as they knew it hasn't changed.

What does the Bible say about the world ending as we know it or in its present form? Again, *nothing*! What did Jesus say about it? *Nothing*! What does the Bible say about an end of time or end of human history? Again, *nothing*! Not a single text, taken in context, declares the world will ever end. As unpleasant as this truth may be for some, the end of the world is simply a false, pagan doctrine that's been dragged into the Church and read into the Bible. This revelation should be a major wake-up call to all endsayers.

But wait a minute! you protest. I've been reading Billy Graham's newspaper column for years and he says the Bible says that "the world will definitely end some day."[1] With all due respect, once again, to this revered man of God, and one with whom we agree on so many points of faith, the emphatic answer to that assertion is, *it does not!*

Moreover, relying on who says what will not settle this matter. Only specific statements from Scripture will do, as we agree to "test everything. Hold on to the good..." (1 Th. 5:21). Nothing is exempt from this scriptural admonishment. And the fact is that there is no clear statement that teaches an end of the world, an end of time, or an end of human history. *None!*[2] Likewise, not one iota of evidence exists that 1st-century Jews, the early Christians, or any New Testament writer (men guided by the Holy Spirit, according to John 16:13) anticipated an end to the human race or the demise of planet Earth. It is not, as some believe, a profound and glorious doctrine of the Church. This terminal belief must be exposed for what it is, a false assumption that has been arbitrarily read into Scripture.

The biblical truth about the end of the world is contained within the biblical phrase "world without end, Amen." The Bible says that the world had a beginning, but is without end.

> ...from the beginning of the world...throughout all ages, world without end. A-men. (Ephesians 3:9, 21 KJV)

The Gloria Patri, the famous doxology and confessional of the historic Church, emphasizes and confirms this biblical truth:

> Glory be to the Father, and to the Son, and to the Holy Ghost. As it was in the beginning, is now and ever shall be. World without end, Amen.

A pastor friend of mine declared in astonishment one day, "I've said this doxology so often in church and never stopped to realize what it meant." He added, "it's tragic that so many of us, so often, have said or sung this biblical phrase in our church services without ever stopping to consider what it means."

What does "world without end, Amen" mean, anyway? It means exactly what it says: the world (or age) is not going to end! Earlier we said that the truth about the end of the world is contained within the biblical phrase. We stated it this way because in the original Greek, the phrase translated as "world without end" in the King James Bible is an idiom and is translated differently in other, more modern translations. Some versions read, "throughout all generations (ages) for ever and ever!" Literally, it's "into all generations of the age of the ages." As an idiom, the actual meaning of the phrase is greater than, and cannot be directly understood, from its literal words. But every translation of this Greek idiomatic phrase contains the same basic truth.

The meaning of the word translated as "age" (*olam* in Hebrew and *aion* in the Greek) is "a long indefinite period of time." In this idiom, however, both the singular age and the plural ages is used. This double use of age and ages intensifies the meaning of an unending future. Therefore, "world without end," and all the other translations, emphasize the concept of permanence, eternalness, endlessness, everlastingness, perpetuity. It clashes with any idea of an end of the world or end of human history.[3] The world and the present new-covenant age simply do not have an end.

... it's not their timing that is wrong. It's their concept that is wrong. As failed prophets of a false premise, they have been continually trying to predict something that's not going to happen.

The translation "world without end" is also a contrapositive. In literary style, a contrapositive is used to make the meaning more emphatic, like John F. Kennedy's famous phrase, "ask not what your country can do for you...." Biblical statements, too, are sometimes made more powerful by using a negative. Are they not? Instead of strengthening a point by using a superlative, the statement is emphasized by using a negative. "I am not ashamed of the gospel of Christ" (Ro. 1:16 KJV) is an example. What it really means is, I am exulting in it, I am proud of it.

The "amen" following "world without end" makes the phrase even more emphatic. Amen affirms the contrapositive proclamation and adds the meaning, "so may it be in accordance with the will of God." What we end up with, then, is a double strengthening and emphasis of the certainty of this Greek idiom that the world (or age) is without end (i.e., is going to continue forever and ever).

Over the centuries, many attempts have been made to evade the plain meaning of certain biblical phrases. This one is no exception. Contrast this message from God's Word to the many voices that keep trying to predict the end of the world. Doesn't this explain the reason why endsaying prophets of doom throughout history have continually been proven wrong? As we've stated before, it's not their timing that is wrong. It's their concept that is wrong. As failed prophets of a false premise, they have been continually trying to predict something that's not going to happen. In their folly, they've ignored or rejected the transcendent truth of the Bible and the historic proclamation of the Church that the world is without end, Amen.

Consequently, endsaying can be compared to crying wolf when there is no wolf. In this case, they've been crying "End! End!" but there is no end of the world. It's a basic foundational flaw of all endsaying and a concept that's headed for the scrap heap of history. We've been programmed by it for too long. The world is never, repeat never-ever, going to end. We live in a never-ending world. How can we be so sure? We can repeat the old rhyme, "How do I know? The Bible tells me so."

Five hundred years ago Christopher Columbus utilized a similar direct statement from Scripture to confront much of the conventional wisdom of his day. Back then, experts disagreed over how big the world was, and no one knew that two continents blocked the ocean route to the Orient. Some believed that the world was flat, had an edge, and that if you sailed far enough, you would fall off and die.[4] This flat concept was soon headed for the scrap heap of history. So how did Columbus become convinced that the world was round, when many of the people of his day thought he was crazy? We can repeat the rhyme, "How did he know? The Bible told him so." In his *Book of Prophecies*, Columbus wrote,

> It was the Lord who put into my mind (I could feel his hand upon me) the fact that it would be possible to sail from here to the Indies. All who heard of my project rejected it with laughter, ridiculing me. There is no question that the inspiration was from the Holy Spirit, because He comforted me with rays of marvelous inspiration from the Holy Scriptures...I did not make use of intelligence, mathematics or maps. It is simply the fulfillment of what Isaiah had prophesied...[5]

Columbus referred to Isaiah 40:22, which declares that the earth is a "circle." Eight centuries before Christ, the prophet Isaiah had written these words. Twenty-three centuries later Columbus verified this truth from the Scripture. With this conviction from the Bible, Columbus set sail and discovered the New World. We're glad he did. Perhaps centuries from now the inhabitants of planet Earth will be glad that we rediscovered the age-old, biblical truth of "world without end, Amen." They will be glad that we stood apart from the conventional wisdom of our day and confidently proclaimed an unending future for the world.

In our day, everyone knows that the earth is a sphere. Columbus confirmed it, and now we've seen pictures from space! But just like some in Columbus' day, many people have trouble accepting new ideas. They raise objections and issue threats against those who bring them. Columbus believed that the world was round because the Bible said it was, and he proved it. We believe the world is without end because the Bible says it is, and we will continue proving it. "World without end, Amen" is a strong, direct statement from God's Word. It cannot be ignored or diminished. We can count on it, Hal Lindsey's opinions notwithstanding.

But we have not exhausted the biblical evidence that the world is without end. Far from it.

God Promised Never Again to Destroy the World

Twice, since the flood in Noah's day, God has promised not to destroy the world. He made these two promises to Noah on behalf of all humanity for all time. They are recorded in the Old Testament and the Torah book of Genesis as a record of his faithfulness and trustworthiness.

> **Promise 1:** Never again will I [God] curse the ground because of man, even though every inclination of his heart is evil from childhood. And never again will I destroy all living creatures, as I have done. As long as the earth endures [remains], seedtime and harvest, cold and heat, summer and winter, day and night will never cease. (Genesis 8:21b-22)

> **Promise 2:** Never again will all life be cut off by the waters of a flood; never again will there be a flood to destroy the earth. (Genesis 9:11b)

For centuries, theologians have debated what these two promises really mean. Most agree they are eternal promises and depend solely upon the reliability of God. But most also surmise that the second one is a disclaimer or qualifier of the first. They assume God placed this later restriction on his first promise, and argue that since God "destroyed" the world once by a flood, the sum total of these two promises is that He has only limited Himself by how He can destroy it the next time. That is, He is supposedly free to use any method other than water (such as fire, colliding planets, nuclear bombs, or even bowling balls) to destroy it all or end it as we know it. Or, is He free? After all, what is the value of a promise?

What is at stake here is the fundamental question of the reliability of God. Nowhere else in the Bible does God take away from any of his other eternal promises. If God or you or I can make a promise and then come back a little while later and diminish what we said, can this be considered trustworthy? Faithful?

Let me illustrate. Suppose I go on a rampage and destroy my house by hacking up all the furniture and chopping holes in the walls with a long-handle ax. Then I promise my wife and kids that "Never again will I destroy all the furniture and the walls, as I have done. As long as the house endures [remains]." A few days later, however, I tell them, "Never again will all the furniture be cut to pieces and holes poked in the walls by a long-handle ax; never again will there be a long-handled ax to destroy the house."

What will I have promised? Would my second promise reduce the commitment of the first? Would the greater promise be diminished by the lesser? Would the first one then be null and void, freeing me to choose any other method (fire, bulldozer, bombs, chainsaw, or bowling balls)? How could my wife and kids ever again trust one of my promises, if all I had to do was come back a little later and change things by making a lesser promise or issuing a qualifying disclaimer? My family would never buy it. Neither would yours, and neither should we. God is trustworthy and faithful. He is not playing games with his promises. We can rely fully on both of them.

Why not just take God's Word at face value here? If we do, his second promise does not compromise his first. He simply made two independent promises about the same topic separated by ten verses of scripture—not one promise plus a disclaimer. Each one stands on its own merits and is subject to its own contingencies.

Granted, God's second promise is contingent upon a flood method. There's no question about that. Special notice should be given, however, to the fact that planet Earth remained intact both during and after the flood. Nor did time end, even though the world was said to have been destroyed.

God's first promise, conversely, is not contingent upon the phrase, "as I have done," but upon the conditional phrase, "as long as the earth endures [remains]." God did not say "as long as I allow the earth to endure." So how long does the earth endure [remain]? The

Bible tells us, "Generations come and generations go, but the earth endures [remains] forever" (Ecc. 1:4).

God's promise is contingent upon the earth's immortality, which is forever.[6] The Psalmist confirms that the earth is established forever (Ps. 78:69) and that the earth and its foundations shall not be removed, ever (Ps. 104:5; see also Ps. 93:1; 96:10; 119:90). This applies to the whole material universe that He created, as well. Both moon and sun are eternally established as faithful witnesses in the sky (Ps. 89:36-37), as are the highest heavens (Ps. 148:4, 6). Eternalness is not only an attribute ascribed to God and his glory, it's also an attribute ascribed to his creation. That's one reason why Psalm 19:1 states, "The heavens declare the glory of God; the skies proclaim the work of his hands."

It is important to note again that God has never diminished any of his promises in the Bible, but only enhanced them. Likewise, no scripture can be used to negate or diminish another scripture. They all fit together in harmony and consistency. We have many corroborating scriptures stating that not only is the world without end, but the moon, the sun, and the heavens endure [remain] forever, as well.

The second stanza of the classic hymn of the Church, "Great Is Thy Faithfulness," picks up on a portion of this great enduring truth from God's first promise to never again destroy the world:

> Summer and winter, and springtime and harvest,
> Sun, moon and stars in their courses above.
> Join with all nature in manifold witness,
> To Thy great faithfulness, mercy and love.
> Great is Thy faithfulness, Great is Thy faithfulness... [7]

The Psalmist further writes, "Your faithfulness continues through all generations; you established the earth and it endures [forever]" (Ps. 119:90).

Moses, in the 14th century B.C., wrote, "Know therefore that the Lord your God is God; he is the faithful God, keeping his covenant of love to a thousand generations of those who love him and keep his commands" (Dt. 7:9).

This passage is to be understood figuratively and as an understatement. But even if we reduce Moses' thousand generations to a literal level and assume that a generation is forty years, that equals 40,000 years. Approximately 3,400 years have transpired since God directed Moses to write these words in the book of Deuteronomy. If our mathematics are correct, that leaves us with at least 36,600

Eternalness is not only an attribute ascribed to God and his glory, it's also an attribute ascribed to his creation.

---

years yet to go. What do you think people 100, 200, 5,000, 7,000 and 10,000 years from now will think of our 20th-century, end-of-the-world musings? Someday future generations may view our 20th century as a primitive and unenlightened time, especially on this topic of the end of the world.

God's plan since the flood has not been to deal with human sin by eliminating the human race or by destroying his creation. If we think otherwise, we've misunderstood his plan of redemption. "For God so loved the world that he gave his one and only Son...For God did not send his Son into the world to condemn the world..." (Jn. 3:16a, 17a). And neither should we condemn it by saying it's going to end, when Scripture clearly states that it's without end and therefore not ever going to end.

Rest assured that the future stability—and everlasting nature of—the earth and the cosmos are secure. They are grounded in the trustworthiness of the Almighty God who created the universe in the first place. As the Creator and Controller of the Universe, He has personally pledged to forever sustain and protect all life from total destruction by his grace and his great faithfulness. This includes all animal life, as well. So, in whom shall we believe? In God's promises, grace and great faithfulness? Or, in Hal Lindsey, Nostradamus, and other endsayers who predict worldwide catastrophe and destruction of all living things, even the universe?

Apocalyptic Language and Its Fulfillment

Falling stars, bloody moons, darkened sun, shaking earth, signs in the sky...this collapsing-universe, cosmic-cataclysm language is employed throughout the Bible. In our modern-day minds it sounds like the end of the world. But scattered throughout biblical history, and mostly overlooked by the popular prophecy writers of today, are numerous fulfillments of this apocalyptic language. Knowing the nature of these previous fulfillments will enable us to make proper sense of this biblical language.

The popular stream of endsayers has assumed that the Bible's apocalyptic language must be interpreted literally and physically, and that since no one has witnessed a cataclysmic, earth-ending event of this nature, its time must lie in the future. The shock value of earthquakes, exploding stars, cosmic eclipses, and nuclear holocausts is awesome. Thus, a literal/physical rendering of the Bible's apocalyptic texts serves the purpose of endsayers, and has become fixed in the minds of millions of Americans.

The problem with this line of thought is that no biblical grounds exist for this assumption. What's worse, it's an obviously flawed method of interpretation. It ignores the biblical precedent and pattern of fulfillment. This is not the way to approach the Scriptures. When we fail to give proper attention to the historical fulfillments, we do a grave injustice to understanding the Bible's use of apocalyptic language.

When we fail to give proper attention to the historical fulfillments, we do a grave injustice to understanding the Bible's use of apocalyptic language.

Let us look at some of the Bible's apocalyptic descriptions of cosmic disaster and how they were actually fulfilled. This type of language has always been associated with another major, Old Testament theme: the coming of "the day of the Lord." Only when we view these poetic figures of speech from within their numerous historical contexts can we properly apply them to our own time. Without this historical perspective, we are guaranteed to misinterpret their meaning, committing the error of eisegesis—reading one's own preconceived ideas back into the text. This is not wise if one sincerely desires to know what the text is talking about.

As we allow the Bible to shed light on itself, we'll see that this type of apocalyptic language always depicted a coming judgment of God. Its use and mindset was in full bloom in Bible times. Jesus used this same language, as did many New Testament writers, and added no disclaimers that they were using it any differently. Its roots are in the Old Testament, and 1st-century Jews were steeped in it, not only from ancient Scriptures but also from inter-testament literature dating back to the 4th century B.C. Consequently, they expected apocalyptic fulfillments to be quite different from what most of us today have been led to believe. Here are some examples from the Old Testament:

Isaiah 13:10, 13. The stars of heaven and their constellations will not show their light. The rising sun will be darkened and the moon will not give its light...Therefore I will make the heavens tremble; and the earth will shake from its place at the wrath of the Lord Almighty, in the day of his burning anger.

Fulfillment. The prophet was *not* speaking of the end of the world, the final judgment, or a solar or lunar eclipse. He was giving a figurative prediction of the literal destruction of Babylon by the Medes in 539 B.C. (Isa. 13:1). The use of cosmic language means the Presence of God was involved and revealed in this judgment upon these people.

Isaiah 34:4. All the stars of heaven will be dissolved and the sky rolled up like a scroll; all the starry host will fall like withered leaves from the vine, like shriveled figs from the fig tree.

Fulfillment. This was *not* the end of the world, or the end of the cosmos, but a figurative description of the coming divine destruction of Edom in the late 6th century B.C. (Isa. 34:5).

Ezekiel 32:7, 8a. ...I will cover the heavens and darken their stars; I will cover the sun with a cloud, and the moon will not give its light. All the shining lights in the heavens I will darken over you.

Fulfillment. This prophecy was God's warning to the Pharaoh of Egypt of his impending fall in the mid-6th century B.C. (Eze. 32:2).

Nahum 1:5. The mountains quake before him and the hills melt away. The earth trembles at his presence, the world, and all who live in it.

Fulfillment. The subject is God's coming in judgment on the city of Nineveh, and not the physical world, in 612 B.C. (Na. 1:1).

Isaiah 40:4. Every valley shall be raised up, every mountain and hill made low; the rough ground shall become level, the rugged places a plain.

Fulfillment. This is not a reference to a giant excavation job, but a description of the 1st-century ministry of John the Baptist (Mt. 3:1-3).

Joel 2:30, 31. I will show wonders in the heavens and on the earth, blood and fire and billows of smoke. The sun will be turned to darkness and the moon to blood before the coming of the great and dreadful day of the Lord.

Fulfillment. Joel was not describing the end of the world. He was giving a figurative description of the actual events accompanying the coming of the Holy Spirit on the day of Pentecost. Peter said it was fulfilled in their day (Acts 2:16-21). We'll see that this "day of the Lord" (actually, "the day of Christ") followed less than forty years later.

The Old Testament pattern of figurative language usage and numerous fulfillments by literal, divine judgments sets the precedent. If the words of these passages were to be taken literally, it would mean that massive changes or destructions of the cosmos and earth occurred numerous times. But the language transcends its literalism and has to be understood figuratively.

Next let's look at some uses found in the New Testament. These prophesied another, soon-coming-judgment event:

Matthew 24:29. ...the sun will be darkened, the moon will not give its light; the stars will fall from the sky, and the heavenly bodies will be shaken.

Fulfillment. Jesus is speaking in the same apocalyptic terms drawn from the language of the prophets cited above, a language very familiar to 1st-century Jews. As we shall see in subsequent chapters, He was figuratively describing the coming judgment and fall of Jerusalem in A.D. 70.

2 Peter 3:10, 11a. But the day of the Lord will come like a thief. The heavens will disappear with a roar; the elements will be destroyed by fire, and the earth and everything in it will be laid bare. Since everything will be destroyed in this way, what kind of people ought you to be?

Fulfillment. Again, Peter is employing the same common apocalyptic terminology of his day (2 Pe. 3:2). His words are no more to be taken literally/physically than are any of the others above. As we shall see, the figurative fulfillment about which he was warning came upon his contemporaries in a way [nature] totally consistent with all the other apocalyptic fulfillments cited above.

What should we learn from the above perspective? One thing is for sure—the Bible's use of this collapsing-universe, cosmic-cataclysm, apocalyptic language is well-developed, consistently employed, and highly pragmatic! No disclaimers, qualifications, or changes are ever recorded or hinted at by Jesus or any New Testament writer who used this identical language. What, then, would cause us to interpret this apocalyptic symbolism differently? If we do so, without legitimate justification, isn't this a violation of proper and honest interpretation?

Many more examples could be cited, but that would belabor the point. Even though it sounds like the end of the world, this apocalyptic language of the Bible is a common and frequently-used linguistic style. It's the language of the prophets and it's employed throughout the Old and New Testaments in an identical manner. It's the Bible's method of metaphorically describing actual, literal events—specifically, God's coming judgments upon nations, peoples, or cities that have been enemies of his people; or his judgment upon his own people, Israel. The physical means employed are always those of invading foreign armies or natural disasters. These many biblical judgments are also events of international and/or eschatological importance. In every instance, the "worlds" (social, political, religious) of those receiving this judgment of God were ended or dramatically changed. So complete and comprehensive was each judgment event that it was appropriately spoken of in world-ending terms. Speaking appropriately does not require that one speak literally. Please note that in none of these historical fulfillments did the physical nature of literal heavenly bodies or the earth change.

We might ask if it is possible that a literal/physical, time-ending, universe-destroying, cosmic-crashing event can be an additional fulfillment? Can apocalyptic language using symbolism and poetic imagery be taken both figuratively and literally? Some theologians argue that they can, terming such a case a double or multiple fulfillment. But is this possible here?

Certainly, a future cosmic destruction could be within the sovereignty and capability of a God who many believe brought the world into existence in the first place (see Ge. 1). But to break the pattern of biblical precedent by suddenly literalizing apocalyptic terms and phrases and applying them to the destruction of the physical universe, *without an expressed biblical warrant to do so*, is to misunderstand the Bible on the Bible's own terms.

The Jews of the 1st century did not understand apocalyptic phraseology as literally ending the world. And neither Jesus nor any New Testament writer amended the common Jewish understanding when employing this linguistic form. Doing so in our day is totally arbitrary and completely reprehensible. It only confuses and leads readers away from what this kind of language always meant and how it was consistently fulfilled when it was used. Nor is a literal rendering in harmony with the scriptures we have cited that proclaim eternalness.

On the other hand, when God wanted to express his blessings upon a nation or a people, the same apocalyptic language is used, but in positive terms. Instead of the earth or the universe pictured as collapsing or destroyed, they're shown to be abundant, flourishing, and more strongly established. Note the following.

Isaiah 30:26; 60:19-20. The moon will shine like the sun, and the sunlight will be seven times brighter, like the light of seven full days, when the Lord binds up the bruises of his people and heals the wounds he inflicted...The sun will no more be your light by day, nor will the brightness of the moon shine on you, for the Lord will be your everlasting light, and your God will be your glory. Your sun will never set again, and your moon will wane no more; The Lord will be your everlasting light, and your days of sorrow will end.

Fulfillment. Portrays the blessings promised to Old Covenant Israel if they submitted to God and were obedient.

Isaiah 35:1, 6. The desert and the parched land will be glad; the wilderness will rejoice and blossom. Like the crocus, it will burst into bloom; it will rejoice greatly and shout for joy...Then will the lame leap like a deer and the tongue of the dumb shout for joy. Water will gush forth in the wilderness and streams in the desert.

Fulfillment. The figurative language describes actual kingdom blessings brought by Jesus. He proclaimed them in like manner when He declared, "'Whoever believes in me, as the Scripture has said, streams of living water will flow from within him.' By this he meant the Spirit, whom those who believed in him were later to receive." (Jn. 7:38, 39a).

Both positive (blessing) and negative (judgment) symbolism were well understood in the synagogues of the 1st century. We Americans use symbols today, too. For example, if I said that I love the Bears, the Bulls, or the Dolphins, would you think I was an animal lover? Or, if I showed you a cartoon of an elephant and a donkey fighting each other, what would that mean to you?

The interpretation of apocalyptic language is taught to us by the Bible itself. This precedent should serve as a caution to any modern-day interpreter toying with the idea of breaking this long-established pattern.[8] With a proper historical understanding of the Bible's consistent use of apocalyptic language in mind, we moderns would be wise to follow it. We must conclude from the Bible itself that God isn't going to destroy the world. That leaves only ourselves. Could we destroy it? In the next chapter, we will look at the possibilities.

4

We Couldn't Destroy the World If We Planned It

Psalm 24:1 declares that "The earth is the Lord's and the fullness thereof" (KJV; see also 1 Cor. 10:26; Ex. 9:29). In Job 38:33, God states that He is the one who has "dominion over the earth." These passages are meant to remind us that we live in God's world, not ours. He created it. He owns it. He sustains it (Heb. 1:3). We are not the owners, but mere stewards, and we're only here for a short stay.

It is legitimately debatable whether we humans, as irresponsible stewards, could destroy the world even if we sat down and planned it. Allow me to illustrate this point by being absurd. We couldn't destroy the world even if we:

- Exploded all our nuclear bombs at one time, or in a chain reaction. It's doubtful that we could blow up the world once, let alone four-times-over,[1] or affect its orbit, axis, or rotation. How much of all life would be permanently impacted? Bikini in the Marshall Islands has recovered rather nicely after 23 nuclear explosions in the 1940s and 1950s.

- Took a direct hit by a massive asteroid. Would that do the job? Jupiter seems to be surviving rather well after massive, multi-comet crashes in 1994.

- Poured our waste directly into the waters, onto the land, or spewed it into the air. Could we really destroy all life?

- Melted the polar ice caps or started a new ice-age. It's arguable how much of humanity would be lost, given our high-tech knowledge and survival capabilities.

- Let the population explosion grow on unabated. How far would it go before contravening variables began to interfere?

Absurd statements? Yes. And the best-case scenarios would be catastrophic. But could we humans really destroy God's world? No. Here's a "top twelve list" of reasons.

Top 12 List
It's because:

12. Most pseudoscientific theories are just that—"less-than-scientific." The so-called scientific warnings of apocalyptic disasters are notorious for using models that don't mesh with reality. Commonly, they don't allow for all contravening variables that come into play, and fail to recognize natural ranges of known variations. Then they run linear projections and trend extrapolations to absurdity. Not only is this bad science, it's unreliable. We have come to expect overstatement and wildly inaccurate paranoia like, "the earth only has a few more decades if current [their latest idea] trends continue."

11. All scientists don't agree. Many reputable scientists disagree with the pessimistic forecasts of self-annihilation. They are highly skeptical about the attention-getting, scare tactics used by some, and the proposed solutions about what we should do. They note the flimsy evidence, contradictory data, and lack of empirical measurements behind many of the predictions paraded as scientific fact instead of theory.

10. The pursuit of power is behind it. Hidden agendas and selfish motivations are behind the frenzied tone and dire predictions of many environmental, apocalyptic motifs. Scare tactics, misinformation and distorted facts have become standard fare. It's the politics of science and government funding. So, we fund to develop a theory. We fund again to debunk it.

9. Progress is made the enemy. Some environmentalists try to make Americans feel guilty, or evil, about our way of life. But anyone who has visited former communist, socialist and third-world nations can see horrendous environmental damage first-hand. It's far worse than anything western, capitalistic countries have ever done.

8. We're so gullible. We've got to protect the planet is the battle cry. More often than not, it's raised to the moral equivalent of war. Who hasn't watched in amazement as the media, celebrities, and politicians accept almost anything that's dished out? Classically, these under- or unsubstantiated scenarios go unchallenged. When challenged, smear tactics, demonization and personal attacks come into play against those who refuse to see the light. The biggest victim is truth.

7. Most pollution arises from natural causes. Other scientists tell us that volcanic eruptions, geysers, and forest fires vastly outdo people in producing major pollutants. The earth has far more power to destroy itself than we do, and the earth has been doing this for eons. It also keeps regenerating itself.

6. Mistakes are rarely admitted. When alarmist assertions are proven wrong, their perpetrators, like street-corner prophets of doom, side-step the blame and find some other scenario to take its place. It's amazing that some environmentalists have any credibility left. Whatever happened to global cooling of the 1970s and 1980s? Is it now global warming? Or cellular phones and power lines causing cancer? Or oil fires in Kuwait producing massive global climatic changes? The Exxon Valdez oil spill in Alaska causing a lifetime of damage? If the alarmists were wrong then, why not now?

5. Human ingenuity could find a way. Let's recognize that human knowledge and technology have advanced to such a level that a sizable portion of the earth's people could probably find a way to cope with any disaster. And the survival of the human race doesn't depend on the survival of all of its members. Nor does the survival of the planet depend on the survival of every tree or stream.

4. Dirt is their god. Far too many environmentalists and scientists make no allowance for a personal God of creation. Environmentalism is their religion. They worship Mother Earth (i.e., dirt is their god) and regard Earth Day as a holy day. To use up or tarnish the *terra firma* is to damage their god. So, seeing people as the earth's biggest problem, they'd prefer that we reduce the quality of life back to a pristine, peasant existence. Any volunteers? It's almost to the point that to save the planet we have to get rid of humanity. Again, any volunteers?

3. The earth's fullness is bigger than we think. The earth's fullness—its immensity and resiliency to heal itself—is so easy to underestimate when we're sitting inside our four-walled buildings. It's not the "little globe" on the shelf. Those who have climbed mountains, sailed the seas, or gazed into spacious skies over fruited plains may have a sense for how impossible it would be for us surface dwellers to destroy this planet, even if we tried.

2. God would thwart our plans. If we human beings ever sat down and attempted to plan "our" planet's demise (assuming we could destroy it), I suspect that God would thwart our plans, just as He confused the builders of the tower of Babel (Ge. 11:1-9). After all, the earth belongs to Him. He has dominion over it. And his stated will and purpose is that the earth be filled with his glory, not destroyed (Nu. 14:21; Isa. 6:3; Hab. 2:14).

1. The Second Law of Thermodynamics can be overridden. Also termed "entropy," this law (actually, it's a theory or conclusion[2]) states that any order in a closed system will eventually wind down, move toward decay and dissipate. Scientists using the Hubble Space Telescope "confirmed" this suspicion for the universe. They reported that the sun is burning out and that we may only have five billion years to figure out what to do about it. But let's think about this further. First, it has not been proven that earth resides in a closed thermodynamic system—nor even our universe, for that matter. "Strong new evidence" presented by other astronomers using the Hubble Space Telescope contradicts this leading theory/law. They claim the universe is expanding and "will continue expanding forever instead of snapping back in a 'big crunch'."[3]

Secondly and most importantly, if it's true that God originally spoke the entire universe into existence—and the majority if not all the scientific evidence points to this type of creation event—then He certainly should be able to transcend the Second Law of Thermodynamics any time He desires, shouldn't He? God is sovereign over the laws of thermodynamics, as He is over everything. If a little more sun or cosmic substance of any kind is someday needed, He will simply speak it into existence. Likewise, if the speed of light slows down too much—as some scientists worry about—He could give it a boost. These divine acts would only be minor sustaining tweaks compared to creating it all in the first place.

The bottom line is that it's legitimately debatable—make that doubtful—that we small specks of dust confined to the earth's massive surface as it spins and flies through outer space could inflict any irrevocable harm in our so-called exploitation of God's world. He created it. He owns it. He sustains it (Heb. 1:3). Contained in its "fullness" is a strongly entrenched resiliency, full of contravening variables. While it's true that earth's limits are finite, we most likely aren't close to pressing against those limits or surpassing the planet's so-called carrying capacity. And contrary to popular opinion, the earth's health is not fragilely balanced, delicately poised, or precariously teetering on a knife's edge.

In the best-selling book and blockbuster movie *Jurassic Park*, the character of Malcolm said it well:

> Let me tell you about our planet...Our planet [has]... a background of continuous and violent upheaval, mountain ranges thrust up and eroded away, cometary impacts, volcanic eruptions, oceans rising and falling, whole continents moving ...Endless, constant and violent change...Even today, the greatest geographical feature on the planet comes from two great continents colliding, buckling to make the Himalayan mountain range...The planet has survived everything, in its time. It will certainly survive us...This planet is not in jeopardy. We are in jeopardy. We haven't got the power to destroy the planet—or to save it. But we might have the power to save ourselves....[4]

In this chapter, we do not intend to send an anti-environmentalist message. Irresponsible stewardship of any type (war, pollution, overuse of resources, short food supplies, etc.) can severely damage the quality and quantity of life on this planet, or on portions of it. But the rain will still fall and the sun will still shine. Life as we know it would be different, inhospitable, perhaps unthinkable, but eventually the earth would recover. It is legitimately debatable and doubtful whether we humans, intentionally or unintentionally, could destroy this amazing sphere on which we live so briefly, even if we wanted to. We can't come close to duplicating the powerful forces of nature which have been polluting and damaging earth's environment for eons of time. The earth has survived it all. More than likely, it will survive you, me, our kids, and endless generations to come.

There is a Latin saying worth noting: *Nemo contra mundum nisi deus ipse*. "Nothing can destroy the world but God Himself," and He has promised not to!

5

What a "World Without End" Message Means to Us

T he recovery of a world that is "without end, Amen" is an idea whose time has come. Its power to influence the human psyche and thus the future course of history cannot be overestimated. In this author's opinion, the unleashing of this truth is destined to change the cultural and theological landscape. Entire schemes of religious and nonreligious teaching focusing on a future end of the world have run their course; their prophecies have not come true. Instead of striving to hang on till the end, we can have a strong reason to undertake dynamic roles in the present, both individually and corporately, for a better future and for the benefit of coming generations.

> There is one thing stronger than all the armies in the world; and that is an idea whose time has come.—Victor Hugo

Pioneering a new idea is rarely a popular work, at least at first. Historically, the "powers that be" have usually reacted angrily whenever confronted with an upsetting truth. Voltaire, the 18th-century French philosopher, hit it on the head when he surmised, "Our wretched species is so made that those who walk on the well-trodden path always throw stones at those who are showing a new road."

Our road is really not new, but so old and so neglected that it seems new. Thus it will suffer the usual reaction of anger and disbelief. But after a reformational idea bursts onto the public scene and awareness spreads, a paradigm shift begins to take place. People at the grassroots level will soon realize how much the value of the new outweighs the detriments of the old.

The New Paradigm Shift

The word paradigm comes from the Greek *pardeigma* (*para*, side by side + *deiknynai*, to show, point out). A paradigm is a model, a pattern, a frame of reference, or a worldview for understanding and interpreting external reality. It's the way we "see" the world, not visually but by perception. It is the mental framework by which we perceive reality, process information, make decisions, and determine actions. For individuals, it brings order and meaning to our experiences. It's also at the very heart of any culture.

Our paradigm answers our most basic question: What is real? If one's paradigm is the correct way of seeing the world, then one's judgments, decisions, and actions will be correlated and productive. If it's distorted or incorrect, they won't be. In practice, a person may not live what he or she professes, but that person will always live in accordance with his or her paradigm. They live out what they truly believe. Consequently, when our paradigm shifts, many things will change.

Our view of the future is a paradigm. As we've seen, millions have been programmed into believing in an end-of-the-world paradigm. Many are simply following the way they have been raised or parroting what they've heard others say. But others are in bondage to this paradigm, venerating it as a religious icon. They are afraid to raise questions. Some actually want the world to end and even imagine it as a wondrous happening. Call it a termination wish. They see the end as God's, and their own, final vindication. They see it as their best opportunity to escape from the toils and responsibilities of this life, even from death itself. For them the idea that "the world's going to end" sounds so right. Few have bothered to check Scripture for themselves, and most are unaware of its clear and concise promises to the contrary.

It's time this future-destroying deception and fear-mongering crime against humanity was stopped. It's time to stand up against it with something of substance. It's time for a paradigm shift—a mental transformation—that offers a new, optimistic, and opportunistic perspective on the future of the future. Based upon confidence in God's Word, we can "set sail" like Columbus. Yet changes of this nature are never easy, often take time, and are usually achieved incrementally. Sometime shortly after the turn of millennium, I predict a paradigm shift away from the tyranny of termination and into the hopeful, scriptural truth of a world without end.

It's time for a paradigm shift—

This new, open-ended paradigm will force us to reexamine and rethink other end-time assumptions, prophecies, and beliefs. Several of these will be addressed in this book, and more in a subsequent book. But if this world is, indeed, a world without end that was eternally established by a Creator God, isn't our role in taking care of it, and of each other, even more significant? Doesn't this provide more reason and responsibility to pass it along to future generations in a better condition than we found it?

What the New Paradigm Means for the Church

For centuries, we in the Church have imposed on generation after generation of believers, and the rest of the world as well, the view that this world is doomed. Like the tobacco industry, we've been pulling the wool over everyone's eyes, including our own. But we must face the biblical fact that what we have done is wrong! The first task we will have is to get our faith back in order. If the Church is to be taken seriously, it must clamp down on the steady drone of endsayers misinterpreting and exploiting Bible prophecy. It must lay aside these distractions and get its faith right. Then we can take that corrected faith to the world and expect much better results.

To begin this next reform process, let's compare the Bible with our traditions on the issues we've been discussing so far.

The Bible Says:	Tradition Says:
World without end, Amen	The world's going to end
The earth remains forever	The earth shall be destroyed
Generations come and go	We may be the last generation

So who's right? A Christian should believe that the Bible is right. But the Bible also teaches that an "appointed time...of the end" will "come," will "not prove false" and will "not delay" (Hab. 2:3). What's this about? How does this relate to a world without end? It might be comforting to know that Jesus understood the difference. The writers of the New Testament understood it, too. But before we can teach a corrected faith to the world, we, as well, will need to understand the true, biblical meaning and fulfillment of Habakkuk's "appointed time...of the end." As we shall see, it's something quite different from the traditionally-posited, cataclysmic end of the world. This revelation takes us to Daniel and the subject of our next three chapters.

6

Don't Monkey with Daniel *

Something was up, back then in Bible times. Something so big and so imminent that it prompted the 1st-century, Spirit-guided writers of the Bible to make or record such startling statements as,

- …the end of all things is at hand (1 Pe. 4:7 KJV)

- …the fullness of time was come (Gal. 4:4 KJV)

- …the time is fulfilled (Mk. 1:15 KJV)

- …the fulfillment of the ages has come (1 Cor. 10:11)

- …the ends of the world [ages] are come (1 Cor. 10:11 KJV)

- …for these be the days of vengeance, that all things which are written may be fulfilled (Lk. 21:22 KJV)

- …the time is short (1 Cor. 7:29)

---

* Much of the material in this and the next chapter was originally presented by the author at the Evangelical Theological Society's Midwestern Region Meeting in March 1996 in Fort Wayne, Indiana.

- ...for the world in its present form is passing away (1 Cor. 7:31)

- ...it is the last hour (1 Jn. 2:18)

What's the scoop? Why were they talking like this? Is it possible that these words literally mean what they say and, therefore, these writers said what they meant? If so, what could have been so monu-mental and so impending, right there and then and in their lifetime, to justify such emphatic and strong claims? The thoughtful answer to that question is the rest of the greatest story ever told.

No question about it, the 1st-century followers of Christ lived in expectation of something big about to happen, very soon. For them, it was the "last hour." But the last hour of what? Was this big event the proverbial end of the world? The end of time? Or, the conclusion of human history? Obviously it was not. So it had to be something else.

No question about it, the 1st-century followers of Christ lived in expectation of something big about to happen, very soon.

If nothing of radical magnitude happened, befitting this language and imminency, then these statements were mistaken. That is exactly the interpretation that has been given to us by many modern interpreters!

The popular method of interpretation qualifies or changes the meanings of these words to remove their imminency from the time period in which they were penned. But this will not do if we believe God's Word is inerrant. Each statement uses common, easily under-stood words. They are not just sayings that could be used at any time, anywhere, under any circumstance, up until the end. They specify an event or events that have a specific time frame. They cannot be dragged out over thousands of years. Instead of being puzzled or resorting to constant qualifying, we'd be well-advised to honor these inspired statements as God-given, clear, and precise. Let's consider the possibility that they meant exactly what they said for that particular time, a most important time when "the time" of something extremely significant had grown very "short."

If the event was that important, and supposed to happen soon, what could it have been?

The Two-age Jewish View of Time

To help us discover what was going on, let's put ourselves inside the 1st-century scene. Foundational to both Judaic and Christian thought in that century was the division of time between two consecutive periods— "this present age," and "the age to come." Back then, they were living in "this present age," the age of Moses, the Old Covenant age of the Temple system. "The age to come" was being anticipated. It was to be a golden age of God in which all of God's promises to Israel would be fully realized, and God's power would operate in a new and better way.

This dual concept of time represented the Jewish expectation for God's plan of redemptive history here on earth. They did not view history as a series of unending ages, but stressed these two distinct and contrasting periods. No parenthetical age, third age, or interruption between the two ages was ever envisioned. The line of demarcation, or transition, between the two ages would be accomplished by a visitation of God. Specifically, it was to be ushered in by the coming of the Messiah (Saviour) into human history, along with a terrible coming of "the day of the Lord," and the establishment of the eternal kingdom here on earth.

Although these two-age expressions are not found in the Old Testament, they are found in the New. Jesus reinforced this Jewish differentiation of time (Mt. 12:32; Lk. 20:35), and especially drew attention to it in his famous prophecy of "the end of the age" (see Mt. 24; Lk. 21; Mk. 13). He also equated "the end of the age" with the harvest of the kingdom (Mt. 13:39), and "the age to come" with eternal life (Mk. 10:30; Lk. 18:30). Paul and the Hebrews' writer also spoke of this age division (Gal. 1:4; Eph. 1:21; Heb. 6:5). These expressions were well known to 1st-century hearers.

The Jewish religious society of that day had been well-schooled, and clearly understood that the Messiah, at his coming, would end "this present age" and usher in "the age to come" (the Messianic age). Most rabbis believed that this period of transition between the two ages would last about 40 years, like the wilderness wandering, like the reigns of David and Solomon, and the three 40-year periods of Moses' life. They believed it would take place within the confines of history.[1] But Jesus didn't usher in this new age during his earthly ministry, or so most traditions have assumed. Therefore, reasoned the Jews—from that day to the present—Jesus could not be the promised Messiah.

Peter, a 1st-century Jew who believed that Jesus *was* the Messiah, penned these basic words naming time and consummation, "the end of all things is at hand" (1 Pe. 4:7 KJV). What did he mean?

Habakkuk's Appointed Time of the End

We modern-day mortals have not been left to wonder about the timing, duration, or nature of this most important, age-changing, transitionary, and consummatory period. It's variously termed the end times, the eschaton,[2] or, biblically, "the last days," "the last time(s)", "the time of the end" or just "the end." Hence, the biblical meaning for "the end" is the place for us to begin.

Two Old-Testament prophets, Habakkuk and Daniel, prophesied the time of the end. They are in agreement, and one prophecy gives light to the other. In the 7th century B.C., God inspired the Old Testament prophet Habakkuk to prophesy:

> For the revelation awaits an appointed time; it speaks of the end and will not prove false. Though it linger, wait for it; it will certainly come and will not delay (Hab. 2:3).

At that time, neither Habakkuk nor any one else had any idea when this "appointed time...of the end" (not "end of time"—big difference[3]) would come, or what events would accompany it. All Habakkuk knew was that there was an appointed time, that it would "not prove false," that it would "certainly come," and that it would "not delay."

One century later, in the 6th century B.C., God supernaturally gave another Old Testament prophet, Daniel, the two most spectacular and explicit time prophecies ever given to humankind. They are "Daniel's 70 weeks," and the "time of the end." You'll find them in Daniel 9:24-27 and 12:4-12, respectively. Like bookends, these two prophetic time periods bracketed the exact time in history for this coming of the Messiah and Habakkuk's "appointed time...of the end." They foretold the climactic events that would signal the consummation of God's redemptive plan for the world.

Daniel's two time prophecies, are some of the most misunderstood and misapplied passages of Scripture.

Unfortunately, much disagreement has arisen among both Christian and Jewish scholars over how and when Daniel's prophecy occurred. Some even say that Daniel's book was a "contemporary" forgery composed after-the-fact in the 2nd century B.C. This, they claim, accounts for its accuracy—it was "predicting" events that had already occurred. This view, however, seems illogical when we note the reverence given to the book of Daniel in Jewish Scripture. It was so prized, revered, and accepted by the 1st-century B.C. scribes in the Qumran community that they made more copies of it than any other Old Testament book. These two factors indicate their regard of Daniel as authoritative.[4]

In a similar fashion, Daniel's two time prophecies, elaborating on Habakkuk's "appointed time...of the end," are (it is almost needless to say) some of the most misunderstood and misapplied passages of Scripture. The popular view among Christian evangelicals in our day is that this "appointed time" has been delayed (or put on hold), and is yet future. But this is in direct contradiction to Habakkuk's text, and invalidates the very inspiration these proponents seek to uphold. As we shall see, there is a better, more fitting, and simpler fulfillment framework that keeps the biblical inspiration intact.

Daniel Is the Key to the End Times

Because Daniel provides the key to understanding the "end times," we will give it close attention. It is the basis upon which all other end-time prophecies and events rise or fall. Our main point is that God is not ambiguous or deceptive with his use of time prophescies or time statements in Scripture, and Daniel proves this point. There are no hidden or secretly encoded meanings in Daniel's two time prophecies. They are plainly written and Daniel got it exactly right. Nothing illustrates the supernatural character of the Bible better than this ability to predict the time and nature of end-time events.

In this chapter and the next, we will examine the historical evidence supporting the literal, exact, chronological, and sequential fulfillment of Daniel's two time prophecies. We will see that:

- God doesn't play word games with these time prophecies. They are his self-imposed boundaries and his framework for the end-times. No artificial interpretative devices such as gaps, interruptions, postponements, delays, elongations, twisted dates, flip-flopped segments, symbolic appeals, non-literal tampering, or esoteric qualifying methods of any kind are required to properly understand this fulfillment. God intended that Daniel's time prophecies be clearly understood, not confusing and divisive.

- They present the "big picture" and central theme of the whole Bible—man's problem and God's solution—i.e., redemption. They contain God's predetermined blueprint for this course of human and redemptive history. Their events lead up to and include Habakkuk's appointed time of the end. It was precisely pinpointed, did not prove false, certainly came, and did not delay (Hab. 2:3).

- Like bookends, Daniel's two prophecies identify the front end (70th week) and the back end (time of the end) of Habakkuk's appointed time of the end. Daniel covers the complete and indivisible transition period between "this present age" and "the age to come," and not the demise of planet Earth or the end of human existence.

- This fulfillment in literal timing and in two unbroken time periods is *the overriding precedent* for the proper interpretation of all other end-time prophecies and time statements, and a *starting point for prophecy reform*.

- God's time trustworthiness throughout his Word is totally consistent. It is the discipline to which all interpretations of the consummation must adhere. It's also *the ultimate apologetic*— the final proof in defense of the faith.

In Daniel's day, the 6th century B.C., this transitional period of history was still in the "distant future" (Da. 8:19, 26). Daniel was told to go his way because "the words are closed up and sealed until the time of the end" (Da. 12:9). In stark contrast, John's 1st-century book of Revelation is left unsealed. The angel tells John, "Do not seal up the words of the prophecy of this book, because the time is at hand" (Rev. 22:10). Note the significant difference.

A word of caution. Over the centuries many scholars have offered a wide variety of conflicting and manipulative interpretations of Daniel's prophecies. Using questionable techniques, they have built a wide array of different end-time expectations and scenarios. The interpretation outline in this and the next chapter is—in our opinion—the most straightforward, historically documentable, and inspirationally impressive. Even a hard-boiled skeptic must be impressed by its unaltered, uninterrupted, and chronological exactness. As you read, keep in mind that it's not all-important to agree with every detail in order to grasp the totality of what exactly transpired during these two interrelated time periods and the transition in between. Keep in mind that if some aspects were not fulfilled and still lie in the future, as most popular views hold, then Habakkuk's "appointed time of the end" failed to arrive on time; it proved false. But such truncated views violate the integrity of Scripture. If it was delayed, then Habakkuk prophesied falsely, for he said it would certainly come, and would not be delayed. We'd be well advised not to monkey with Daniel and his two time prophecies. Instead, let's see how they can be understood in a straightforward sense.

Daniel's Time Prophecy of 70 Weeks

Around the year 538 B.C., some 2,500 years ago, the Israelites were in captivity in Babylon. At this time the prophet Daniel prayed to the God of Israel for his people. He knew that God had decreed beforehand, through the prophet Jeremiah, a precise 70-year period of captivity (Da. 9:1-2; Jer. 25:11-12; 29:10).[5] Since Daniel and a first group of captives were deported in 605 B.C., he realized that Jeremiah's prophecy was near completion. It was time for their release and return to their homeland. As he prayed, the angel Gabriel appeared to him. In answer to his petition for the forgiveness and restoration of a repeatedly rebellious Israel, Gabriel gave Daniel a powerful prophetic vision. He was to have clear "insight and understanding" (Da. 9:22) of the extended future that God had determined for the Jews. Part of that vision was the time prophecy of "seventy sevens," or 70 weeks of years (Da. 9:24-27 [KJV]):

> Seventy 'sevens' are decreed [determined] for your people and your holy city to finish transgression, to put an end to sin, to atone for wickedness, to bring in everlasting righteousness, to seal up vision and prophecy and to anoint the most holy.

> Know and understand this: From the issuing of the decree to restore and rebuild Jerusalem until the Anointed One, the ruler, comes, there will be seven 'sevens,' and sixty-two 'sevens.' It will be rebuilt with

streets and a trench, but in times of trouble. After the sixty-two 'sevens,' the Anointed One will be cut off and will have nothing. The people of the ruler who will come will destroy the city and the sanctuary. The end will come like a flood: War will continue until the end, and desolations have been decreed [are determined]. He will confirm a covenant with many for one 'seven,' but in the middle of that 'seven' he will put an end to sacrifice and offering. And one who causes desolation will place abominations on a wing of the temple until the end that is decreed [determined] is poured out on him.

The Hebrew word (*sha bu'a*), translated above as "sevens," or "weeks" in some versions, literally means a unit, a period or a group of seven of something. It's akin to our English word *dozen*, which means a unit of twelve of something. The word by itself does not tell us what the units are. Most interpreters agree that Daniel's sevens of something was sevens of years. They have two good reasons:

1) Jeremiah's original prophecy of "seventy" was an explicit period of 70 years of Babylonian captivity. This time of deportation was to serve as both the setting (2 Ch. 36:21) and an uninterrupted archetype for Daniel's 70 weeks.

2) This concept of time was not new. God had used the same biblical concept of "weeks of years" from the beginning of Israel's history under Moses (Lev. 25:8). He had equated days to years for determining their period of wandering in the wilderness (Nu. 14:34). He had divided the Hebrew calendar into seven-year periods with every seventh year being a sabbatical year. Also, the seven years that Jacob worked for Rachel was called "the fulfilling of her week" (Ge. 29:27, 28 KJV). We agree with the standard interpretation that "seventy sevens" means "seventy times seven years, or a total time span equating to 490 years.

The angel Gabriel further stated that both the duration and contents of this divinely fixed time period of 490 years were "decreed [or determined] for your people (the Jews) and your holy city (Jerusalem)." This time period's express purpose was to reveal the exact time in human history when God would send the "Anointed One, the ruler" or "Messiah the Prince" to Israel, begin his public ministry, and confirm a covenant for one week of years (seven years). Thus, Daniel's 70 weeks prophecy historically links the Old Covenant, Judaic period to the New Covenant, Christian period.

The total elapsed time of 490 years further demonstrates that the course of events was already decided. It had a specific starting and finishing point, and was subdivided into three time segments: 1) an initial period of "seven sevens" (49 years), 2) a period of "sixty-two sevens" (434 years), and 3) a final period of "one seven" (7 years).

the God of the Bible is the God of exactness and history told in advance.

Scripturally, we can examine this prophesied 490-year period and verify its determinism and accuracy. Historically, we can see it transpire as a firm, unbroken sequence of chronological time and events. For those accustomed to a postponement tradition, the following exposition may be disturbing or even threatening. For others, it will be quite illuminating. For all, it is important validation of the biblical faith that must not be overlooked or truncated. The hope is that you'll be convinced that this explanation demonstrates that the God of the Bible is the God of exactness and history told in advance. As the one, true, and proven God (Isa. 44:6-8; 41:22-29; 42:9; 45:21-22; 46:9-10; 48:3-6; Am. 3:7), He has spoken through his prophets to all humanity. The sincere seeker of truth will surely recognize and understand the precision and drama of Daniel's prophecy.

Beginning at 457 B.C. and using the ancient dating chronology of Ptolemy,[6] we present, section by section, the historic fulfillment of Daniel's 70 weeks, with no gaps and no gimmicks:

The Starting Point

457 B.C. ...from the issuing of the decree to restore and rebuild Jerusalem... (Da. 9:25).

The Bible records three decrees by Gentile kings that affected the restoration and rebuilding of Jerusalem (Ezra 6:14):

- Cyrus' Decree in 538 B.C. (recorded in Ezra 1:2-4)

- Darius' Decree around 520 B.C. (Ezra 6:3-12)

- Artaxerxes' Decree, dated by the majority of historians and Bible scholars at 457 B.C. (Ezra 7:11-26).

Which is the right one for the starting-point of Daniel's 70 weeks of years?

The decree and date which best begins the grand countdown of 490 years is the last one, Artaxerxes', in 457 B.C. (see footnote 6 above). It is the best for three reasons:

1) In retrospect, dating from the first two decrees has no literal, future, or chronological significance, or historical prophetic value. But dating from Artaxerxes' Decree does.

2) Some interpreters feel Cyrus' Decree should be the starting point, since the prophet Isaiah, a century and a half before, had foretold that a man by that name would decree the rebuilding of Jerusalem and the Temple (Isa. 44:26-28; 45:1-4). But for some unknown reason, both Cyrus' and Darius' decrees, as recorded in Scripture, only called for the rebuilding of the Temple in Jerusalem and made no mention of the city or the restoration of Israel as a people.[7] Big difference. A rebuilt Temple would enable the Jews to offer sacrifices and pray for the well-being of the king (Ezra 6:10). But a rebuilt city would provide the Jews with a military fortress. They

could then rebel again, and this was a concern of Israel's enemies, as seen in the letter to the king of Persia (Ezra 4:12,15). Using the 538 B.C. date as the starting point would require either a time gap or a symbolic reading of the numbers for the time period to come out with any significant meaning. Note that 538 B.C. plus 490 literal years only works out to 48 B.C., and nothing of significance occurred then.

3) Artaxerxes' Decree, nearly one hundred years later in 457 B.C., and his subsequent letters of passage issued in 445-444 B.C. (mentioned in Nehemiah 2:5-8), covered everything.[8] This is the latest possible date for the beginning of Daniel's 70 weeks. In addition, these associated letters specifically mentioned both the rebuilding of the city and the Temple.

The First Segment: the Seven Sevens

457 - 408 B.C. ...*It will be rebuilt with streets and a trench, but in times of trouble...* (Da. 9:25).

The first segment of 49 years spanned the restoring and rebuilding of Jerusalem under the administration of Ezra and Nehemiah. You can read about it in the book of Nehemiah, especially chapters 2-6. Nehemiah records how the Jews returned from captivity and worked "in times of trouble," just as Daniel had prophesied. Carrying materials with one hand and a weapon in the other, returning Jews rebuilt the walls in 52 days (Ne. 4:17-18; 6:15). This was only part of the restoration. They also restored the streets and houses (Ne. 7:4); instituted laws, civil ordinances (Ne. 7:5), and religious reforms (Ne. 13:30); and finished settling in Jerusalem within this 49-year time segment (Ne. 11:1).[9]

The Second Segment: Sixty-two Sevens

408 B.C. - A.D. 27 Sixty-two sevens, (i.e., 434 more consecutive years) pass. Note that no interval or interruptive gap between the 7- and 62-week segments is suggested in the text. Toward the close of this second segment, messianic expectations began running high in the Promised Land, and for good reason. Daniel's time prophecy was well known, and its fulfillment was being anticipated. In addition, Jesus Christ was born, most probably in 4 B.C., not A.D. 0, as is sometimes assumed. (Mistakes made in transposing dates into the commonly accepted Christian calendar by the 6th century A.D. Roman monk, Dionysius Exiguus, account for this dating discrepancy.)

The Third Segment: One Seven—the First Half

A.D. 27-30. ...*until the Anointed One, the ruler, comes, there will be seven 'sevens' and sixty-two 'sevens'...* (Da. 9:25).

This one week is the most significant and the most misunderstood. It will require special attention. To help our understanding, we have divided it into four sections: first half, middle, second half, and finishing point.

An "anointing" event marks both the conclusion of the second 62-week segment and the beginning of Daniel's 70th and final week of unbroken and uninterrupted years.

Again, there is no suggestion in the text of any interval or interruptive gap between the 62- and 1-week segments. Simple arithmetic shows 483 years (49 + 434 years) had elapsed since Artaxerxes' Decree in 457 B.C. It's now A.D. 27. Jesus Christ, "the Anointed One, the ruler" (or "Messiah the Prince"),[10] who had emptied Himself of his glory, authority, and power to become like other men (Php. 2:27-8; Heb. 2:17), is hereby publicly identified as the Messiah with his baptism in the Jordan River. At that moment he is *anointed* by the Holy Spirit. No previous or subsequent event in Jesus' earthly life could be taken as the fulfillment of these words of Gabriel to Daniel (see Ac. 10:38; Heb. 1:9). Luke reports that Jesus was 30 years of age at that time (Lk. 3:22-23). As was the Jewish custom, the 30th year was the age at which men of Israel were permitted to become active in temple or tabernacle service. Next Jesus departed and went into the wilderness for a period of forty days (Lk. 4:1-2). Luke 4:13-21 then records that after Jesus had been tempted in the wilderness, He went to Nazareth where He had been raised, stood up in the synagogue, and read the messianic prophecy from Isaiah 61:1-

2 regarding the coming of an "anointed one" and "the year of the Lord's favor." Then Jesus said, "Today this scripture is fulfilled in your hearing."

Something else, however, is especially noteworthy about Jesus' quotation from Isaiah. He stopped in mid-verse. He did not quote the last half of Isaiah 61:2 concerning "the day of vengeance of our God." Why not? Because the time period for the fulfillment of that day of judgment was not yet present. Its fulfillment awaited the future time of Daniel's "time of the end," which we'll cover in the next chapter.

From the day of his anointing, Jesus moved in the power and authority of the New Covenant. During the next 3¹/₂ years of his earthly ministry, Jesus taught and demonstrated the new in-breaking kingdom of God (Da. 2:44; 7:14, 18, 22, 27) and modeled its "powers of the age to come" (Heb. 6:5). Also, He trained and commanded his followers to do likewise. Thus, "Jesus came into Galilee, preaching and manifesting the gospel of the kingdom of God, and saying, the time is fulfilled..." (Mk. 1:14-15 KJV). What time was He talking about? It was the fullness of Daniel's 70 weeks time prophecy. The 70th week was upon them, precisely, right on time. Next we must read closely. What is to happen *after* the sixty-two sevens is crucial to our understanding.

> After sixty-two 'sevens' the Anointed One will be cut off and will have nothing. The people of the ruler who will come will destroy the city and the sanctuary. The end will come like a flood: War will continue until the end, and desolations have been decreed [determined]...And one who causes desolation will place abominations on a wing of the temple until the end that is decreed [determined] is poured out on him. (Da. 9:26 [KJV])

The only time restriction here is "after" sixty-two sevens (the 69th week, 483 years). It is not predicting that all this will happen during the 70th week of years. It is simply saying "after" the 69th week. Nor does it say how long after—just after. However, we know that the final week began with Jesus' anointing 3 years earlier.

So, the Messiah being "cut off"[11] so as to "have nothing" meant He was crucified and had nothing befitting the Messiah. This did occur during the middle of that 70th week in A.D. 30. He was without his messianic kingdom. This event is time-restricted in the next verse, and will be addressed in our next section on the middle of the 70th week.

Hence, we have separated the "cutting off" (the crucifixion), which is time-restricted to the middle of the final week, from the other events of Daniel 9:26, which are not so restricted, but only named as coming "after" the sixty-two weeks. We know from history that these events occurred 37 years after the crucifixion.

The other events that were to come "after" the sixty-two weeks are the destruction of Jerusalem and the Temple, and desolations and abominations. They were "decreed" or "determined" (meaning fixed and unable to be changed) *within* Daniel's 70th week, when most of Israel did not or would not recognize the time of its visitation by Messiah, just as Jesus had warned (Lk. 19:41-44). These decreed events (the destruction, desolations and abominations) did not take place until the decade of A.D. 60 - 70 because they were part of *the end* and were associated with Daniel's other time prophecy, the *time of the end*. In Daniel's last chapter, Gabriel gave Daniel this second time prophecy for the chronological fulfillment of those predetermined, time-of-the-end events. As we shall discover, it has its own, separate time frame, different time parameters, and different terminology.

How can we be so sure these end-time events were only "decreed" or "determined" *within* Daniel's 70th week and not fulfilled in that time segment? The answer is found in the way the Hebrew word is used elsewhere. In Daniel 11:36, the same Hebrew word [*charats*], translated as "decreed" or "determined," is used in a future fulfillment sense, "...for what has been determined must take place." Hence, "decreed" or "determined" [past tense] does not require that all events "happen" during that same time frame, although some did. Others were set, or locked into motion (determined) for future fulfillment. This distinction must be understood. It enables us to maintain the integrity of Daniel's two interrelated and interconnected time frames without resorting to gaps or gimmicks.

The Middle of the Final Week

A.D. 30. ...*He will confirm a covenant with many for one 'seven,' but in the middle of that seven, he [Jesus, the Messiah] shall put an end to sacrifice and offering...* (Da. 9:27).

Note that this later event is in the middle of the last week, the same time as the previous "cutting off." The crucifixion of the Messiah is time restricted to the middle of the 70th week, and so is the end of sacrifice and offering. Even though the Jews continued the practice of animal sacrifices and offerings for another 40 years, Christ's death and resurrection ended the Old Covenant obligation. It no longer had value and acceptability. It had been superseded by the "once-for-all...sacrifice" of Christ (Heb. 9:26, 10:10; 1 Pe. 3:18). What's more, it sealed or "determined" the fulfillment of all six of the redemptive purposes and promises for Daniel's 70 weeks time prophecy stated in verse 24:

1. To finish transgression
2. To make an end of sin
3. To atone for wickedness
4. To bring in everlasting righteousness
5. To seal up the vision and prophecy
6. To anoint the most holy (place)

Hence, "decreed" or "determined" [past tense] does not require that all events "happen" during that same time frame, although some did.

This is restoration language. It speaks of the final portion of God's plan for redeeming humankind from the consequences of sin. With his death on the cross, Jesus set in motion this restorative and consummatory process. But, as we shall see throughout this book, the new could not fully come, nor all six of these puposes and promises be fully brought in and totally fulfilled, until the old was completely removed at the "time of the end." That time was still in the future for those living in A.D. 30. But it would "not prove false, it would "certainly come," and would "not delay," just as Habakkuk had prophesied.

The Second Half

A.D. 30 - 34. After the Messiah was "cut off," or crucified, as the prophet Isaiah had also foretold (Isa. 53:8), his disciples and followers obediently stayed in Jerusalem awaiting and then experiencing the events of Pentecost (Lk. 24:49). But after Pentecost they did *not* yet disperse and "Go...and teach all nations" or "make disciples of all nations," as Jesus had commanded (Mt. 28:19 KJV - NIV). Why didn't they? Because the covenant was to be confirmed for "one seven" (one week of years), first and exclusively upon the Jews (Da. 9:24; Ro. 1:16; Jn. 4:22). The purpose and focus of Daniel's last week of years was to be a 7-year period of covenant confirmation for the Jews. Half of this final "one-seven" segment still remained. The covenant to be confirmed was the one promised through the prophet Jeremiah (Jer. 31:31-33). The first half of $3^{1}/_{2}$ years was fulfilled by the earthly ministry of Jesus Christ and his disciples. That meant that $3^{1}/_{2}$ more years were to be fulfilled before Jesus' followers would be free to take the Gospel outside the Jewish realm. To this day, most Jews don't recognize that their prophet Isaiah said the Servant (the Messiah) would also be sent to the Gentiles (Isa. 49:6 f).

The biblical fact of Jewish preeminence is frequently emphasized throughout the gospels. God set it up that way. Remember, Jesus did not minister to the Gentiles (with a few notable foreshadowing exceptions). He had commanded his disciples, "Go not into

the way of the Gentiles, and into any city of the Samaritans enter ye
not; but go rather to the lost sheep of the house of Israel" (Mt. 10:5-
6; 15:24 KJV). Is Jesus' command here in contradiction to his Great
Commission command to go and teach [make] disciples of all nations (Mt. 28:18-29)? No, it is not. Why? Because there was a
time-restricted waiting period in which the New Covenant was to
be confirmed with the Jews exclusively. That time was during the
seven years of Daniel's 70th and final week.

Jesus' disciples knew this. How did they know? Quite simply; in
Luke we are told that Jesus expounded and explained in all the
Scriptures the things concerning Himself. He began at Moses and
proceeded through all the prophets (Lk. 24:27). Jesus' teaching
would have most certainly included Daniel, the Jews' most copied
book, and Daniel's prophecy of 70 weeks pertaining to the Messiah.
Further, "He opened their minds so they could understand the Scriptures" (Lk. 24:45). The Bible says that Jesus' teaching caused their
hearts to burn within them (Lk. 24:32). This is how they knew that
they were prohibited in where and to whom they could go until
the time restriction ran its course. Consequently, they remained in
Jerusalem and preached exclusively to the Jews until the time
was up.

The Finishing Point

A.D. 34. Toward the end of A.D. 33, Jewish persecution of Christians in Jerusalem reached a climax with the stoning death of Stephen
(Ac. 7:54-60). The Bible says that all except the apostles were
scattered throughout Judea and Samaria (Ac. 8:1).

The event that documents the finishing point of Daniel's 70th
week occurred when "Philip went down to a city in Samaria, and
proclaimed Christ there" (Ac. 8:5). How could he do this? Hadn't
Christ forbidden it? What's more, the apostles in Jerusalem sent
Peter and John to Samaria as a support team to build on what Philip
had started (Ac. 8:14f). Were they disobeying Jesus' prohibition on
going to the Gentiles? The answer is no, because it was now
A.D. 34.

The time restriction for confirming the New Covenant exclusively for the Jews was now chronologically over.[12] The Gospel of the New Covenant had come first to the Jews, then to the Samaritans, who, as half breeds, were despised by the Jews (Ac. 8), and finally to the Gentiles (Ac. 10; 11:18-20) and the whole world. In this manner, the mystery of God uniting Jew and Gentile in one body was phased into human history (Jn. 4:22; Eph. 3:3-6, 9; Col. 1:26-27; 2:2; 4:3; Ro. 3:29-23; 15:26-27). God's grand purpose was never to make boundaries between peoples or nations, but to make all into one.

In retrospect, then, the prophecy of Daniel's 70 weeks:

- *Commenced* in 457 B.C. with the decree of Artaxerxes,

- Was *determined* in A.D. 30 at the cross.

- Was *confirmed* by the New Covenant for $3^1/_2$ years before and $3^1/_2$ years after the cross.

- *Concluded* in A.D. 34 when the Gospel had been preached to the Jews and was now freed to go to the Gentiles.

The entire prophecy transpired in an uninterrupted 490-year period. No valid rationale exists for interrupting the time segments, splitting apart the years, inserting gaps, elongating weeks, or postponing, delaying, minimizing or tampering with the fixed time period in any manner. Thus, the front bookend of the end-time, age-changing transition period—Daniel's 70th week—certainly came and was perfectly fulfilled. Perfectly! It's a mainstay of messianic authentication, a mathematical demonstration for the divine inspiration of the Bible, and an unanswerable argument for critics of the faith.

Even so, all was not complete. More that had been "decreed" or "determined" remained to be accomplished, a fact which brings us to our back bookend, our final time period, and the grand finale of the end that would shortly come to pass. *(See Appendix A for a timeline of the events outlined in this chapter.)*

7

Daniel's Time of the End

We find Daniel's second time prophecy in his chapter 12, verses 4-13. It serves as the back bookend or boundary of the age-changing transition we call the "end times." The biblical term is the "time of the end" (Da. 12:4, 9; 11:35; 8:19), not the "end of time." Big difference! The Bible never speaks of an end of time. Changing the order of these words has led many into gross error, such as end-of-the-world misconceptions.

But you, Daniel, close up and seal the words of the scroll until the time of the end. Many will go here and there to increase knowledge.

Then, I Daniel, looked, and there before me stood two others, one on this bank of the river and one on the opposite bank. One of them said to the man clothed in linen, who was above the waters of the river, "How long will it be before these astonishing things are fulfilled?"

The man clothed in linen, who was above the waters of the river, lifted his right hand and his left hand toward heaven, and I heard him swear by him who lives forever, saying, "It will be for a time, times and

half a time. When the power of the holy people has been finally broken, all these things will be complete."

He replied, "Go your way, Daniel, because the words are closed up
and sealed until the time of the end. Many will be purified, made
spotless and refined, but the wicked will continue to be wicked. None
of the wicked will understand, but those who are wise will
understand.

"From the time that the daily sacrifice is abolished and the abomination that causes desolation is set up, there will be 1,290 days. Blessed
is the one who waits for and reaches the end of the 1,335 days.

"As for you, go your way till the end. You will rest, and then at the
end of the days you will rise to receive your allowed
inheritance."

In his previous 70-week prophecy, Daniel referred to some of
the events that would take place during this "time of the end,"
including the fall of Jerusalem, the destruction of the Jewish Temple,
and many other desolations of war (see Da. 9:26). But these events
were only "decreed" or "determined" within Daniel's 70th week. Their
actual occurrence (fulfillment) lies outside that time period. But
how can we be sure this interpretation is correct?

In his last vision, Daniel sees two others (angels) standing on
the bank of a river and talking. One asks the other, "How long will it
be before these astonishing things are fulfilled?" (Da. 12:6b). The
asking of this time question subsequent to Daniel receiving his 70
week prophecy strongly suggests that the events of this fulfillment
were not included in that previous time period. This is evidently
why Daniel is given another time prophecy for another sovereignly
determined time period. Note that this one uses different time terminology, which differentiates it from the 490-year time span covered
by Daniel's 70 weeks.

This second prophecy speaks in terms of straight days (1,290
and 1,335) instead of "sevens" or "weeks" of years. The two sets of
days are not two separate time periods, but rather the shorter

period is inclusive within the longer. This can be legitimately surmised since it was also specified that the "time of the end" would be "for a time, times and half a time," or approximately a year, two years, and half a year. It links back to the same terminology used in Daniel 7:25-28 and was the standard Jewish interpretation contained in their rabbinical writings and commentaries. Further, it compares with the 2,300 evenings and mornings (Da. 8:14) of temporary cessation of Temple services occurring during the three-year and two-month period of occupation by Antiochus Epiphanes in 167-164 B.C. (covered in chapter ten).

Daniel's "time of the end" would be a time of intensified trouble (Da. 12:1) and divine judgment. That judgment would be poured out upon Daniel's people (Israel) "in the latter days" (Da. 10:14 KJV), because of their continual breaking of the covenant, and their rebellion against God and his plan of redemption by the Messiah. The climax would occur "when the power of the holy people (the Jews) has been finally broken." At that time, "all these things" concerning

---

... judgment would be poured out upon Daniel's people (Israel) "in the latter days"

---

the "time of the end" would "be complete" (Da. 12:7). So, what was this "power of the holy people?" It was the biggest power anyone could have—the power of biblical Judaism (i.e., their exclusive relationship with God) as manifested by the Temple complex (Isa. 2:2-5; 56:7). The final breaking of this power was to be both the historical setting and defining characteristic for Daniel's "time of the end." Note that this distinguishing element was *not* to be the demise of planet Earth, the end of human existence, the removal of believers from the world, a 1,000-year reign of Christ or any of the other traditional end-time notions.

In contrast, however, to the wealth of Scripture supporting the fulfillment of Daniel's 70-weeks time prophecy, none exists concerning the fulfillment of Daniel's "time of the end." Why not? A strong case can be made that all the books later included in the New Testament canon were written before the "time of the end." However, with the help of Josephus (A.D. 37 - 100),[1] the 1st-century Jewish priest and renowned historian who was an eyewitness to the end time, we have authentication for the fulfillment of Daniel's final, "time-of-the-end" prophecy—again, no gaps and no gimmicks, but literal, exact, chronological and sequential fulfillment:

The Starting Point

A.D. 66. (Da. 12:11) ...*from the time that the daily sacrifice is abolished...*

In July of A.D. 66, Josephus records that, as part of the Jewish rebellion against Rome, Jewish Zealots stormed Jerusalem and burned the palace of Agrippa and Bernice (the Roman ruler and his sister). They also burned the palace of the Jewish High Priest, Ananias, and killed him in retaliation for his liberal affiliation with the Romans. Next, they massacred a garrison of Roman soldiers. And to top it off, they stopped performing the twice-daily Temple sacrifices for Caesar and the Roman people. Josephus states that this cessation of the daily sacrifice was the true beginning of the Roman-Jewish War.[2] Both the Romans and the revolting Jews viewed it as a formal declaration of war. The total cessation of all sacrifices didn't take place until the Jews ran out of priests and animals in August of A.D. 70, just prior to the fall of Jerusalem and the destruction of the Temple by the Roman army.

1,290 Days Later   (Da. 12:11) ...*and the abomination that causes desolation is set up, there will be 1,290 days.*

Earlier, Daniel had referred to "desolations" (note the plural) that had been "decreed" or "determined" (Da. 9:26b), and stated that "one who causes desolation (note the singular) will place abominations on a wing of the temple until the end that is decreed is poured out on him" (Da. 9:27b).[3] "Wing" refers to a pinnacle or an extreme point of abominations. Again, the determination was done during the 70 weeks, but their fulfillments were not a chronological part of the 70 weeks' time frame. As we saw in the last chapter, the only restriction was "after" the second 62-week segment, and not "during" that third segment.

Early in the year of A.D. 70 (approximately—if not exactly—three years and six months, or 1,290 days, after the cessation of the twice-daily sacrifice for Caesar and Rome), Josephus reports that a major abomination that all in Jerusalem could see took place in the Temple. While the Roman Army (under the leadership of Titus) was encamped in Caesarea on the Mediterranean Sea, approximately 55 miles northwest of Jerusalem, and marshaling its forces for the final campaign against Jerusalem, civil strife between three rival, Jewish factions inside the city walls reached a climax. Rival Zealot factions defiled the Temple's innermost courts with murders as fierce fighting raged between the Jews struggling for control. The Temple was their battleground and was defiled with carnage at every corner. Even worshipers were killed while trying to offer their sacrifices.[4]

There can be no doubt that the warring of the three Jewish factions inside the city walls (and particularly in the Temple area) was one of the many abominations and desolations spoken of by Daniel. But even this was not the worst or the pinnacle. Josephus details how the Jews frequently and blatantly desecrated their own Temple during the time of the Roman-Jewish War. As a Jewish priest himself, and speaking from a priestly point of view, he felt that these Temple atrocities and their impact on the rest of the Jewish people were what eventually led to the complete desolation of Jerusalem and the Temple by the Roman legions.

A strong argument can be made that the Jews brought the final desolation upon themselves. When all the facts are known, the Jews were "the people of the ruler [i.e., the people of Jesus, and not the Roman army under Titus' command or some future Antichrist ruler] who will come and destroy the city and the sanctuary" (Da. 9:26). The question of who destroyed Jerusalem has been equated with the age-old question of who crucified Christ?" In both cases, the Romans tried to avoid the final action. But the Jews' abominable and self-destructive activities forced the Romans to act. You can read about it in Josephus' eyewitness accounts of the Jewish rebellion and the subsequent Roman-Jewish War in A.D. 66 - 73.[5]

The Finishing Point
1335 Days Later

A.D. 70 (Da. 12:12) *Blessed is the one who waits for and reaches the end of the 1,335 days.*

Jesus warned his first followers, "When you see Jerusalem surrounded by armies, you will know that its desolation is near...For this is the time of punishment in fulfillment of all that has been written" (Lk. 21:20, 22; see also Lk. 19:43-44).

Shortly before Passover in the spring of A.D. 70 (approximately— if not exactly—45 days following the previously-cited Temple desecration),Titus' Roman legions advanced toward Jerusalem from the Northwest through Samaria (the invader from the "north" of Ezekiel 38 and 39). He "set up" three encampments within three miles of the walls on the hills surrounding and overlooking Jerusalem. This was the fourth and final encampment of armies around Jerusalem during the Roman-Jewish War period. Although it is not possible to know the final "day or hour" (Mt. 24:36; 25:13), this "setting up" occurred precisely within the 1,335-day time period prophesied to Daniel. The "time of the end" was now at hand. And, as we'll see in chapter ten, Jesus had given the Jews ample signs and warnings that this end was coming upon them within their lifetime. And come it did. In April of A.D. 70, the Roman army began the fourth and final siege of the war. In September, it was over. Not only the city and the Temple but the whole of biblical Judaism was utterly destroyed and left desolated. This Roman siege, using 1st-century warfare technology, was precisely the form of judgment

Jesus had promised was coming (Lk. 19:41-44). It was also the fulfillment of "the day of vengeance of God." This was the portion of Isaiah 61:1-2 which Jesus, 43 years earlier, auspiciously did not quote while reading the scroll in the synagogue (Lk. 4:13-21). But at just the right time, the "appointed time of the end" had "certainly come," it did "not prove false," and did "not delay," just as God's prophet, Habakkuk, had prophesied almost eight centuries earlier.

... both the historical setting and defining characteristic of Daniel's "time of the end" achieved fulfillment in A.D. 70 when the "the power of the holy people" was "finally broken."

All the events cited in this and the last chapter as fulfillment of Daniel's two time prophecies (the 70 weeks and "time of the end") took place literally, exactly, chronologically, and sequentially within their two respective time periods, and precisely as foretold, with no gaps or gimmicks. As a result, both the historical setting and defining characteristic of Daniel's "time of the end" achieved fulfillment in A.D. 70 when the "the power of the holy people" was "finally broken." The Jews' exclusive relationship with God, as manifested by the Temple complex, was finally terminated. Ever since and yet today, rabbis speak about the destruction of the Temple in A.D. 70 as "the end of biblical Judaism." Even they recognize that something extremely significant happened back then. Since then, it has not been reversed and, contrary to popular Jewish and Christian views, will never be restored.

However, we will miss the greater significance of these events if all we see in them is the destruction of a local city and its Temple.

As we shall see throughout the remainder of this book, the time of the end involved much more. "All these things," including the accomplishment of Daniel's six purpose clauses (Da. 9:24), were fully "completed" (Da. 12:7). Plus, the transition between the two ages was finished at the fall of Jerusalem in A.D. 70.

Thus, the end the Bible proclaims is *past*. Habakkuk's "appointed time...of the end" certainly came and is over. It did not demand the end of human history, the end of time, or the destruction of the physical creation. This end, its end times, and the biblical last days are behind us, not ahead of us. They are in the past, not in the future. Note especially that every New Testament reference to the "last days" or equivalent "last times, last hour," refers to the time its writers were living in—the 1st century. They weren't the last days of planet Earth, or the end of time. They were the last days of the Old Covenant Jewish system and age. There are no exceptions (see Heb 1:2; Ac. 2:17; 1 Ti. 4:1; 2 Ti. 3:1; Jas. 5:3; 2 Pe. 3:3; 1 Pe. 1:5, 20; Jude 18; 1 Jn. 2:18).

Like two bookends, Daniel's two time prophecies provide the front and a back for the end-times period. Like a picture frame, they provide the framework in which all end-time events took place and the appointed time of the end certainly came.

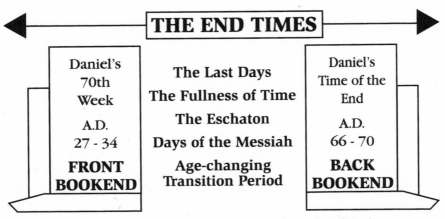

THE END TIMES

Daniel's 70th Week	The Last Days	Daniel's Time of the End
A.D. 27 - 34	The Fullness of Time	A.D. 66 - 70
	The Eschaton	
	Days of the Messiah	
FRONT BOOKEND	Age-changing Transition Period	**BACK BOOKEND**

(See Appendix A for a complete timeline.)

8

Is God's Word Trustworthy?

One of the most divisive elements in recent Christian history…
Few doctrines unite and separate Christians as much as eschatology
[end-time prophecy].[1]

After reading many books on the end times and realizing that
there are so many different views coming from the same Bible,
one must conclude that there is a glitch somewhere. Not only have
the endsayers misled generations of people about the end of the
world and the time of the end for the world, they have seriously
compromised the integrity of God's Word on other related matters
as well. The result is that many Christians and non-Christians don't
really know what to believe about Bible prophecy!

But God is not the author of confusion, nor of this confusion
(1 Cor. 14:33). His Word is trustworthy—totally trustworthy:

- God's Word says the earth is a "circle" (Isa. 40:22). Columbus
  counted on it and set sail.

- God's Word declares, "Generations come and generations go,
  but the earth remains (endures) forever" (Ecc. 1:4). We can
  count on it.

- God told Noah, "Seven days from now I will send rain on the earth for forty days and forty nights" (Ge. 7:4). We can rest assured that these were two precise time frames.

- God's prophet, Jeremiah, prophesied the duration of Babylonian captivity at 70 years. That was its exact length— no gaps, no gimmicks.

- God commissioned the angel Gabriel and the Lord Jesus Himself to show Daniel the beginning and ending of the period we call the end times. The coming and cutting off of the Messiah, the cessation of the daily sacrifice, the power of the holy people being finally broken, and much more were prophesied to occur during that time frame. We can trust the precise timing and integrity of this prophecy as well. It is God's Word.

God is not ambiguous. He doesn't play word games with any of his Word, and certainly not with his time statements. No artificial interpretative devices of any kind—gaps, gimmicks, interruptions, postponements, delays, or tampering of any type—are required to understand the intended meaning. All of God's time periods given to humankind are reliable, accurate, and literal. They each commenced, transpired, and were fulfilled in chronological and sequential exactness.

For further proof, God also set his end-time events into the definite context of world history. Daniel was given the famous apocalyptic view of four world kingdoms. In two parallel dream-visions, Daniel isolated, this bookended age-changing, end-time period to be *within* the days of the old Roman Empire (which ended in A.D. 476):

- In Daniel 2, Daniel both declared and interpreted the king's dream of a statue with four sections (head of gold, chest and arms of silver, belly and thighs of bronze, and legs and feet of iron and clay) to symbolize four earthly kingdoms.

- In Daniel 7, Daniel's prophetic dream of four beasts (a lion, a bear, a leopard, and a ten-horned beast) symbolizes the identical scenario—four earthly kingdoms.

All of God's time periods given to humankind are reliable, accurate, and literal.

We agree with the majority of scholars that these two dream-visions portray the same thing. Four—not five—Gentile kingdoms or world empires would transpire during this divinely predetermined course of history. They began in Daniel's day and successively unfolded. They were Babylon, Medo-Persia, Greece, and the old Roman Empire, respectively.[2] Because Daniel prophesied the rise and fall of these kingdoms so accurately, some scholars insist that these sections must have been written after-the-fact, in the 2nd century B.C. Even if that were true, it still leaves a two-hundred-year-plus foretelling factor to explain (see footnote 4, chapter six).

Daniel records that during—not after—the time of the fourth beast/kingdom (the old Roman Empire) one like the Son of Man (the Messiah) was to come on the clouds and establish his everlasting kingdom. It would happen "in the times [days] of those kings" (Da. 7:13-14; 2:44). This divine placement in world history perfectly harmonizes with the fulfillment of Daniel's 70 weeks and time of the end prophecies we presented. Twice in these dream-visions, and more than 600 years in advance, Daniel unerringly foretold the general time when the Messiah would come and God's appointed end for Israel would be carried out by the power of Rome. It all happened in the 1st century A.D. exactly *as* and *when* it was supposed to happen, and precisely *as* and *when* it was expected (Jn. 16:13).

What Should We Learn from This Perfection?

We of biblical faith could solve many of our disagreements by reconsidering the time-integrity of Daniel's time prophecies, and by becoming better acquainted with the nature and historical accuracy of their fulfillment. To help us further, here are seven principles for "making sense" of God's time trustworthiness.

Principle 1.   When the Normal Sense Makes Sense, Seek No Other Sense.

Doesn't a straightforward approach to Daniel's prophecies and the preciseness of their literal, exact, chronological, and sequential fulfillment make more sense than a view that interrupts the time context? By the straightforward method, Daniel's prophecies were fulfilled long ago. Only by tampering with the text can we get a yet-future fulfillment.

Most Christian endsayers insist that the prophetic time clock stopped ticking when the Jews rejected the Messiah and crucified Him on the cross. So they interrupt Daniel's 70 weeks and insert a time gap of indeterminable length between the 69th and the 70th week. Next, they lift the 70th week out of its 1st-century time period, stretch it like a rubber band over 19 centuries and counting, and plop it down somewhere out in the future. This seven-year period, which was designated by the text as the time the Messiah would confirm a covenant with the Jews, is now recast into a future 7-year period of tribulation upon the Jews. In this bizarre scheme, the Antichrist rises from one of the nations of a so-called revived Roman Empire and confirms a supposed covenant with the geopolitical nation of Israel.

No scriptural warrant or valid biblical precedent exists for such abusive treatment or manipulative handling of God's Word. No imposition of gaps, interruptions, or delays can be scripturally or historically justified.[3] This type of tampering with Scripture has crippled the Church and resulted in erroneous and disastrous date-setting.

Oddly, the futurist-literalists themselves have a good phrase: "when the normal sense makes sense, seek no other sense." It's unfortunate that those who subscribe to this bit of good sense are doctrinally and/or emotionally committed to violating it here. But times are changing. A new reformation is underway.

Principle 2. The "Once For All Delivered" Faith.

...Contend for the faith that was once for all delivered to the saints. (Jude 3)

The vast majority of Christians and Jews don't do this. Many are woefully ignorant of the past-fulfillment heritage of our once-and-for-all-delivered faith. Through the Jewish prophet Daniel, God provided four clear time parameters—two specific and two general—for when the time determined upon the Jews would be over, when the Messiah would come, and when Habakkuk's "appointed time...of the end" would take place. Both biblical Judaism and Christianity spring from these same deep roots and shared scriptures. And there is no Messiah apart from Israel's Messiah.

The literal, exact, chronological, and sequential fulfillment of Daniel's historical time prophecies presents a powerful argument that Jesus of Nazareth was and is Israel's promised Messiah, the Christ. He came at "the appointed time" (Ro. 5:6), or He is not the Messiah. The renowned Jewish historian, Josephus, believed that Jesus was the Messiah:

> About this time lived Jesus, a wise man, if indeed one ought to call him a man. For he was the achiever of extraordinary deeds and was a teacher of those who accept the truth gladly. He won over many Jews and many of the Greeks. He was the Messiah.[4]

When "the appointed time of the end" is taken out of its 1st-century context, the biggest victim is truth. Part of God's grand purpose was to draw Jews and Gentiles into one people. This He accomplished during this divinely-determined, fixed end-time period. It cannot be changed, amended, or protracted to an unscriptural "end of time." Nor can we ignore it, suppress it, or hold it in contempt. The stakes are too high. Both Christians and Jews dilute and diminish the credibility of their separated faiths by failing to recognize the historical fulfillment outlined in our last two chapters. Let us now sincerely reconsider our full, joint, and historical heritage, and stop deferring it as a yet-future hope.

Principle 3. The Foolishness of Antichrist Speculation.

It's almost unbelievable how some Christians speculate that some future and final Antichrist is the one who confirms the covenant in Daniel's 70th week. What is their textual proof? There is none.

First, in Scripture, there is no such thing as a "final Antichrist." Antichrists (note the plural, 1 Jn. 2:18) were present in the midst of 1st-century saints, and have been present ever since (1 Jn. 2:22; 2 Jn. 7). Moreover, they don't confirm covenants. Only God makes and confirms covenants. If anything, antichrists break them. Speculation about some future final Antichrist is just that—pure speculation that has been read into prophecy.[5]

Second, Jesus was the One who, through his crucifixion and resurrection, put a stop to the Jewish sacrifices. It was not some future Antichrist in some distant revived Roman Empire inside a rebuilt Jewish temple in Jerusalem. There is no need to reconstruct the same socio-political conditions of that 1st century, or revive the days of Rome, or reestablish any of the obsolete institutions of the old Judaic system (Heb. 8:13) in order for them to be destroyed again. There is no need to forecast these repetitions of fulfilled end-time prophecy. It need never again be repeated.

This redundancy idea is terrible scholarship. The Bible says nothing about the Jews building a third temple in our day or in the future. Let's call this theology for what it truly is—the re-Judaizing of biblical faith (Christianity). Sadly, it has great appeal, if not a strange hypnotic power, over many who claim they are the ones who are "rightly dividing the Word of truth" (2 Ti. 2:15). If we have ever wondered how "the elect" could possibly be deceived in our day (Mt. 24:24), here's one way. This view does not serve the work of the Church or the purposes of God.

Principle 4. Shifting the Burden of Proof.

The chronological exactness of Daniel's two time prophecies is thought-provoking. Their prophetic fulfillment has perfectly come to pass (see Dt. 18:22). Isn't this just like God? When this realiza-

If we have ever wondered how "the elect" could possibly be deceived in our day, here's one way.

tion becomes better known, then the burden of proof, or rather disproof, will shift. Rightly, it must fall on those who argue that these scriptures and their fulfillment should be interpreted in unique ways:

- Those who insert a gap on their own initiative and maintain that Daniel's time prophecies are not successive, but interrupted, and who break off the fixed 70th week, leap over a gap of at least two millennia, and stick it out in the future somewhere. Although this disjointing tactic provides material for sensational preaching, it has no known scriptural justification.

- Those who arbitrarily stretch out Daniel's final week, or its last half, to embrace a long period of time termed the Church age (i.e., between Christ's supposed first and second comings).

- Those who tell us that the fulfillment of these end-time events cannot be found anywhere in known history—and therefore must be yet future.

- Those who claim that the timing for end-time events cannot be known by man and place it just before the proverbial and unscriptural end of the world.

- Those who believe that God's Word does not communicate with us in terms of time tables and time contexts which we can understand or trust, and that He is therefore not limited by our understanding of their normal-sense meanings.

- Those who say that we moderns are now living in the end times, or biblical last days, and who attempt to fit present-day world circumstances and events into their end-time scenario.

- Those who shrink the 490 years to a lesser time span, or use a starting point prior to 538 B.C. (the date when Daniel received this vision) in order to make these prophecies fit into a 2nd-century B.C. fulfillment in the time of Antiochus Epiphanes and the Maccabean rededication of the Temple. If this was the true fulfillment, how could all six purpose clauses of Daniel 9:24 possibly have been fulfilled in those events?

- Those who claim that Daniel's time prophesies should not and cannot be pressed to yield literal exactness or chronological reliability.

The bottom line is that no interpreter has the freedom to weave in and out of time-restricted contexts at will. What God has put together, let no man presume to put asunder, divide, or separate (Mt. 19:6). Let us also heed Jesus' warning that "the Scriptures cannot be broken" (Jn. 10:35).

Principle 5.   Only One "End" and One Indivisible "End Time."

Some may be wondering, "which end was up at the time of the end?" They've been led to believe that there may be two ends, or one end split in half and only partially fulfilled.

The Bible consistently proclaims only *one end* (from the Greek word t*elos,* meaning "goal" or "destination," not termination) and *one indivisible end-time*, or age-changing period. It may have different names, such as "the last days," "the fullness of time," "the eschaton," or "the days of the Messiah," but it is the same end. It was the time God completed his plan of redemption for humankind. Its historical setting and defining characteristic was "when the power of the holy people has been [was] finally broken" (Da. 12:7). Note, it was not the end of the material world or human civilization, but the end of biblical Judaism. This end was covenantal, not cosmic in nature. As promised, it was a "short work" (Ro. 9:28; Isa. 10:22, 23), and is long past.

Today, we have nothing to fear from the end that's behind us—only positive things to gain. For one, it's the foundation for understanding all end-time prophecy and the whole of biblical faith as well. No longer can we credibly preach a pre-end message in a post-end world. The end the Bible proclaims lies within history rather than outside of history or at history's conclusion. Outside this finished end-time framework, neither the Bible nor the end can be properly understood. This explains why we have so many conflicting and competing views today. They naturally arise whenever the foundation of eschatological and redemptive history is torn from its God-ordained, 1st-century setting and forced into a time frame God never intended. The acceptance of this fulfilled truth is a starting point for a new reformation. All promised end-time events were fulfilled and all redemptive realities fully established within this time context.

No longer can we credibly preach a pre-end message in a post-end world.

Principle 6. *Exact Timing Demonstrates God's Sovereignty Better Than Gaps and Gimmicks.*

The God of the Bible accurately foretold and time-restricted the course of human history through the arrival of the time of the end. This exactness demonstrates his existence and sovereignty. It reveals the God of the Bible as the one, true, and proven God, Who is wise, powerful and orderly. This should be comforting, not disturbing. The precise fulfillment of a predetermined end secures our faith and lends credibility and superiority to the Bible's claim of supernatural origin. No other faith, religion, or philosophy has this authenticating quality and quantity of evidence.

Honest readers will concede that exactness glorifies God more than postponement gaps and other side-stepping gimmicks. As we shall soon see, it also honors and secures our trust in the words of Jesus and in the writings of the New Testament. By its clear and conclusive proof, exactness certifies that the Bible is the inspired, infallible Word of the living God, that the world is governed by divine providence, and that biblical faith is the most reliable of all faiths. God kept all his promises, right on time. That's the *ultimate apologetic* for biblical faith.

Principle 7. *The Harmony of Consistency as a Standard for Agreement.*

A truly amazing harmony of consistency runs throughout end-time Bible prophecy. Daniel's time prophecies are in perfect synchronization with the literal rendering of Peter's consummatory statement, "The end of all things is at hand," (1 Pe. 4:7). They agree with all the verses cited at the start of chapter six, and many more yet to be cited. All were literally fulfilled in that 1st-century time context "when the power of the holy people has been [was] finally broken" (Da. 12:7). But that harmony is lost when fulfillment is deferred to the 20th or 21st Century. It was biblical Judaism whose time was "short" and ending, not the end of planet Earth, of human existence or the end of time.

Biblical faith is not a blind faith, a confused faith, or an ambiguous hard-to-understand faith. It's true, clear, technically accurate, and perfectly harmonized when kept in its 1st-century fulfillment context. We can stand firm on the trustworthiness of God's Word and his literal, exact, chronological, and sequential linkage between two covenants, the Old Covenant and the New Covenant.

2,500 years ago, the Bible precisely foretold Jewish history— from Babylonian captivity to the cross, the destruction of Jerusalem, the end of the Old Covenant system, and the consummation of the new in A.D. 70. That's the way God said it through the prophets in the Bible and did it in history. All the parts fit together in one harmonious whole, with no gaps, no gimmicks, and no inconsistencies. Again, isn't that just like God?

In our next chapter, we'll discover how Jesus' amazing predictions of the end of the age *directly* and *perfectly* tied into and connected the time between Daniel's two time prophecies. Once again, we implore you not to dismiss anything you read here without first testing the Scriptures and the evidence presented (1 Th. 5:21).

9

Jesus' Most Dramatic Prophecy

Not long before He died, Jesus made some startling statements about the end. He left no doubt that something truly significant was about to happen. His prophetic words are paramount to understanding end-time prophecy. Although they have puzzled and perplexed us for nearly 2,000 years, they need not. We have only to compare his prophecy with Habakkuk's and Daniel's—and take Him at his word—to arrive at his meaning.

While sitting on the Mount of Olives, looking across the valley at the beautiful Jewish Temple, Jesus stunned his disciples by prophesying that this entire complex of buildings, an awesome structure "famous throughout the world" (2 Maccabees 2:22 NRSV), would be totally destroyed. "I tell you the truth, not one stone here will be left on another; every one will be thrown down" (Mt. 24:2).

His disciples asked, "When will this happen?" (Mt. 24:3) and He answered, "I tell you the truth, this generation will certainly not pass away until all these things have happened" (Mt. 24:34). Not only was something significant about to happen, it was to happen in their lifetime. To top it off, He told them about many other end-time events that would take place within that same time period. Included in Jesus' "all these things" were:

- The end of the age and the sign of his coming (*parousia*) (Mt. 24:3)

- The gospel preached in all the world…to all nations (Mt. 24:14)

- The end will come (Mt. 24:14)

- The abomination of desolation standing in the holy place (Mt. 24:15)

- The hearers fleeing for their lives (Mt. 24:16-20)

- A great tribulation, unequaled in history before or after (Mt. 24:21)

- False Christs and false prophets appearing, performing great signs and miracles and deceiving even the elect—if that were possible (Mt. 24:24)

- The coming (*parousia*) of the Son of Man (Mt. 24:27)

- The sun and the moon darkened, stars falling from the sky and the heavenly bodies shaken (Mt. 24:29)

- The sign of the Son of Man appearing in the sky (Mt. 24:30)

- Them seeing the Son of Man coming on the clouds (Mt. 24:30)

This passage of Scripture is recognized as Jesus' longest, most dramatic, and most problematic teaching. Scholars call it the Olivet Discourse, since Jesus gave this end-time prophecy while sitting on the Mount of Olives during the last week of this life. We suggest you read Jesus' prophetic words for yourself before continuing this chapter. Three similar but slightly different versions are recorded in Matthew 24, Mark 13, and Luke 21.

Today, millions of Bible readers and scholars continue to be baffled and confused by Jesus' allegedly cryptic words and his emphasis that those who were there with Him at the time would witness "all" these climactic end-time events. Most of the debate has centered on what generation Jesus was really talking about when He referred to "this generation." Let's also note that He emphatically warned his first hearers, "Watch out that no one deceives you" (Mt. 24:4). As we shall soon see, his warning is just as relevant today as it was back then. So, if we take Jesus at his literal word (as they did) and hold to an inerrant view of Scripture, "all these things" must have occurred within the lifetime of his disciples exactly *as* and *when* He said. Nothing short of the credibility of Jesus Christ is at stake. Surely Jesus didn't make a mistake or intend to mislead his disciples. The only other alternative is that He spoke truly—just as He said He did.

Nothing short of the credibility of Jesus Christ is at stake.

Skeptics contend that Jesus' Olivet Discourse is an empty prophecy, since neither Jesus' generation, nor any generation since, has seen its "complete" fulfillment. However, his prophesied stone-by-stone destruction of the Temple complex is historical fact. It occurred in A.D. 70 - 73, precisely within the time period Jesus said. Yet most people of the world have been led to believe that the rest, or most, of Jesus' prophetic words are still to be fulfilled. To sidestep the plain meaning and utmost importance of Jesus' words, prophecy teachers have found many devices.

Five Side-stepping Devices

Traditionalists assure us that when Jesus returns at some point in the future, He will fulfill the rest of his prophecy and destroy this physical world. But is this really what Jesus taught? For those raised in postponement traditions, most have never considered that Jesus might have been speaking of events (note the plural) which were *all* to transpire during the lives of his 1st-century hearers. Consequently, to cover up for Jesus' apparent failure to produce what He promised, and to defend their futuristic-deferment positions, they have employed one or more of five side-stepping devices.

These interpretative techniques usually fall under the guise of traditional explanations. And many of us have naively accepted one or more of them as orthodox. Each device, however, is a ploy born of theological necessity. None is textually, exegetically, or grammatically justifiable. They are simply "necessary" in order to evade, finesse around, or distort the plain, face-value meaning and clear relevance of Jesus' prophetic words and time restriction. In other words, they are tied to agendas, and therefore "absolutely demanded." Here they are:

Device 1: "Generation" must refer to a future generation. Interpreters in the most popular of the postponing traditions (premillennial dispensationalism) try to escape the plain meaning of Jesus' time-restrictive phrase "this generation" (and also the "you" who would experience "all these things") by claiming that Jesus' words meant some other, yet-unborn generation in the distant future. They maintain that the phrase "this generation" is qualified by the phrase "not pass away until all these things have happened." The latter phrase, they say, governs the timing of the former. Since they can't fathom how "all these things" could possibly have occurred during the lifetime of Jesus' contemporaries or been fulfilled in any subsequent generation, they conclude that they must occur in the lifetime of some future generation—now almost 2,000 years and counting away from when Jesus' spoke these words.

This postponement device was popularized by C.I. Scofield in the 1900s. In the reference notes for Matthew 24:34 in his Scofield Bible, he writes:

> The word 'generation' (Gk. genea), though commonly used in Scripture of those living at one time, could not mean those alive at the time of Christ, as none of 'these things'—i.e. the world-wide preaching of

the Kingdom, the tribulation, the return of the Lord in visible glory, and the regathering of the elect—occurred then. The expression 'this generation' here (1) *may mean* that the future generation which will endure the tribulation and see the signs, will also see the consummation, the return of the Lord.... (italics are mine)

Hal Lindsey, today's best-known end-time prophecy writer of this same tradition, claims that Jesus'"this generation" began in 1948 with the rebirth of the nation of Israel. This means that in Lindsey's vernacular, our current generation is "the terminal generation." Several red flags wave against this popular but misleading interpretative device.

First, it's circular reasoning and double talk to say that whatever generation sees these things happen will be Jesus'"this generation." What must rightly be emphasized is that at the time He spoke these words, Jesus was sitting face-to-face with his disciples on the Mount of Olives. He spoke directly to them. He naturally used first-person speech (now printed in red letters in some Bibles) and the commonly used, normally understood language of ordinary people of that time: "And the common people heard Him gladly" (Mk. 12:37 KJV). His strong sense of directness and imminence would not have led them to believe that He was addressing distant matters or a future, far-removed generation of people. Furthermore, Jesus expected them to "understand" (Mt. 24:15).

Second, no other or future generation is mentioned anywhere in this chapter's context or in any of the chapters leading up to or following Jesus' prophecy. That's why the demonstrative pronoun used is *this* and not *that*. Since "this" has no textual antecedent, the generation Jesus was speaking to personally is its first-person object. Hence, "this generation" carries the grammatical idea of present existence. To divorce this time-indicator phrase from its natural first-person context is both grammatical abuse and an interpretive violation.

Third, a simple word study of the seventeen other New Testament uses of the identical word construction reveals that "this generation" always means the generation then living.[1] Since no textual justification exists for abandoning its consistent use, its standard, natural, and plain grammatical meaning should be the one accepted.

Fourth, Jesus' many uses of the personal pronoun "you" always relate to the same time period and group of people He is speaking to. His "yous" consistently refer to the ones living then and there, and the ones hearing his words. Jesus told them, "*you* will be handed over and put to death…" (Mt. 24:9; see also Mt. 10:16-23 and Paul's similar words in 1Th. 3:3-4). "*You* will see…" (Mt. 24:15), "*Your* flight…" (Mt. 24:20), "I have told *you* ahead of time" (Mt. 24:25), "*You* know…" (Mt. 24:32,33), and "I tell *you* the truth…" (Mt. 24:34). He used "you" in a personal way, a factor that must not be ignored or denied. Jesus was not trying to misguide those early Christians to keep them in line. They were the "you" He meant. To *them* He applied the fulfillment of his prophecy. Their generation would be the one that would not pass away until "all these things" took place. They would personally witness and experience all these end-time events. Furthermore, while Jesus' prophetic words were spoken and written *to* them, and not to us or some future generation, they were certainly written *for* us. Big difference!

Device 2: "Generation" must mean "race," "nation," or "a kind of people." Some Bibles add a footnote next to Jesus' word "generation"[2] indicating that the word could mean "race or nation (Israel)." The Scofield Bible's reference note for Matthew 24:34 gives this possibility as a second meaning:

> …it may be used in the sense of *race or family*, meaning that the nation or family of Israel will be preserved "until all these things have happened.…

This device stretches Jesus' words "this generation" from a contemporary group to a long line of successive generations. All time

Could there be any more blatant evidence of bias-interpreting among translators?

relevance is gone. But note that the *only* place the word "genera-tion" is footnoted with this alternative meaning is in the three gospel accounts of Jesus' Olivet Discourse. In all its other, thirty-three iden-tical uses in the New Testament, *no footnote* is attached and no alternative meaning added! In these other verses, generation is never interpreted race, nation, Israel, or the Jewish people. Could there be any more blatant evidence of bias-interpreting among transla-tors? This arbitrary device is a classic example of the inconsistencies some will resort to in order to defend their agenda-driven, futuristic, postponing, end-time-scenario schemes. No scriptural warrant exits for this intrusive and distortive attempt to make generation mean race or nation.

Others attempt to avoid the temporal meaning of the word "gen-eration" by claiming that it refers to a kind of people possessing similar attributes (such as unbelief and bad character and headed toward judgment). Some warrant does exist for this application. This possible meaning is recognized as a secondary one in most Greek reference books. Like most words, generation has more than one meaning. Even English dictionaries today list ten or more possible meanings. This other meaning, however, is not its primary meaning.

A simple word study of the Greek word *genea*, translated "generation," should clear things up. The primary meaning of *genea* is a people living at the same time. Most scholars agree that *genea's* use in the Bible refers to a chronological association, and not ethnicity or personal characteristics. The Bible says that forty-two "generations" were between Abraham and Christ (Mt. 1:1-17), and these obviously are not forty-two races of Israel or forty-two kinds of people carrying Abraham's blood. Likewise, in the Old Testament, God's chronological timing for Israel to come out of Egyptian bondage was in the "fourth generation" of exiled Israelites, and not in some elongated unknowable time of a race or kind of people (Ge. 15:16). Similarly, God told Noah to get himself and his family into the ark "because I have found you righteous in this generation" (Ge. 7:1). Conclusively and consistently, the Bible reckons a generation to be a contemporary group of people. Scripture also implies that the length of a biblical generation is forty years (Heb. 3:9-10).

If Jesus had meant to convey any other meanings, the inspired writers of his words could have chosen from several more appropriate Greek words such as *ethnos* (translated as "nation" in Mt. 24:7, 9, 14), or *genos* (translated as "generation" in 1 Pe. 2:9 and having more of a meaning of "kin" or "kind"), or *suggenes* (translated as "race" in Ro. 9:3 NIV and meaning "kinsmen, fellow countrymen or a relative by blood)," or *gennema* (translated as "generation" in the KJV and as "brood" in the NIV in Mt. 3:7; 12:34; 23:33 and meaning a type or progeny of people with like character and attributes).

If we are so lax or willing to be so undisciplined that we'll allow some hard-pressed postponement interpreters and Bible translators such latitude and freedom in changing the meanings of simple words, why don't we just change the meaning of some other words, too? What would happen if we changed the definite article "the" to the indefinite "a" in "I [Jesus] am *the* way and *the* truth and *the* life..." (Jn. 14:6)? What would be the justification for this change? It would be the same as changing "generation" from a definite contemporary group to an indefinite "race" or endless type of people. There is no justification for this device—absolutely none.

In all honesty, the biblical phrase "this generation" should cause no difficulty. After all, Jesus was answering a *when* question from his disciples (Mt. 24:3). These proposed other meanings would be non-answers and basically leave the disciple's question unanswered. But Jesus consistently used this same phrase elsewhere. In Matthew 23, Jesus sets the stage and context for his Matthew 24 prophecy. He pronounces seven "messianic woes" on the Pharisees. He calls them "You snakes! You brood of vipers!" (Mt. 23:33). He says, "upon you will come all the righteous blood that has been shed on earth..."(Mt. 23:35). Then He makes the identical time statement, "I tell you the truth, all this will come upon this generation" (Mt. 23:36). What generation did He mean? The answer is, the same one He intended in all his other identical uses of the word and phrase. Here are a few more examples:

- The same "wicked and adulterous generation" who was asking for a sign (Mt. 12: 39; 16:4).

- The same one He calls an "unbelieving and perverse generation" and asks "how long shall I stay with you? How long shall I put up with you?" (Mt. 17:17).

- The same one that would reject God's only Son: "But first he must suffer many things and be rejected by this generation" (Lk. 17:25).

- The same one to whom John the Baptist came and about which Jesus lamented, "To what shall I compare this generation?" (Mt. 11:16-24).

- The same one who would crucify Him: "Therefore, this generation will be held responsible for the blood of all the prophets that has been shed since the beginning of the world... Yes, I tell you, this generation will be held responsible for it all" (Lk. 11:50, 51b).

- And the same one Peter warned his contemporaries about: "Save yourselves from this corrupt [perverse] generation" (Acts 2:40; from Dt. 32:5, 20).

The Pharisees knew that Jesus was speaking to them and prophesying a judgment that was to come upon them (Mt. 21:45; 23:29-38; Mk. 12:12). They were the generation who shouted out, "Crucify him...crucify him" and "let his blood be on us and on our children" (Mt. 27:22-25). They were the ones who would personally experience the horrors of the end-time events. They were the ones upon whom would "come all the righteous blood shed upon the earth..."

(Mt. 23:35), not some unborn yet-future generation or people of the Jewish race in a far distant time. Jesus further told them, "Look, your house is left to you desolate" (Mt. 23:38). There is no need to explain away Jesus' use of the word generation, or mutilate its normally understood, consistent meaning. Nor is there a need to extend it beyond a scriptural forty-year period. History records that in A.D. 70 exactly forty years and within one generation after Jesus gave his powerful end-time prophecy, Jerusalem, the Temple, and the whole of biblical Judaism were utterly destroyed and left desolated.

Only one generation in history was Jesus' "this generation." That generation was a contemporary group who had become the most evil, ungodly, rebellious generation of Jews ever. That generation of Jewish people filled up their cup of iniquity by rejecting and crucifying the promised Messiah and persecuting God's emerging new people. No other generation comes close. No other generation makes sense of the time-limited and time-sensitive meaning that Jesus gave it.

Who are we to add some 19 centuries and counting? The Bible defines its own limitations. And no interpreter has the freedom or the right to weave in and out of time contexts at will. Jesus' "this generation" must be taken literally, consistently, and within the com-

---

Only one generation in history was Jesus' "this generation."

---

monly used and normally understood meaning of his words. Outside this historical context, the end that the Bible proclaims, with all its associated events, cannot be understood. Therefore, postponement beyond the generation in which Jesus lived must be called what it truly is—unscriptural.

Device 3: Dividing Jesus' prophecy into two sections. Reformed, amillennial, and postmillennial circles use another side-stepping device. It likewise causes great harm to the intended understanding of Jesus' prophetic truths. And it bears a striking resemblance to the interruption and dismemberment treatment of Daniel's 70 weeks that we exposed in chapters six and eight. To their credit, most reformed scholars agree that Jesus' "this genera- tion" means exactly what it plainly says. But then they divide his prophetic words into two sections. One section is associated with events fulfilled in A.D. 70. The fulfillment of other events, however, is ascribed to a second, yet-to-be-fulfilled "end of time" (a phrase the Bible never uses) section, which is equated to be the "real" end of the age (i.e., the Christian age, but it is without an end—see Eph. 3:21; Lk. 1:33; Is. 9:7). How can they do this?

They allege that Jesus did not structure his Matthew 24 discourse according to the three questions asked by his disciples (Mt. 24:3). Rather, these reformers contend, He "clearly separated" his answer to their first question about the destruction of the Temple and the fall of Jerusalem from their two other questions regarding his com- ing (return) and the end of the age. They concede, of course, that the first part occurred in A.D. 70. But they argue that his return and the end of the age (i.e., the end of the Christian age and not the age of Moses) still await the end of the physical world and the end of time. Thus, the whole of Jesus' predicted events must span two different end-time periods separated by a 19-centuries-and-count- ing gap of time. Sound familiar? Although totally unannounced in the text, and without any clear biblical authorization, the dividing line between the two time sections is usually placed between verses 34 and 35, or 35 and 36, and for *some very strained reasons*. Those reasons, followed by rebuttals, are:

1. *Verse 36 begins with the word "but" (in some translations) and is, obviously, a transitional verse.* The word "but" is used here as a conjunction, not a preposition. It joins and *does not* change subjects, alter context, or contrast with what Jesus has just said. If the use of the word "but" at the begin- ning of a phrase *does* introduce a new subject—and we insist on consistency—then there are at least 15 subject changes in Matthew 24 and 25. This is clearly ridiculous!

2. *Signs are given in the first section but not in the second.* This is an argument from silence and therefore proves nothing. Why must Jesus repeat what He's already stated? Isn't it possible that He had given all the signs He intended to give at that point?

3. *The text "demands" this division, but the events described in verses 14 and 27 belong in the second section.* There is no scriptural authorization for making such an exception. While clinging to their two-end program, Reformed dividers seem to have no qualms whatsoever about cherry-picking verses from one time section and applying them to the other.

4. *Or, the parousia mentioned in the first section (verse 27) is metaphorical and occurred in A.D. 70 but the one in the second section (verses 37 and 39) refers to another coming or the final return of the Lord at the end of time.* That means there are two *parousias,* two returns. The former one Jesus' disciples could know about. The other they could not. Then why in the second section would Jesus, by inspiration, command his disciples there with Him to "watch" (Mt. 24:42) and "be ready" (Mt. 24:44) for something that wasn't to take place until more than 1,900 years after their deaths? Or, why would He confuse them—and us—by telling his disciples about two comings when they only asked about one (Mt. 24:3)?

The truth is, Jesus' Olivet Discourse (Matthew 24) cannot be divided. He did not jump millennia in one breath or suddenly change subjects in midstream. Nor did He introduce a different coming, or ambiguously discuss a local minor coming versus a universal major coming centuries later. His terminology never changed. Nowhere does the text support this division. It's purely a devised and imaginary dividing line.

There's yet more proof that every attempt to identify an unannounced point of division between any two verses is scripturally in error. Notice that neither of the accounts found in Luke 21 and Mark 13 lend themselves to any such division, nor does the parallel teaching in Luke 17:20-37. While it covers the same end-time events, it speaks of them all happening in one time period, "on the day the Son of Man is revealed" (Lk. 17:30). Like the others, this passage cannot be divided into a two-section format. But, most interestingly, its listing of events is in a totally different and intermingled order from that of Matthew's account. The graphic in Appendix B illustrates the fallacy of attempting to divide the events of Matthew 24 and Luke 17 into two different, time-separated sections.[3]

There is no escaping the obvious truth that the integrity and prophetic unity of Jesus' Olivet Discourse (Mt. 24, Mk. 13, Lk. 21) must stand undivided. His powerful prophecy is a united, end-times discourse discussing only *one* subject and *one* fulfillment. No announced or unannounced time division exists. Jesus plainly intended it to be one interconnected, interrelated, interdependent context. Contextually, "all these things" were to occur within Jesus' time-indicator phrase of "this generation" (i.e., the contemporary "you" group at the end of that Jewish age).

Isn't it time we ceased putting asunder, separating, or dividing what God (in Christ) has joined together (Mt. 19:6; Mk. 10:9)? Let's affirm that "the Scripture cannot be broken" here, too (Jn. 10:35). Also worth mentioning is the biblical lesson of the two women who argued over possession of a baby. The proposed solution was a division—cutting the baby in half (1 Ki. 3:16-28). But this was unbearable. Let's keep this story in mind the next time someone suggests dividing Matthew 24 into two parts. Lastly, let's honor "rightly dividing the word of truth" (2 Ti. 2:15), with our emphasis on "rightly," not on "dividing."

Device 4: Change the meaning of the apocalyptic language.
Again, without any scriptural justification, Jesus' descriptive phraseology of the sun and moon darkening, of stars falling from the sky,

and heavenly bodies shaken (Mt. 24:29) is suddenly declared to mean something different from its time-honored figurative usage and its many historical fulfullments.

As we saw in chapter three, this figurative language is the language of the prophets. In all its numerous uses and fulfillments throughout the Bible, never once was the physical creation ever altered or affected. Instead, this vivid cosmic-collapsing, earth-shaking language always prophesied a coming divine judgment and destruction of wicked nations. Here, in his New Testament prophecy, Jesus is quoting from the prophet Isaiah (Mt. 24:29; from Isa. 13:10; 34:4). Let's recall that Isaiah used this same phraseology and apocalyptic imagery in foretelling a coming "day of the Lord" in judgment against Israel in the 7th century B.C. (Isa. 13:10) and another against Babylon in the 6th century B.C. (Isa. 34:4). Jesus gave no indication He was using this figurative language any differently.[4] In a similar fashion, He was announcing the coming judgment and destruction upon Jerusalem and the Temple, and the passing away of the Judaic system and age. The imagery and parallel are far too striking and strong to avoid.

For some strange and unknown reason, the postponement interpreters arbitrarily declare that this type of language now means something it has never meant before (i.e., a literal and catastrophic end of the world). Such a shift in meaning, however, without any legitimate textual justification, betrays an ignorance of biblical history and the nature of its many historical fulfillments. This fourth device is another serious interpretive error that's in opposition to the entire witness of Scripture. Almost verbatim, Jesus appropriated this apocalyptic language. Its scriptural precedents demand that we understand it in exactly the same way as it was fulfilled many times before in Old Testament history.

Device 5: Jesus was mistaken or never said these words.

To their credit, atheists, critics of Christianity, and liberal-tradition Christians alike recognize the time limitation of Jesus' "this generation" and his pronounced emphasis on the fulfillment of all end-time events within the lifetime of his hearers. They rightly conclude that if "all these things" did not take place *as* and *when* Jesus said, something is dreadfully amiss.

This nonoccurrence factor is a legitimate complaint and an inescapable dilemma for Christians. It has opened the door for liberal Christians to invent some equally strained but disastrous twists in an attempt to discount or explain away the implications of Christ's Olivet Discourse. They handle the supposed nonoccurrence problem by contending that Jesus was mistaken and made erroneous pronouncements. Or, they contend that He never spoke most of the words attributed to Him, theorizing that these words must have been added to Scripture later by his zealous followers.

This nonoccurrence factor is a legitimate complaint and an inescapable dilemma for Christians.

Thus, Jesus' embarrassing time and imminency statements in his Olivet Discourse became the crack that let the liberals in the door in the 19th century. Once in, they systematically began questioning and dismantling all of Scripture. Their assumption was, and still is that if the Bible is wrong here, it's surely wrong elsewhere. They even called into question the divinity of Jesus and attempted to discredit large portions of his teachings and ministry by searching for the real historical Jesus. What's even more amazing, is that conservative evangelicals have had no effective response to these liberal assertions and discrediting inroads, except to say that someday Jesus will come back and finish the job, which only proves the liberals' point.

The imminence of Jesus' "this generation," and whom He meant by "you," lie at the heart of his message on the Mount of Olives. These two chronological keys are indispensable to the proper understanding of his prophecy, and all New Testament end-time statements as well. His words were not vague or ambiguous. They were clear and time-sensitive. They qualified the context and nature of fulfillment, and therefore absolutely demanded a 1st-century fulfillment. It's the most natural way of reading and understanding the text.

If, however, Jesus was mistaken, or even partially mistaken, about something this central and this dramatic, how can we trust anything else He said? Or, if we allow that He never made these statements, how can we defend the Bible as inerrant? Moreover, if the Bible is wrong here, might it not also be mistaken on any number of spiritual matters? The problem is a serious one. If any of these liberal assertions is true, biblical faith becomes extremely vulnerable. And this is precisely where the liberal methodology of historical criticism logically leads. All liberals in the Christian tradition need to squarely face the consequences of their approach—the bankrupting of the faith. All conservative evangelicals, on the other hand, need to squarely recognize that their cover-up attempts won't work. There is only one credible and effective solution to the dilemma of nonoccurrence. It's *occurrence*. Perhaps this book will help both groups wake up.

In sum, the five side-stepping devices are nothing more than exegetic gymnastics designed to evade, explain away, cover up, or undermine the relevance and force of Jesus' prophetic words. They are desperate ploys born of theological necessity from those compelled by their particular traditions. At best, these avoidance and tampering techniques are serious errors. At worst, they constitute "handling the word of God deceitfully" (2 Cor. 4:2 KJV). None of these devices should be tolerated by responsible handlers of God's Word. When undisciplined manipulation of Scripture like this is allowed, any number of conflicting and confusing fulfillment claims can be advanced. This is precisely how most prophetic disagreements and confusion have come about. These devices have plagued the field of end-time Bible prophecy for far too long. They prevent an honest reader from grasping the true meaning and relevance of

Jesus' powerful prophetic words. We must guard against their destructive tendencies and allow the Bible to speak plainly for itself.

Restoring Jesus' Original Meaning

Any time someone has to create new definitions of familiar words, find exceptions to normal meanings, discount the reliability of Scripture, or go to any of the lengths outlined above, something is wrong. If allowed to stand, these traditions of men cast aspersions on Jesus' other sayings, destroy the authenticity, authority and inerrancy of Scripture, and make the Word of God of little or no effect (Mt. 15:6; Mk. 7:13). It's time we stopped reading the text of Jesus' Olivet Discourse through the distorted eyes of these traditions and restored his powerful prophetic words to their original meaning. Consider these attributes of Jesus:

He is clear and emphatic. How could Jesus have been any more clear or emphatic? What other words or phrases could He have used to communicate any better? Moreover, how could He have expected his original hearers and readers to understand (Mt. 24:15) if He was being deceptive? Why don't we sincerely consider the possibility that maybe, just maybe, Jesus *said what He meant and meant what He said?* As we shall see, most but not all of his followers understood exactly what He literally intended and the utmost importance of his words in their lives.

Simplicity is the key for solving the majority of our end-time confusions and conflicts. In the words of the old hymn,

> Tis so sweet to trust in Jesus,
> Just to take Him at His word,
> Just to rest upon His promise,
> Just to know, "Thus saith the Lord."

Why should it be so hard for us to believe exactly what Jesus and the Bible say? What a contrast this presents to the inconsistencies, abuses, and errors of the five contrived, side-stepping devices used by most traditional views.

He is in perfect harmony. The literal time frame of Jesus'"this generation" perfectly correlates with the literal, exact, chronological, and sequential fulfillment of Daniel's two time prophecies previously covered. (Again, see the timeline in Appendix A.) This transition period transpired over exactly forty years—one biblical generation. It perfectly connected Daniel's last week to his 1,290 - 1,335 days "time of the end." That's why Jesus tapped directly into Daniel's time of "unequaled distress" or "tribulation" (Mt. 24:21 from Da. 12:1) and the coming of "the abomination that causes desolation" (Mt. 24:15 from Da. 12:11). The end in Jesus' prophetic discourse and the end in Daniel 12 are the *same end.* They speak of an identical scenario—"when the power of the holy people has been finally broken all these things will be completed" (Da. 12:7). This breaking is the defining characteristic of the nature and historical setting for the only end the Bible proclaims. It can refer to no other time or event other than the fall of Jerusalem in A.D. 70. What's more, this perfect harmony of literal prophetic convergence in that 1st-century time period is beyond coincidence and human manipulation. Its pinpointed perfection should conclusively demonstrate that the end-focus of the Bible was covenantal change, not cosmic catastrophe.

Furthermore, Jesus' words are in perfect harmony with the other time and imminence statements made by New Testament writers (or perhaps we should say that they are in perfect harmony with Him.) Guided by the Holy Spirit into all truth, and shown the things that were to come (Jn. 16:13), the New Testament writers spoke of the same end-time events and soon-coming end. Peter spoke in plain terms and in a 1st-century context when he warned that "the end of all things is at hand" (1 Pe. 4:7) and "it is time for judgment to begin with the family of God" (1 Pe. 4:17). How much more perfectly must the time prophecies and imminency statements of Scripture agree and harmoniously align before men and women of faith bow to their authority? Postponing fulfillment of "these last days" (Heb. 1:2), or "last times" (1 Pe. 1:20) beyond the generation in which Jesus lived must be seen for what it truly is—unscriptural.

He is an infallible Prophet. According to the standards of Deuteronomy 18:22:

> If what a prophet proclaims in the name of the Lord does not take place or come true, that is a message the Lord has not spoken.

This was the acid test for prophets in Israel. If "all these things" didn't come to pass *as* and *when* Jesus said, He should be considered a false prophet, or, at the very least, a fallible prophet, as many atheists, critics of Christianity, and liberals maintain. There is no other alternative. Conversely, we must give the name "false" to the failed prophets of our generation. The remainder of the verse from Deuteronomy says that such a prophet has spoken presumptuously, and that no one need fear him.

We are therefore left with two options: 1) continue with our various side-stepping devices, or 2) take a positive approach as we seek to understand the possibility of 1st-century fulfillment. Let's take the latter and submit to the absolute authority of Jesus in his prophetic words and to the full and complete inspiration and inerrancy of the Bible. In so doing, we challenge you, as we have been challenged, to search the scriptures carefully for the real fulfillment of Jesus' most dramatic prophecy and its real "end time."

10

The End that Was, the Last Days that Were

History records that in A.D. 70, exactly forty years after Jesus prophesied on the Mount of Olives and within the span of one biblical generation, Roman armies led by Titus destroyed the city of Jerusalem and the Jewish Temple. This was the same Temple that was standing when Jesus foretold its destruction—not some third, rebuilt temple centuries removed.

Make no mistake—Jesus was no false or fallible prophet. He was the greatest Prophet of all. And even though many may have dealt loosely, if not treacherously, with Jesus' words, He set a definite time limit for the "last days" of biblical Judaism. Every New Testament reference to the "last days" or to equivalent terms such as "last times" or "last hour," confirms the same. Without exception, they literally refer to that 1st-century time frame in which these writers were living there and then. Hebrews 1:1-2 clearly affixes Jesus' earthly ministry to the period termed the "last days:"

> In the past God spoke to our forefathers through the prophets at many
>
> times and in various ways, but in these last days he has spoken to us by

131

his Son.... (see also Ac. 2:17; 1 Ti. 4:1; 2 Ti. 3:1; Jas. 5:3; 1 Pe. 1:5, 20; 2 Pe. 3:3; Jude 18; 1 Jn. 2:18).

This time-restricted period was to encompass the full redemptive work of the Messiah: his birth, anointing, teaching, ushering in of the everlasting kingdom of God, death, resurrection, sending of the Holy Spirit, ending of the Jewish age, and much more, as we shall see.

These biblical "last days" were never to be the last days of the world, planet Earth, human history, or the Church. They were the beginning days of the Church. But they *were* the last days of the biggest thing that was ending—the age of biblical Judaism. That's why the Apostle Paul reminded his contemporaries that "...this world in its present form is [was] passing away" (1 Co. 7:31) and that "the time is [was] short" (1 Co. 7:29). For Paul the end was very close. Was he wrong? Or did he understand exactly what he was saying?

Crucial to our understanding of end-time Bible prophecy is the proper identification of this end-time period. Daniel had said that its historical setting and defining characteristic would be "when the power of the holy people has been [was] finally broken" (Da. 12:7). This is what happened in A.D. 70. Jesus' prophecy fits this scenario exactly. Forty years—one biblical "this generation"—had been given to the Israelites to repent and accept their Messiah. Many did. Many didn't. But when the time of God's grace was over, "it is [was] time for judgment to begin with the family of God" or "at the house of God" (1 Pe. 4:17 NIV-KJV). This age-ending judgment certainly came during the final portion of Israel's "last days." After A.D. 70, the "last days" were over.

As we saw in chapter seven, the events leading up to and following this historic period are well-documented in the eyewitness accounts of Josephus, the 1st-century Jewish historian and Pharisee who led the Galilean army during the revolt of A.D. 66. His account of the terrible sieges and the fall of Jerusalem is one of the most fascinating and reliable that can be found anywhere. Other accounts were written by Tacitus, the Roman historian; Eusebius, the 4th-century Christian historian (A.D. 263 - 340.); and in the Talmud.

Crucial to our understanding of end-time Bible prophecy is the proper identification of this end-time period.

The existence of these historical accounts often comes as a surprise to many Christians. Let's especially note that Josephus was not a Christian, nor was he sympathetic to Christianity. He was a Jewish general who was captured by the Romans and later prophesied that Vespasian would become Emperor. When this happened, Josephus gained favor with the Romans and was released from prison. They appointed him their historian, so he wrote to please the Romans rather than the Christians. It is amazing how closely Josephus' recorded history illuminates and reflects the various details of Jesus' Mount Olivet prophecy as recorded in the three gospel accounts (Mt. 24, Mk. 13, and Lk. 21). Below are eight confirmatory insights into key events fulfilling Jesus' prophesy of "all these things" within a literal time-constraint of "this generation." Keep in mind that though not one word of Jesus' end-of-the-age prophecy was written *to* us, every word was written *for* us.

Eight Confirmatory Insights

1. **Early confirmations.** Jesus told his 1st-century disciples that they would be the ones to see "all these things" take place. Three early Church fathers confirmed that these things did indeed occur:

- Historian and church leader Eusebius (A.D. 260 - 340), in his patristic writings of the early 4th century, is our source for much information about the first three centuries of the Christian community. He understood that the "great tribulation" of Jesus' Olivet prophecy was fulfilled in the events leading up to and culminating in A.D. 70:

> All this occurred in this manner, in the second year of the reign
> of Vespasian [A.D. 70], according to the predictions of our
> Lord and Saviour Jesus Christ...[1]

> The abomination of desolation, according to the prophetic dec-
> laration, stood in the very temple of God...which was
> approaching its total downfall and final destruction
> by fire.[2]

- St. Augustine, writing about this same topic, stated:

> For Luke (Lk. 21:20) very clearly bears witness that the proph-
> ecy of Daniel was fulfilled when Jerusalem was overthrown.[3]

- Athanasius wrote:

> ...in accordance with the injunction of the Apostles, let us go
> beyond the types and sing a new song of praise...For no longer
> were these things to be done which belonged to Jerusalem
> which is beneath...the things pertaining to that time were ful-
> filled, and those which belonged to shadows had passed away.[4]

2. Those who correctly read the signs and fled. Jesus spoke
of a whole catalogue of signs (events) which would herald
the coming of the end (Mt. 24:5-12, 21-25). Many modern-
day interpreters call these "signs of the times" and argue that
we are just now seeing them occur, or are seeing them
occur with greater intensity and frequency. These signs include: social decay, wars, rumors of wars, famines, diseases,
natural catastrophes, earthquakes, false prophets, and apostasy. While it's true that these signs are prevalent in our day,
they were also prevalent in A.D. 60 - 69. In fact, they are
continually characteristic of depraved humanity, human history, and/or the earth's physical dynamics. In and of

themselves, Jesus said that they do *not* indicate the end. They were only "the beginning of sorrows" or "birth pains" (Mt. 24:8 KJV - NIV). So we must not be misled by the presence of these same signs today; rather we should focus on the two certain, recognizable and indisputable signs of the end to which Jesus gave prime importance over all the others:

Prime sign #1: *The abomination that causes desolation ... standing...."*

So when you see standing in the holy place 'the abomination that causes desolation' spoken of through the prophet Daniel—let the reader understand—then let those who are in Judea flee to the mountains (Mt. 24:15-16; Mk. 13:14).

The Jews of Jesus' time were the "you" group He was warning. He expected them to "understand" what He was talking about without his having to explain. How could they? Quite simply, most of them were well-schooled in Jewish history, like most Americans are, or use to be, about ours. They knew that the last abomination of desolation that "stood" or took place in the holy place was the Temple desecration and temporary cessation of religious rites caused by Antiochus Epiphanes in 167 - 164 B.C.

During the intertestament times, the Jews were taught that all of Daniel's prophecy concerning the abomination of desolation had been fulfilled by Antiochus Epiphanes. Jesus, to the contrary, prophesied that all had not yet been fulfilled. Rather, this 2nd-century B.C. abomination, as prophesied in Daniel 8 and 11, was a type and was going to happen again, as prophesied in Daniel 9 and 12. This next time, as before, the very "standing" or presence of pagans in the holy place would be the abominating offense. But unlike before, this next time would bring more than a temporary three-year period of desolation. It would bring the permanent and everlasting desolation. Here's a brief synopsis of what transpired.

Early in the decade of A.D. 60 - 69, an unqualified Jew was appointed to the position of high priest. Prior to that time, nothing secular or unholy was allowed in the Temple. This high priest and his staff of other priests failed to properly perform the daily sacrifices and many other required Temple duties. Instead, they made a mockery of the holy ordinances. In A.D. 66, priests and Zealots fought each other in the Temple courts. Josephus reports that the floors swam with the blood of more than eight thousand who stabbed each other. Many more atrocities (abominations) between the Zealots and other Jewish factions occurred in the holy place between A.D. 66 - 70. The final abomination that caused the final desolation was similar to that of Antiochus Epiphanes. What happened before, happened again. It came in the same way, when another foreign Gentile army, the Roman army, stood in the Temple, and raised and worshipped its standards, as was the custom. But then the Romans destroyed the Temple and tore it down stone-by-stone.

Prime sign #2: Jerusalem surrounded by armies.

Luke's parallel account of Jesus' prophecy tells us exactly what the nature of this final abomination of desolation would be (was) by adding Jesus' words:

> When you see Jerusalem surrounded by armies, you will know that its desolation is near. Then let those who are in Judea flee to the mountains, let those in the city get out, and let those in the country not enter the city. For this is the time of punishment in fulfillment of all that has been written (Lk. 21:20-22).

We must note that "...all that has been written" would include Daniel's "time of the end," Isaiah's new heavens and new earth, and much more (see Lk. 24:44).

Again as in 167 B.C., foreign armies were God's instrument of judgment. Early in the decade of 60 - 69 A.D., skirmishes between Jews and Romans began to break out. Many false Christs appeared among the Jews. "Wars and rumors of wars" were rampant. When the twice-daily sacrifice for Caesar and the Roman people was stopped, the dye was cast. Then, *four times*, shortly following this time-frame-starting event and just as Jesus had warned, Jerusalem was surrounded by armies.[5]

First Time. In A.D. 66, Roman armies commanded by Cestius Gallus came to put down the Jewish rebellion. After surrounding Jerusalem, they began their siege. But for no apparent reason, Cestius withdrew his troops and left in retreat. The Jews pursued the Romans, slaughtering many and capturing their abandoned war machinery. This humiliating withdrawal by the Romans gave the Jews a false sense of being undefeatable. In addition, it helped create an atmosphere of having "peace and safety" before the destruction of the day of the Lord which was soon to "come on them suddenly" (1 Th. 5:3).

Second Time. When news of Rome's defeat at the hands of the Jews reached Nero, he was most upset with Cestius' "poor generalship." He ordered Vespasian, a veteran general, back to Jerusalem in A.D. 67 to completely crush the Jewish uprising and avenge Rome's humiliation and the damage to its ruling prestige. Vespasian advanced into Galilee, a region north of Jerusalem. He conquered its major cities and subdued the land. After his Galilean campaign in the north, he marched south and encamped around Jerusalem. But when word came of Nero's death, Vespasian delayed his plan for taking Jerusalem, withdrew his troops, and returned to Rome to become Emperor. Again, the Jews prevailed.

Third Time. In A.D. 68, at the request of the Zealot faction inside Jerusalem, Idumaeans from the territory south of Judea camped outside the walls. The Zealots inside let the Idumaeans into the city to join their forces. In the ensuing battle, over 8,500 were killed in the Temple area. Shortly afterwards, the Idumaeans withdrew from the city, but the cruelties and killings of Jews by other Jews continued.

Fourth and final time. Shortly before Passover in A.D. 70, Titus, the son of Vespasian, arrived with his legions at the northern outskirts of Jerusalem to finally put an end to the Jewish revolt and finish the insurrection. He had marched south through Galilee and set up three camps overlooking the city. During this final siege, those who sought to flee were either prevented from doing so, killed by the Jewish factions inside, or captured, tortured, and crucified by the Romans at the city wall so all could see. By this time, it was too late to flee. All inside the walls were entrapped by Titus and his Roman legions. Josephus details how the Romans encircled and built an embankment or rampart to breach the city walls, just as Jesus had foretold (Lk. 19:43-44). He further notes that 500 or more were captured daily and that "the soldiers out of rage and hatred amused themselves by nailing their prisoners in different postures; and so great was their number, that space could not be found for the crosses nor crosses for the bodies."[6]

It's more than coincidental that sometime around A.D. 63, and prior to the arrival of the first army, the Apostle Peter announced that judgment was about to begin at "the house of God" (1 Pe. 4:17 KJV). And John twice proclaimed, "it is the last hour" (1 Jn. 2:18). Even John the Baptist in A.D. 27 warned his generation to "flee from the coming wrath" (Lk. 3:7). There is no need to side-step or try to explain away these passages. Nor should we believe that we have been living in this "last hour" for almost 2,000 years. Also, contrary to another very popular end-time notion, the king or invader from the north spoken of in Daniel 11 and Ezekiel 38 and 39 is not a modern-day Russian or Iraqi army invading from countries located directly north of Israel. Rather, it was the Roman army of that 1st century. In all three campaigns against the Jews, the Roman army came from the "north" and fought many battles as it systematically marched south. It's both historically and prophetically significant that the Romans chose to invade from the same direction from which Babylon invaded in 579 B.C., just as Ezekiel and Daniel had prophesied.

Josephus recounts how Jewish war refugees and defeated defenders fled Israel's northern territories for the south and the "safety" of Jerusalem's high walls. They continually carried with them news of the fighting and the defeats of the fortified cities. Great mourning and fear swept over the inhabitants of Jerusalem as they prepared the city for the impending siege. Many Jerusalem Jews, however, felt that the city—with its massive fortifications—could never be taken.

During the persecutions and the time between the four sieges, a great temptation arose for many to abandon the new Christian faith and return to the old ways of Judaism. Others remembered Jesus' solemn warning to "watch out no that one deceives you" (Mt. 24:4) and heeded his life-saving instruction to "flee" (Mt. 24:16). They were watching, and did what Jesus had told them to do. Around A.D. 66, when the two prime signs began to occur in tandem (Mt. 24:32-33), they didn't wait until the final stages but began fleeing from Jerusalem and Judea while they still could. This is the reverse of what the Jews normally did in troubled times before an impending battle. Always before, they had fled to the city and the protection of its walls. But as A.D. 70 drew near and anticipation of the end intensified, fleeing the city became more and more difficult. Then it became impossible. The days of grace were gone. Judgment was upon Jerusalem and the rebellious Jewish people.

But everyone should have known this. Jesus had emphatically warned that this destruction would happen in their "this generation." Those who believed Him and his time frame were watching and were not taken by surprise. They escaped the slaughter, the horrors, and the total catastrophe that befell others inside the city walls. No one (including Jesus and the angels) knew or could know the final "day or hour" (Mt. 24:36; 25:13). But that did not mean that they, and we, could not know the time. This prohibition on knowing was only against knowing the day or hour, not the week, month, year, or generation. Therefore, knowing was not and is not a futile task. That's the reason He gave these two prime signs.[7]

Jesus' followers, in obedience, watched for these two signs and knew when the end was near. And because they correctly recognized these signs and the urgency for flight, that day and hour (time) did not overtake them as a thief (1 Th. 5:4-6); at various times during the several sieges and times in between, they left in obedience to the Lord's instruction. Eusebius records that many Christians fled to Pella in Transjordan around A.D. 68 after the first siege and before the second one.[8] Others fled to Alexandria in Egypt, and still others to Asia Minor. In this way, "Jerusalem will be [was] trampled on by

the Gentiles [armies] until the times of the Gentiles are fulfilled"
(Lk. 21:24b), permanently ending the apostate Jerusalem. Hence,
"the times of the Gentiles" have been fulfilled.[9]

Our explanation here is in stark contrast to the popular, modern-day view that these signs and warnings apply to a yet-future,
time-ending, earth-destroying, great tribulation period. If this latter
application were correct, Jesus' instruction to "flee to the mountains" would be meaningless. How could one flee from the
traditionally posited end-of-the-world scenario if that was what Jesus
had in mind? To mishandle Jesus' teachings in this way is to
eliminate what He said to his disciples in answer to their three
questions (Mt. 24:3). Flee is what his Jewish and Gentile disciples
did in that 1st-century time period. Remember, this instruction to
flee was given to them, not to us. They properly read the two prime
signs and were spared from the horrors of the fall of Jerusalem.
There is therefore no longer a need to flee to the mountains if Jerusalem becomes surrounded by armies in our day. This was not and is
not a worldwide phenomena, but was a local and time-sensitive
instruction.

Jesus kept his word. The Roman army was God-ordained to
destroy Jerusalem and bring about the end. One of the most
remarkable and documented facts surrounding the fulfillment of
Jesus' end-time prophecy is that none of his disciples is known to
have perished in the siege and destruction of Jerusalem. The
historian Eusebius actually recorded that no Christians were trapped
and destroyed in the siege of Jerusalem which concluded in
A.D. 70.[10] Others weren't so fortunate.

3. **Those who failed to read the signs.** Two groups experi-
    enced the horrors of the fall of Jerusalem: the unbelieving
    Jews and former followers of Christ who were zealous for
    the law and fearful of being put out of the synagogue. Both
    groups chose to remain inside Jerusalem and failed or re-
    fused to read the signs. Members of both groups suffered
    the judgment, and many physically perished. Let's take a
    closer look:

The unbelieving Jews. Having rejected Jesus as the Messiah, this group naturally refused to follow his prophetic warnings. In their minds, Jesus was a disgrace and a failure. Since the Temple in Jerusalem was the only place in all the world where acceptable worship could be offered (again this was "the power of the holy people" which would finally be broken—Da. 12:7), the Jews wanted to continue their exclusive relationship with God, and viewed equality with the Gentiles as an insult. They also believed that God would someday make Israel politically supreme over all the nations. So they held fast to their supremacy hopes, and steadfastly believed to the end that God owed them deliverance from their current enemy, the Roman army. They had a good reason. As descendants of Abraham and God's chosen people, the Jews had a long history of deliverance from their enemies—but not this time.

An unknown number of law-zealous followers of Christ who were unwilling to give up the old ways. For this group, the presence of the Temple, the priesthood, the daily sacrifice, and the appeal of the city itself were too much to leave. So they turned

---

There is therefore no longer a need to flee to the mountains if Jerusalem becomes surrounded by armies in our day.

---

their backs on the crucified Messiah and reverted to their old faith. This end-time apostasy is mentioned in several of Paul's letters and was forecast by Jesus Himself (Mt. 24:10, 12, 24). As "foolish virgins" (Mt. 25:1-13), they failed to heed Christ's warnings and to follow his instructions to flee.

There were other warnings as well, and some were spectacular. Josephus writes of several strange, if not bizarre, oracles that appeared in the sky and in the city before the final siege and foretold its impending devastation: a star in the shape of a sword that stood over the city; a comet that continued for a year; a brilliant light around the altar at night; a cow that gave birth to a lamb; the sighting of chariots and armed soldiers (angelic armies) in the sky; and the hearing of voices in the inner court of the Temple, saying, "We are departing hence."[11] These signs were also reported by the Roman historian Tacitus.[12] When those inside the city disregarded the prophesied signs (Ac. 2:19; Joel 2:30), ignored or misread the portending warnings, and rejected this final call from God, their fate was sealed. According to Josephus, 1.1 million Jews were killed in the fall and destruction of Jerusalem.[13] This tally does not include those killed in countless skirmishes against the Jews in foreign cities, or in the Galilean campaign, or those who died in the Diaspora of disease, famine and persecution. Ninety-seven thousand more Jews went into foreign captivity. Thus, members of both groups held onto false hopes, rejected Jesus as the Messiah, disregarded his prophetic words, and stayed in the city. They personally received the judgment of "the time of the end" in apt fulfillment of Jesus' words:

> This is how it will be at the coming of the Son of Man. Two men will be in the field; one will be taken [into captivity] and the other left [to die in the destruction]. Two women will be grinding with a hand mill; one will be taken and the other left (Mt. 24:39b-41; see also Lk. 17:34-36).

4. **The Temple complex torn down stone by stone.** God set Jerusalem "in the center of the nations, with countries all around her" (Eze. 5:5), for a definite purpose (see Eze. 5:8-17). The city's centerpiece was the Temple complex. Its grandeur was "famous throughout the world" (2 Maccabees 2:22 NRSV), and powerfully manifested the Jews' exclusive relationship with God. Again, this relationship was "the power of the holy people" which the Jews held over all the nations. But the prophet Daniel had prophesied that at "the time of the end" this power would be "finally broken" (Da. 12:4, 7).

The earthly life of Jesus took place during the time of this magnificent second Temple. Isaiah had prophesied of this time, "In the last days the mountain of the Lord's temple will be established as chief among the mountains; it will be raised above the hills and all nations would stream to it" (Isa. 2:2ff). The small country of Israel sat strategically located in a geographic corridor at the crossroad of three continents. The expansion of the Roman Empire had brought peace (*Pax Romana*) and the Roman road system (Isa. 2:3-5). This enabled traders, travelers, and messengers throughout the ancient world to pass through Jerusalem.

The Jews thought their privileged position with God would never end, and that He would always protect them and their Temple. They therefore believed that it would remain the exclusive center of worship forever. But someday they expected God to remove the Romans and make their nation chief among the nations. Sadly, their expectations were not accurate and never fulfilled. Rather, they were dramatically altered when Titus and the conquering Roman legions removed every building stone from the Jews' second Temple, just as Jesus had perfectly prophesied when He warned, "I tell you the truth, not one stone here will be left on another, every one will be thrown down" (Mt. 24:2; also Lk. 19:44). After this occurred, the Temple on the Holy Mountain in Jerusalem was no longer the exclusive center of acceptable worship, just as Jesus and Jeremiah had perfectly prophesied (Jn. 4:19-26; Jer. 51:25-26). But why did the Romans go to such an extreme effort to dismantle the Temple stone-by-stone and raze the whole city to the ground?[14] They had four reasons:

- They were so enraged by the humiliations they had suffered during the $3^1/_2$ year campaign against the Jews and feared that news of this Roman weakness could trigger other uprisings in their empire.

- They were driven by their hatred of the Jews and had sworn to make an example of them.

- They were concerned about the tenacity of the Jews and felt they would never cease their rebellion as long as the Temple stood as a focus of nationalistic pride, and the city provided a rallying point and a fortress to which they might return some-day in times of trouble.

- They were hoping to find melted gold. The Jews used gold to decorate the walls, furniture and fixtures in the Temple. During the intense heat from the fires which destroyed the Temple, this gold ornamentation melted and flowed down between the cracks of the huge stones.

After burning the city and removing the stones one-by-one over the next three years, the Romans plowed up the hill of the sanctuary. Thus was typologically fulfilled the prophecy of Micah: "Zion will be plowed like a field, Jerusalem will become a heap of rubble, the temple hill a mound overgrown with thickets" (Mic. 3:12; also Jer. 26:18).[15] Josephus described the utter destruction and desolation of Jerusalem as follows: "Caesar gave orders that they should now demolish the entire city and temple.... the city was so completely leveled to the ground as to leave future visitors to the spot no ground for believing that it had ever been inhabited. Such was the end to which the frenzy of revolutionaries brought Jerusalem, that splendid city of world-wide renown."[16]

Amazing, isn't it? Jerusalem and its magnificent Temple complex, known throughout the world, had been utterly destroyed, and biblical Israel had ceased to exist. It all happened exactly *as* and *when* both Jesus and Daniel had prophesied. Nevertheless, we must not fall into the trap of thinking that the fall of Jerusalem was only a "localized" judgment, or nothing more than the insignificant end of another ancient city. This was no more the case than Jesus' crucifixion was only a "local" execution or simply the end of another life on earth. These times were truly of paramount importance to the whole world. It was the "time of the end" of the Jewish age. The rebellious Jewish nation had filled up their "measure of sin" (Mt. 23:32; 1 Th. 2:15-16; Isa. 30:1). Her role in prefiguring the new people of God—the Church—was over. God's age-ending "last days" judgment came. It was a powerful witness! News quickly spread to all the nations that something very significant had changed. The city and the Temple, the invincible centerpoint of Jewish religion and political clout—"the power of the holy people"—was, indeed, "finally broken" (Da. 12:7). And so, "in the sight of the nations" (Eze. 5:8), another end-time prophecy was fulfilled: (Israel was made) "...a ruin and a reproach among the nations around you, in the sight of all who pass by. You will be a reproach and a taunt, a warning and an object of horror to the nations around you when I inflict my punishment on you...." (Eze. 5:14-15).

5. **Christianity no longer a Jewish sect.** In these "last days" of biblical Judaism, God through his Messiah was calling out a new people for Himself. John, in the book of Revelation, recorded it this way, "Then I heard another voice from heaven say: 'Come out of her, my people, so that you will not share in her sins, so you will not receive any of her plagues" (Rev. 18:4). True, this passage speaks of Babylon the Great. But Babylon is a sign and a symbol in a book filled with signs and symbols. It points to the 1st-century city of Jerusalem. How do we know this is the correct interpretation? First, recall that at the time Revelation was written (A.D. 65 to 68), the ancient city of Babylon was nonexistent, having been destroyed several centuries earlier. Next, compare the instruction of Revelation 18:4 with Matthew 24:16; and the description of Revelation 18:24 (also 16:6; 17:6) with Matthew 23:34-38. Then compare the "O great city" of Revelation 18:10, 16, 19 with the one in Revelation 11:8. Only one city in the world, at only one time in history, ever matched or will match this instruction and these descriptions. It was the city in which the "Lord was crucified." That city—and the religious system it represented—was the city God was calling his people to "come out of."

Prior to A.D. 70, Christianity was regarded by the Jews, the Romans, and all other nations as a sect of Judaism (Ac. 24:14; 28:22). The Temple and all it stood for had proven to be a stumbling block to many early followers of Jesus. Therefore, the destruction of the Temple was not only a judgment against an institution that had become "obsolete" (Heb. 8:13) and was being superseded by something better (Heb. 8:1-6; 9:8-14; 10:9), it was also a practical necessity for preventing God's new people from wanting to go back. Does this seem so far-fetched? Today this same attraction and re-judaizing tendency is still quite prevalent. Many modern-day Christians, along with orthodox Jews, long for a future time when, supposedly, the temple will be rebuilt in Jerusalem, its rituals reestablished, and its interior divinely re-inhabited. But this desire to go back is unworthy, and an insult to Christ. It's similar to the desire of many Israelites who followed Moses out of Egyptian bondage and yet wanted to return to Egypt (Ex. 16 and 17). God's anger burned against them (Ex. 32:10-14), and they were not allowed to enter the Promised Land (Nu. 14:22-23).

Likewise, a return to the old Judaic law system is not going to happen unless God is schizophrenic. Basically, schizophrenia is a condition of showing markedly inconsistent or contradictory quali-

Today this same attraction and re-judaizing tendency is still quite prevalent.

ties. In this case, God could be said to be schizophrenic if, after going from a lesser to a better system, He decided to go back to the lesser (i.e., if He decided to go from the types and shadows of the Old Covenant to the better substance of the New, and then decided to go back to the types and shadows of the Old—see the whole book of Hebrews). Since God is consistent and "does not change like shifting shadows" (Jas. 1:17), we can safely say He's *not* schizophrenic!

After A.D. 70, Christianity and Judaism were never again to be confused. Christians who had read the "signs" and heeded Jesus' warning to flee were never again considered to be a sect of the Jews. They had distinguished themselves from Judaism, and no longer served God under the Law of Moses. On the other side of the coin, unbelieving Jews who survived the destruction cut off all connections with any of their countrymen who named the name of Jesus, and banned them from the synagogues. Christianity was thereby liberated from Judaism, freed to become its own worldwide movement, and compelled to develop—mostly among the Gentiles. Thus was fulfilled God's Word through the prophet Hosea, "I will say to those called 'Not my people,' 'You are my people;' and they will say, 'You are my God'" (Hos. 2:23b).

Without a doubt, the destruction of Jerusalem and the Temple was the single most decisive and powerful "manifestation of the Sons of God" (Ro. 8:17ff.). It was "a new creation...the Israel of God" (Gal. 6:15-16). This divine act of judgment fulfilled Jesus' words, "Therefore, I tell you that the kingdom of God will be taken away from you [Old Covenant Israel] and given to a people who will produce its fruit" [the Church] (Mt. 21:43).

6. **The final abomination that caused desolation.** Daniel's reference to a single "the abomination that causes desolation" (Da. 11:31; 12:11) contrasts with his earlier plural reference to multiple "desolations" and "abominations" (Da. 9:26-27). His two different usages have proven to be most difficult for many modern-day interpreters to understand. Jesus, however, only used the singular in his Olivet Discourse (Mt. 24:16). As we've seen, both during and after the Roman-Jewish War [A.D. 66-70] there were many different acts of abomination and desolation. But Daniel tells us that there was to be a pinnacle (one) (Da. 9:27; 12:11). Here's a historical recap that should help us gain greater understanding into this apocalyptic phrase:

Abominations. The Jews clearly understood the meaning of all Hebrew words translated as "abomination," "detestable practices," and "desecrated," especially in reference to their city and Temple. In Jewish terminology, an "abomination" was anything that involved the worship of false gods or the false worship of their God in sacred places (see: 1 Ki. 11:7; 2 Ki. 23:13; Jer. 4:1; 13:27; Eze. 5:11; 8:5-18; 22:1-16):

- The abomination which set the historical precedent and type for the final one was committed by the Syrian king Antiochus Epiphanes in the Maccabean period between 171-164 B.C. In 171 B.C., in fulfillment of the 2,300 evenings and mornings spoken of in Daniel 8:9-14, Antiochus Epiphanes replaced the Jewish high priest with Menelaus, who was not a priest, and began a severe oppression of all religious and political freedom. In 167 B.C. he captured Jerusalem, massacred many of its occupants, plundered the Temple and stopped the practices of the Jewish religion under the pain of death. In addition, He profaned the Temple by dragging in a pig—an unclean animal—and sacrificing it on the Jewish altar. He set up an altar to Zeus and erected a statue in the Holy Place. Licentious heathen rites were also conducted in the Temple courts and the Jews were required to take part. During this time, many Jews were put to death (1 Maccabees 1:29-64). Antiochus Epiphanes' abomination(s), however, only caused a three year and two month, temporary period of desolation (Figuring: 2,300 evenings and mornings as 1,150 evenings + 1,150 mornings = 1,150 days [see Ge. 1:5f; Lev. 6:9, 12, 20; 24:3;]). In 164 B.C., the Jews revolted and drove Antiochus out of Jerusalem. They reconsecrated their Temple and reinstituted their religious practices.

Daniel had precisely prophesied both the length of this time period of desolation and the time in human history during which these events would occur—the time of the third world empire, the Grecian Empire, symbolized by a goat (Da. 8:5-8).

All this occurred after the Grecian Empire of Alexander the Great had been divided into four smaller kingdoms, symbolized by Daniel's four horns. One of those horns, a "little horn," caused this temporary abomination of desolation. History shows that the little horn was Antiochus Epiphanes, not a future "Antichrist." Two centuries later, Jesus would point back to this time and tell his disciples that a similar, but far worse, abomination would take place in their generation.

An irony of ironies is the modern-day Jewish Festival of Lights, or Hanukkah. It commemorates and celebrates the reconsecration of the Jewish Temple and the reestablishment of the faith, following the temporary abomination of desolation caused by Antiochus Epiphanes. Ironically, however, most Jews to this very day ignore or deny the significance of Daniel's pinnacle of abomination and desolation, and Jesus' "abomination that causes desolation" which occurred in A.D. 70. Nineteen centuries ago and counting, this last and worst abomination ended the practice of biblical Judaism.[17]

- Prior to A.D. 64, Christians were persecuted primarily by religious Jews, both in Jerusalem and throughout the Roman Empire (Gal. 1:13, 23). After A.D. 64—the year of the burning of Rome—the emperor Nero took over the persecution of Christians whom he blamed and sought as a scapegoat for this embarrassment. James, Peter, Paul, and others were martyred.

- Before, during, and after the Jewish rebellion there was a great falling away or apostasy from both Judaism and Christianity. Many forsook the better things in Christ and returned to Judaism. And biblical Judaism itself became grossly defiled in its last days. Even the Apostle Paul was accused of bringing Greeks (Gentiles) into and defiling the Holy Place (Ac. 21:28).

- Animal sacrifices, made obsolete by Christ's crucifixion in A.D. 30, continued in the Temple until July 17, 70, when a lack of priests to offer them and animals to be offered forced discontinuance. God's attitude toward this detestable abomination was prophesied by Isaiah:

> But whoever sacrifices a bull is like one who kills a man, and whoever offers a lamb, like one who breaks a dog's neck; whoever makes a grain offering is like one who presents pig's blood, and whoever burns memorial incense, like one who worships an idol. They have chosen their own ways, and their souls delight in their abominations; so I also will choose harsh treatment for them and will bring upon them what they dread. For when I called, no one answered, when I spoke, no one listened. They did evil in my sight and chose what displeased me (Isa. 66:3-4).

- The Temple was repeatedly desecrated by the corruption and bloodshed of the Zealots. First, they murdered Ananias, the high priest; then they chose a new high priest by casting lots. The new priest was so unworthy and ignorant of his priestly duties that he and his cohorts made a mockery of the Jewish law and observances of Temple sacrifices and worship. Ceremonially impure, polluted, and bloodstained feet frequently invaded the sanctuary. Later, the Temple areas were turned into an armed fortress and headquarters for tyranny among the Jews.

  Josephus reports another high priest, Annanus, as saying, "Certainly it had been good for me to die before I had seen the house of God full of so many abominations, or these sacred places that ought not to be trodden on at random, filled with the feet of these blood-shedding villains."[18] Concerning the "lawlessness" and "abominations" of the Zealots, Josephus himself said, "These men, therefore, trampled upon all the laws of man, and laughed at the laws of God; and for the oracles of the prophets, they ridiculed them as the tricks of jugglers."[19]

- The bitter strife that split the Jews into warring camps produced many brutal atrocities and thousands of killings within the Temple areas. Jews betrayed Jews and persecuted each other. Priests were even killed as they worshipped and administered their sacred duties. And, in violation of Jewish religious practice, the dead bodies were not buried, but thrown outside the city to rot. Obviously, this was part of the apostate Jews filling up their "measure of sin" (Mt. 23:32). Yet in spite of these ongoing abominations, Temple worship, daily sacrifices, and the celebration of the religious festivals continued.

- During their internal battles, the apostate Jews not only killed and wore each other down, they also set fire to their own stocks of grain, other siege provisions, and even the Temple itself. Josephus says that it was "as though they were purposely serving the Romans by destroying what the city had provided against a siege and severing the sinews of their own strength."[20]

- The famine and starvation forced Jews trapped inside the city walls to eat their own children. Josephus documented this abomination, which fulfilled Moses' dire prophecy in Deuteronomy 28:56-57 (also see Eze. 5:10). Josephus tells of a certain woman named Mary who was at one time well-to-do, but whose house had been plundered several times and who was now dying of hunger. When no one would put her out of her misery, she killed her baby son, roasted his body, ate half of it and buried the remainder. Jewish rebels, smelling the odor, rushed into her house and demanded that she show them what she had cooked. She uncovered the baby's second half and offered it to them.[21]

- The pinnacle and final abomination began when the Roman soldiers, driven by their hatred of the Jews, rushed into the Temple and set it on fire, in direct disobedience to the orders of their commander. Everyone they caught was butchered. Josephus says, "Around the altar a pile of corpses was accumulating; down the steps of the sanctuary flowed a stream of blood, and the bodies of the victims killed above went sliding to the bottom."[22]

- After the Temple was in ruins, the Romans paraded their emblems of deity into the Temple grounds and worshipped and offered sacrifices to their pagan standards—a straight staff with a metallic eagle on top and a graven image of Caesar just below. In the Jews' Temple area, they proclaimed Caesar as God (previous Caesars, but not Vespasian, demanded and claimed to be divine). Later, they stripped the Temple treasury of its money, its raiment, and other spoils, such as the golden, seven-branched candlestick, the Menorah. This booty of war was carried off and later triumphantly paraded down the streets of Rome.

- In A.D. 75, a Roman temple was erected on the site where the Jewish Temple had stood. The Temple area was thereby transformed into a heathen shrine.

- In A.D. 361- 363., the Roman Emperor Julian unsuccessfully attempted to rebuild the Jewish Temple at Jerusalem in order to cast doubts on the Christian claim to be the true Israel and discredit Jesus' divinity by proving false his prophecies that "not one stone here will be left on another" (Mt. 24:2), and that "Look, your house is left to you desolate" (Mt. 23:38).

Desolations. These abominations above produced desolations:

- God had written consequences of disobedience into his covenant with Israel. If they broke the covenant, the greatest penalty would be the desolation of their land and sanctuary, and the scattering of their citizens among the nations (see Lev. 26 and Dt. 28). God kept his word. In 722 B.C., the ten northern tribes were taken captive into Assyria, although later they returned in obedience. In the 6th Century, the

Babylonians destroyed Jerusalem and the first Temple, and took its citizens into captivity. They also returned in obedience. On the "last day" of the "last days," most likely some time in August or September of A.D. 70, the end had come. Three years later desolation became complete when the stones had been removed and the ground plowed up.

- All Judea became a scene of plunder and ruin. In their search for wood to build the earthworks against the city walls, the Romans stripped the beautiful suburbs outside the city of their trees and reduced them to "an utter desert."[23] Malachi had prophesied this desolation:

Surely the day is coming; it will burn like a furnace. All the arrogant and every evildoer will be stubble, and that day that is coming will set them on fire," says the Lord Almighty. "Not a root or a branch will be left to them.... (Mal. 4:1).

The Jews knew that this time was coming. They frequently sang "the song of Moses" (Dt. 32:1-43) to remind them what would befall a "perverse generation" (vv. 5, 20) "in the latter days" or "end" (v. 29). It would be their destruction by a consuming fire (v. 22; see also Lk. 3:8, 17; Heb. 12:29), "famine," "plague," and "bitter destruction" (v. 24).

- Sometime during the many abominations, God forsook the Temple, thus fulfilling Ezekiel's tragic and midexilic vision of God's Glory and Presence departing from the Jerusalem Temple (Eze. 10:18-19; 5:11).[24] Perhaps this also reflects Jesus' tragic pronouncement, "Look, your house [the Temple] is left to you desolate" (Mt. 23:38; also see Mt. 21:13). Josephus writes, "Wherefore I cannot but suppose that God is fled out of his sanctuary, and stands on the side of those against whom you fight."[25]

- Biblical Judaism (not rabbinical Judaism) was so thoroughly destroyed that it has never been, nor ever will be, reestablished. Many rabbis refer to A.D. 70 as "the end of biblical Judaism." God's judgment had to so completely destroy the Temple, the city, the genealogical records—everything—in order to demonstrate his repudiation of Judaism as a religious system. There was, however, one exception to this destruction—a very important thing which God gave the Jews and Jesus said would never pass away—the ancient Scriptures (Mt. 24:35).

- Matthew 24:28 says, "Wherever there is a carcass (body), there the vultures (eagles) will gather." Although this and its parallel verse in Luke 17:28 and Revelation 19:21 have puzzled commentators for centuries, their meaning can now be guessed. Perhaps this refers to physical vultures that gathered to feast on the dead of the Jewish-Roman War. Or, figuratively, it may have been the Romans who were the vultures. They circled outside the walls of Jerusalem and awaited their dying prey as the Jews killed and wore each other out on the inside. Or it could be a reference to the eagles on the Roman standards which they literally planted in the soil of a destroyed Jerusalem (now a carcass or corpse of itself) and which were objects of worship. All three possibilities are quite descriptive!

- For over fifty years the entire country was left desolate and devoid of most of its inhabitants. The people had been killed, had died, or were sold into slavery. Everything was utterly destroyed—"to the uttermost" (1 Th. 2:16 KJV). Sixty-five years after the fall of Jerusalem, the Roman army returned again and wiped out the entire state of Judea.

- No country or people ever suffered the magnitude of God's wrath and judgment as that which befell Old Covenant Israel. Not only did Israel cease being the nation of the living God, it ceased being a nation for 19 centuries until its rebirth as a secular nation in 1948. The world of biblical Judaism, however, perished forever. It all happened forty years from the time Jesus told his disciples that "not one stone shall be left on another." This fulfillment is more than coincidence.

"The power of the holy people" had "been finally broken"

Without question, Josephus held his own countrymen responsible for the destruction they had brought upon themselves. He writes, "The flames...owed their origin and cause to God's own people."[26] Titus gave the Jews numerous opportunities to spare themselves, the Temple, and the city. Josephus pleaded with them personally. But the rebellion spread "a madness" among the Jewish people, who appeared eager to go up against Rome and felt that their God would protect them as before. But He didn't.

Daniel 9 prophesied that the destruction of the city would be caused by "the people of the prince" or "the ruler" (Da. 9:26). As discussed in chapter seven, most likely Jesus Christ is "the Messiah the Prince" (Da. 9:25 KJV), and "the people" were the Jews. The Jews brought on the judgment, and the Romans carried it out.[27] And so abominations and desolations came upon God's chosen people. In a collective fashion, the Jews' rejection of Jesus as their Messiah, their internal battles, and their desecrations of the Temple were some of the "abominations" spoken of by Daniel that culminated in the pinnacle (one)—the "wing" of "desolation" at the hands of the Roman army. What stronger proof could there be that "the time of the end" in Daniel 12 is identical to "the end of the age" in Matthew 24 and to Peter's "the end of all things is at hand" in 1 Peter 4:7 KJV? "The power of the holy people" had "been finally broken" (Da. 12:7). It all fits together perfectly. And it all took place before Jesus' "this generation" had passed away.

Consequently, the abomination of desolation standing in the Temple is a thing of the past. It's not prophesied to occur again. Those words were written to them, not to us, but for us. No future Antichrist is necessary to erect a statue or instigate abomination(s) of desolation(s) in a rebuilt temple in Jerusalem during a cut-off 70th week of tribulation. A Jewish temple does not need to be destroyed again. God utterly destroyed the Temple centuries ago. It was the one that was standing when Jesus prophesied its destruction and desolation. The whole of biblical Judaism became obsolete (Heb. 8:13). It had ceased to shine for God and was darkened. A rebuilt temple someday in the modern-day secular city of Jerusalem would serve no eschatological or redemptive purpose whatsoever. None!

7. **The great tribulation objection.** One objection which has prevented some from accepting a 1st-century fulfillment as the time of "great tribulation" or "great distress," is that Jesus said it would be "unequaled" (past) and "never to be equaled again" (future) (Mt. 24:21; also Da. 12:1). Such critics are quick to point out that the Jewish Holocaust in the 20th century produced five times more Jewish deaths (5-6 million) than the A.D. 70 fall of Jerusalem. There are three valid responses to this objection.

1) The problem might be said to lie with the numerical assumption. The severity and significance of what happened to the Jews in the 1st century was greater than the death toll figure alone indicates. Indeed, it was and is unequaled and never to be equaled again in Jewish history. It was even worse than Noah's flood that destroyed all life on earth (Ge. 9:11). Its consequences and ramifications did "come upon the whole world to test those who live on the earth" (Rev. 3:10). They still do. The Jewish race has suffered many tribulations since the destruction of Jerusalem, yet these other times of persecution and distress—as horrible as they have been—

cannot compare with the utter destruction of Israel as the nation of God, and the abolishment of biblical Judaism in A.D. 66-70. If this "great tribulation" is not yet fulfilled, then an awful catastrophe still lies in the future for the Jews.

2) Others dilute the force of Jesus' words by explaining that this was stock-and-trade language or common dramatic speech (see Ex. 11:6; 2 Ki. 18:5; 23:25; Eze. 5:9).

3) A far better explanation, in our opinion, is that many equate or confuse the "great tribulation" with God's judgment and wrath. Contrary to the popular notion, Jesus' "great tribulation" or "great distress" did not come upon the rebellious Jewish nation. It came upon the early Church. Divine judgment and wrath came upon the apostate Jews; Jesus called it the "days of vengeance" (Lk. 21:22 KJV). Big difference! Jesus also said, "for the sake of the elect those days will be shortened (Mt. 24:22). "The elect" were not the Jews upon whom Jesus pronounced seven "woes," and called "snakes" and "brood of vipers" (Mt. 23). "The elect" were the newly emerging people of God, or the Christians (both Jews and Gentiles) whom Jesus warned to get out of Jerusalem.

The term "unequaled" recognizes that the 60s, and especially the Jewish-Roman War of A.D. 66 - 70, was a totally unique and unparalleled time of tribulation for the Church. Never before and never again was the very existence of God's people (now the Church) more vulnerable and imperiled. The unbelieving Jews had been the greatest enemy of the early Church. They wanted to stamp out the rival Christian sect not only in Jerusalem, but in the other cities and countries of the Roman Empire as well (2 Th. 1:4). That time had to be cut short "for the Church's (elect) sake." But after the destruction in A.D. 70, neither the Jews, nor anyone else, has mounted such a threat to the very existence of "the elect"—the Church. Nor will they ever again.

8. The whole-world objection. Jesus emphatically specified that "this gospel of the kingdom will be preached in the whole world as a witness to all the nations, and then the end will come" (Mt. 24:14). There is no way around it. This condition was a prerequisite for "the end."

How could the end possibly have come in A.D. 70, when the gospel had not yet been preached in the Western Hemisphere? The great missionary movement of the 18th and 19th centuries hadn't taken place, worldwide communications hadn't been developed, and many nations and people groups in remote tribes had yet to hear the gospel. This fact alone, critics contend, should stop dead in its tracks any idea that the end came in A.D. 70.

As we've seen before, the Bible must be understood on its own terms, in the context of its original hearers. Only then can we properly understand what any portion really means. Let's carefully note that the inspired writers of the New Testament confirmed that Jesus' prerequisite was accomplished in their day:

- Using hyperbole and in the context of the Jewish worldview, "every nation under heaven" was assembled on the day of Pentecost (Ac. 2:5).

- The Apostle Paul, 31 years later, confirmed that "all over the world this gospel is producing fruit and growing..." (Col. 1:6) and "the gospel that you heard...has been proclaimed to every creature under heaven" (Col. 1:23), and that "your faith is being reported all over the world" (Ro. 1:8). This was not Paul's opinion. It is inspired Scripture. A few years after Paul said these words, the end came.

- For more confirmations, read: Ro. 10:18; 16:26; Ac. 1:8; 24:5; Jude 3; also compare with Da. 2:39; 4:1, 22; 5:19; 7:23; Lk. 2:1, 30-32; 24:47; Rev. 3:10.

Why is this scripturally-documented fulfillment of Jesus' prerequisite so hard to believe? The answer is simply the power of the traditions of men over the Word of God (Mk. 7:13; Mt. 15:6). According to the Bible itself, and prior to A.D. 70, the gospel was preached to all nations and to the world. The Greek word translated "world" in Matthew 24:14 is *oikoumene*, meaning land (i.e., the [terrene part of the] globe, specifically the Roman Empire).[28] In this commonly used and restricted sense, the then-known Roman world, or the civilized world that they knew at the time, was also the "world" of the Jews into which they had been scattered. If the entire global earth was meant, the Greek word *kosmos* would have been used, as it is in Matthew 24:21. But it wasn't. Hence, Jesus' end-coming condition has been scripturally met. Early Church father Eusebius clearly confirmed that both the world-wide preaching of the gospel and this end of biblical Judaism were fulfilled:

> Moses had foretold this very thing and in due course Christ sojourned in this life, and the teaching of the new covenant was borne to all nations, and at once the Romans besieged Jerusalem and destroyed it and the Temple there. At once the whole of the Mosaic law was abolished, with all that remained of the Old Covenant....[29]

We further note that the fulfillment of this world mission was an absolutely necessary part of God's plan. Since Jews had been scattered over the world (Jas. 1:1), they all had to have the opportunity to accept the gospel or reject it and persecute its proclaimers. It was in this way that they would "fill up, then, the measure of sin of your forefathers" (Mt. 23:32; Isa. 65:6-12). That's why the gospel had to go out into "the whole world." The previously-cited verses verify this accomplishment. They cannot be lightly dismissed. So let's just believe what inspired Scripture writers said. God had allowed one generation of time—Jesus' "this generation"—for the completion of this missionary task. Once completed, the stage was set. The end could now come. It did. It was the end of the Old Covenant, biblical Judaic system, and not the physical creation.

A Caution: Many Christian evangelists and preachers fear that the recognition of this scripturally-documented and 1st-century fulfillment of Jesus' worldwide, gospel-preaching prerequisite will cause the Church to lose motivation for evangelism and we'll fail to complete its task in our day. But is the mission mandate a completable, once-for-all task? Let's recall that it neither originated nor terminated with Jesus' Matthew 24:14 statement or with his Great Commission "to make disciples of all nations" (Mt. 28:18-20). Why not? The mission mandate for world evangelism has always been the responsibility of those who are called to God, and always will be.

Four thousand years ago God called Abraham and made a covenant with him. Not only did God promise to bless Abraham, and all families of the earth through him (i.e., through his seed), He also instructed him (and his descendants) to actively be a blessing to others (Ge. 12:1-4). God's covenant with Abraham was the origin of the mission mandate. It is frequently referred to and enlarged upon throughout the Old Testament. For example, God's people were to

---

The mission mandate for world evangelism has always been the responsibility of those who are called to God, and always will be.

---

be priests and to minister to others (Ex. 19:4-6). Make "your [God's] ways known on earth, your salvation among all nations" (Ps. 67:2; also Ps. 98:3; Isa. 49:6; Ac. 13:47). Be "a light for the Gentiles" (Isa. 42:6). "You are my witnesses" (Isa. 43:10, 12; 43:8), and "they will proclaim my glory among the nations" (Isa. 66:19). "Make known among the nations what he has done...tell of all his wonderful acts...proclaim his salvation day after day. Declare...his marvelous deeds among all peoples" (1 Ch. 16:8-9, 23-24). Thus, Israel's mandate to witness was grounded in her covenant with God and applies to every child of Abraham (Gal. 3:7)—by blood and/or by faith—and never ceases (Gal. 3:15-19f).

Sadly, the Old Covenant Jews failed to take God's blessings to the Gentiles. Instead, they hoarded these blessings for themselves. In our day, if God's people desire his promised Abrahamic blessings through Christ, we must not keep his blessings for ourselves either. We, like them, are responsible to pass them on, to be a blessing to others and all nations, to be "witnesses" (Ac. 1:8), to be "fishers of men" (Mt. 4:19), and to "produce the fruit" of the kingdom we've been given (Mt. 21:43). This missionary mandate hasn't changed since the days of Abraham. What has changed is that God's blessings are greater and the known civilized world is much bigger. We are to bless all the nations with "the eternal gospel" (Rev. 14:6), just as Jesus' contemporaries did in their time.

One More Biggie

Anyone seeking truth should hesitate to embrace any tradition that tampers with the words of Jesus Christ, that takes issue with his imminency, or that even hints that He might have been mistaken or never said these things. Let's also be cautious of accepting any method of biblical interpretation or listening to any end-time prophecy "expert" who un-anchors and lifts "last days" events out of their 1st-century, historical, and covenantal context and assumes that they are just beginning in our day. It's all too easy to drift off in any direction and attach speculative and subjective meanings that are grossly wrong. Let's also be aware that the greatest threat to the Word of God comes not from without but from within the Church. Jesus lived, spoke, and died during the biblical "last days" or "last times." These were the "last days" of the biggest thing that was then ending: biblical Judaism, and not the cosmos.

In conclusion, if Jesus was an infallible prophet, if we truly value the integrity of our faith and the inerrancy of Scripture, then *everything* contained in Jesus' homogeneous prophecy of "all these things" *must have happened within the time span* He specified—"this generation." The destruction of Jerusalem and the Temple, and the end of the Judaic age are historical facts. But *there's one more end-*

time event that also must have occurred during that generation. It's a biggie! We'll devote our next three chapters to it. If we can prove that it also was fulfilled back then, then all futuristic postponement traditions will fall to the ground.

11

Didn't Jesus Return When He Said He Would? *

The fall of Jerusalem in A.D. 70 does not stand alone as an isolated event of history. Nor does it compare with catastrophes like the siege of Troy, the downfall of Carthage, the demise of the Roman Empire, or even the collapse of Communism. Behind its visible events is an unseen significance that is just as real and even more relevant and more important than any other major event in history. Until now, only a few scholars have recognized and appreciated what we will discuss in this and the next chapter. Why is it so important? Because God's Word tells us that "My people are destroyed from lack of knowledge" (Hos. 4:6a). Lack of this knowledge has destroyed much and hindered many. As a result, the Church has squandered much of its true heritage and traded in its sure foundation for a bowl of postponement pottage (Ge. 25:19-34).

---

* Much of the material in this and the next chapter was presented by the author at the Evangelical Theological Society's 48th Annual Meeting in November 1996 in Jackson, Mississippi.

In addition to his astonishingly accurate prediction in A.D. 30 of the destruction of the Temple, the fall of Jerusalem, and the end of the age, Jesus included one other major eschatological event in his prophecy, his parousia, or "coming on the clouds:"

- *What will be the sign of your coming (parousia)...?* *(Mt. 24:3).*

- *For as the lightning comes from the east and flashes to the west, so will be the coming (parousia) of the Son of Man (Mt. 24:27).*

- *At that time the sign of the Son of Man will appear in the sky, and all the nations of the earth will mourn. They will see the Son of Man coming (erchomai) on the clouds of the sky, with power and great glory (Mt. 24:30).*

With three short words, Jesus proclaimed that "all these things," everything from verse 3 through 33, would transpire before "this generation...passed away" (Mt. 24:34). At face value, these words of Jesus are so plain and grammatically precise that they should preclude any possibility of misunderstanding, especially of the timing issue. If not, then his words have no obvious or definite meaning. Like it or not, Jesus' Olivet Discourse is one continuous and homogeneous prophecy. And no interpreter has the freedom to weave in and out of its time-limited context at will. No justification exists for either postponing fulfillment to some distant future or exempting and extracting any of the things He said would happen from the restriction of his "this generation."

If Jesus meant what He said, said what He meant, and was an infallible Prophet, all the components of his prophecy must stand or fall together. These certainly include his coming on the clouds with power and glory. The failure of any one component to occur within that existing generation would disqualify Jesus as a prophet and call into question the truth of Scripture. If He did not return when He said He would, we have a dilemma of huge proportions.

The Enigma and Dilemma of "Nonoccurrence"

No subject in the Bible generates more interest, speculation, or debate than the coming again, the return, or the second coming of Jesus Christ, as it is variously called. Yet for nearly 2,000 years the vast majority of Christians has been eagerly expecting and predicting his "soon-and-any-moment" return. Meanwhile, we've struggled with the enigma and dilemma of "nonoccurrence," as we try to maintain a pretense of inerrancy, infallibility, and inspiration of Scripture—an impossible and harmful balancing act.

Conservative scholarship postulates that Jesus' coming again has been delayed or postponed. This makes Jesus' time-frame references and the imminency expectations of the early Church major embarrassments that must be explained away. Liberal scholarship reckons that Jesus and the New Testament writers were simply mistaken or deluded. Some think that the statements were altered or added later by his frustrated followers. These questionable conclusions dismiss the authenticity of Christ and the whole issue of Bible inerrancy.

If He did not return when He said He would, we have a dilemma of huge proportions.

Most Christians don't seem to realize the predicament we are in if Jesus Christ didn't fulfill his many promises to return within the time parameters He specified. Informed critics of Christianity, on the other hand, have no trouble seeing right through the strained attempts of church leaders to explain away nonoccurrence and to protect the credibility and divinity of Jesus in the face of his supposed failure to return. These critics have a legitimate complaint if Jesus did not do something that He said He would. They are quite aware of the enigma and dilemma that nonoccurrence presents for the Christian Church and the impossibility of escaping it without being disloyal to Christ.

- **Bertrand Russell.** Atheist Bertrand Russell, in his book *Why I Am Not A Christian*, discredits the inspiration of the New Testament by saying:

  > I am concerned with Christ as He appears in the Gospel narrative...He certainly thought that his second coming would occur in clouds of glory before the death of all the people who were living at the time. There are a great many texts that prove...He believed that his coming would happen during the lifetime of many then living. That was the belief of his earlier followers, and it was the basis of a good deal of his moral teaching.

- **Albert Schweitzer.** In his 19-century book, *The Quest of the Historical Jesus,* Schweitzer summarized the problem of "Parousia delay" as follows:

  > The whole history of Christianity down to the present day...is based on the delay of the Parousia, the nonoccurrence of the Parousia, the abandonment of eschatology, the process and completion of the 'de-eschatologizing' of religion which has been connected therewith.

- **Jewish Critics.** Jewish critics contend that Jesus didn't complete the whole mission of the Messiah, although many admit that He fulfilled some of it. That's why, in their opinion, He was definitely not the Messiah, though some allow that He may have been the Messiah for the Gentiles. This is the Jews' primary excuse for rejecting Jesus and belittling Christianity.

- **Muslim Critics.** Many Muslims paint Christianity as a failed and false religion. They acknowledge that Jesus was a prophet, but discredit his divinity and destroy the credibility of the faith He presented by pointing out alleged errors and inconsistencies concerning his *perceived* nonreturn. They rightly recognize the logical implications of the Bible's time statements as having a direct bearing on the messianic and divine claims of Christ. They believe that Jesus and the Apostles either lied about his imminent return and other eschatological matters, or Jesus prophesied things that were not fulfilled when He said they would. Either way, He was a false prophet. These arguments naturally seek to undermine the inspiration and inerrancy of the Bible and open the door for the acceptance of the Koran and Islam.

- **Scoffers.** In New Testament times, Jewish scoffers acknowledged the link between Jesus' return and the destruction of the Temple. They pointed to the continuation of everything—the Temple, city, and priesthood—as evidence that Jesus hadn't come back as He promised. No visible changes were evident. These scoffers doubted the sureness of Jesus' promise, viewed Christianity as a perversion of Israel's future, and mockingly asked, "Where is this coming He promised?" (2 Pe. 3:3-4; Jude 16-19). Back then, Jesus' prophecies were only thirty-some years old. Currently, the "delay" is 19 centuries long and counting. The arguments of those early scoffers are looking pretty good now. If there was a delay, hasn't history proven those 1st-century scoffers were right after all?

- **Complicity in the Christian Camp.** Most Christian traditionalists have not faced or answered the challenge of Jesus' nonreturn. In essence, they have aligned themselves with the 1st-century scoffers and become unwitting accomplices of Christianity's critics. Most agree that Jesus didn't return *as* and *when* He promised, in that generation or in that century. Standard Christian explanations posit that Jesus' coming has been delayed or postponed, or that the timing was misunderstood, and that He will come again (return) someday "soon" and finish the job. Sadly, these rebuttals only prove the critics' point that Jesus was incorrect about his time-restricted predictions and therefore cannot be the Messiah. The bottom line is that postponement theories directly contradict the teachings of Jesus, and nonoccurrence leaves Christianity vulnerable to all manner of critical and skeptical assaults. It gives critics all the license they need to blaspheme Jesus as not only a false prophet, but a deceiver as well. It opens wide the door to the dismissal of all Christian claims.

Even C.S. Lewis, the respected Christian apologist and author, we are embarrassed to report, said in 1960:

> Say what you like, the apocalyptic beliefs of the first Christians have been proved to be false. It is clear from the New Testament that they all expected the Second Coming in their own lifetime. And, worse still, they had a reason, and one which you will find very embarrassing. Their Master had told them so. He shared, and indeed created, their delusion. He said in so many words, 'this generation shall not pass till all these things be done.' And He was wrong. He clearly knew no more about the end of the world than anyone else. It is certainly the most embarrassing verse in the Bible.[1]

As we shall see, the embarrassment belongs to C.S. Lewis.

- **Funeral Eschatology.** Christian preachers who don't believe that Jesus has already returned and has received his first disciples into heaven (Jn. 14:1-3; also 3:13; 13:33, 36), assure the family and friends at a Christian funeral that the departed believer is in heaven with Jesus, right now. Call it "funeral eschatology," but while comforting, it's totally inconsistent. Many educated Christians rightly recognize this no-one-in-heaven-yet dilemma in the classroom. Yet they conveniently choose to ignore it at the funeral home. Which is it? Do believers today immediately go to heaven upon physical death? Or, do they still have to wait in Hades or some-where else until Jesus finishes preparing a place and returns to receive them?

Are we so blind to the implications of nonoccurrence? These attacks from informed critics should stir some sober reflections (1 Pe. 3:15; 2 Ti. 4:2-4).

First and foremost, let us affirm that the foundational doctrine of the return of Jesus Christ is non-negotiable. The very credibility

---

Many educated Christians rightly recognize this no-one-in-heaven-yet dilemma in the classroom. Yet they conveniently choose to ignore it at the funeral home.

---

of Jesus and the authority of Scripture are at stake. But we must come to grips with the inspired time-frame parameters and Jesus' inclusion of his *parousia* return within the context of his "all these things." Only one time in human history is, was, or will be the cor-rect time, and only one generation is, was, or will be the generation to experience the return of Jesus.

Is it possible that there is a relatively simple and greatly over-looked solution to the discrediting enigma and dilemma of nonoccurrence? Perhaps the most obvious has been staring us in the face all these centuries. In our next chapter, we'll examine seven demanding, scriptural evidences why Jesus *did return* within the generation which was alive during his earthly ministry, *just as and when He said He would,* and *as and when every New Testament writer and his first followers expected—under the guiding of the Holy Spirit* (Jn. 16:13). Is this too frightening to consider? Truth is often frightening. But again, the divinity of Jesus and the trustworthiness of Scripture hang in the balance. So, "Come now, let us reason together" (Isa. 1:18). As we do, we implore you not to dismiss any of this evidence prematurely. Read through it all. Ponder it. Test it thoroughly (1 Th. 5:21). As we reexamine what the Bible actually says and teaches, be prepared to unlearn anything you've received by tradition which won't stand up to the test of *sola scriptura*, or "only the Scriptures."

12

*Seven Demanding Evidences of Jesus' Timely Return**

If it were true that Jesus is a failed prophet, then his critics have won the day. But if there is evidence that Jesus did return *as* and *when* He said He would, then we *should* be speaking loudly in his defense, not blindly following the blind. There is demanding evidence to be considered.

Evidence 1. The Emphatic Time Statements of Jesus. The strongest possible evidence that Jesus returned within the lifetime of his contemporaries is his own time-restrictive statements. He left no doubts. Frequently, He confirmed the certainty and faithfulness of his end-time coming and set its time parameter. His words were clear, concise, and unequivocal. He didn't say "maybe" or "possibly" or "someday" or "one day" or "in 2,000 years" or "in 10,000 years." Jesus spoke in a plain, straightforward manner to the

---

*_Much of the material in this and the last chapter was presented by the author at the Evangelical Theological Society's 48th Annual Meeting in November 1996 in Jackson, Mississippi._

ordinary people of his day, not in a complex manner only understood by trained theologians or linguists. When taken at face value,
his words concerning his coming are some of the clearest in the
New Testament. If forced to mean something else, they become
puzzling. As you read the following verses, imagine yourself to be a
1st-century disciple. How would *you* have understood Jesus' words,
especially concerning the *time* of his coming?

Matthew 26:64. Quoting from the prophet Daniel, Jesus responded to and forewarned Caiaphas, the high priest, and the
Sanhedrin saying, "...*In the future you will see the Son of Man
sitting at the right hand of the Mighty One, and coming on
the clouds of heaven.*" When Jesus said "you," He meant the
people He spoke to. He spoke in the first person directly to
Caiaphas, the high priest, and all present. They were familiar
with this apocalyptic language, and would be the ones who

Jesus spoke in a plain, straightforward manner to the ordinary people of his day, not in a complex manner only understood by trained theologians or linguists.

---

would "see" his return in catastrophic judgment. How could
Jesus possibly have been describing an event coming some 2,000
years in the future? The text demands fulfillment in their lifetime, not deferment to hundreds or thousands of years later. That
would have meant nothing to them.[1]

Matthew 10:23. While talking with his disciples, Jesus promised, "*When you are persecuted in one place, flee to another, I
tell you the truth, you will not finish going through the cities
of Israel before the Son of man comes.*"

Was Jesus lying or misleading them here? Was this part of a
clever way of keeping them faithful and devoted by giving them

false hope? Or were these words spoken to real people in that "you" group living in the 1st century? They were the ones Jesus instructed to evangelize those cities of Israel. Jesus' obvious intent was not to deceive but to assure his disciples that during the persecution that was soon to come upon them, they would not run out of places to flee for safety before He returned. Furthermore, didn't Jesus' words have to be fulfilled before Israel ceased to exist as a nation in A.D. 70? If He was inspired and telling the truth, they were.[2]

Matthew 16:27-28. He informed his disciples, *"For the Son of Man is going to come in his Father's glory with his angels, and then he will reward each person according to what he has done. I tell you the truth, some who are standing here will not taste death before they see the Son of Man coming in his kingdom."* Here again, Jesus is describing the same, singular event with a definite time-frame limitation. A 40-year period was to transpire between his ascension into heaven and coming back in his kingdom (2 Ti. 4:1). During that time some of his disciples died, but others remained alive. If this event has yet to take place, then shouldn't we have people living today who are almost 2,000 years old? But this is ridiculous. Why not accept Jesus' words at face value and leave this coming in the time-context in which He clearly and emphatically placed it? Yet many Bible commentators have violently resisted the plain and common-sense meaning of these words.[3]

Matthew 24:3, 27, 30, 34. As we've seen, Jesus divinely linked the time of his coming to the destruction of the Temple. *" 'Tell us,' they said, 'when will this happen, and what will be the sign of your coming and of the end of the age'...so will be the coming of the Son of Man...At that time the sign of the Son of Man [Jesus] will appear in the sky, and all the nations of the earth will mourn. They will see the Son of Man coming on the clouds of the sky, with power and great glory... I tell you* *the truth, this generation will certainly not pass away until all these things have happened."*

Jesus inseparably named his coming as a part of "all these things." He used the very same time phrase his disciples had just heard Him speak to the scribes and Pharisees when He told them the guilt of the blood of the righteous would fall upon "this generation" (Mt. 23:35-36). In all its seventeen other uses in the New Testament, the phrase "this generation" is consistent in its meaning. Jesus meant his contemporaries, not some un-born generation centuries removed, and not a race or type of people. There are no exceptions.[4] And no justification exists for excluding his *parousia* (coming/return) from the context of "all these things."

John 21:22. *"Jesus answered, 'If I want him to remain alive until I return, what is that to you? You must follow me'."*

Here Jesus suggested that the Apostle John could be, but not necessarily would be, alive when He returned. It's yet another confirmation that a 1st-century time frame is the only one Jesus ever intended. As far as is known, John was the only original Apostle who survived beyond the destruction of Jerusalem. The point is clear. Can you seriously doubt that any of Jesus' disciples or hearers would have placed his coming in glory outside of the lifetime of some then present? A well-established pattern and consistency of 1st-century imminency dominates Jesus' words. It perfectly harmonizes with the literal, exact, chrono-logical, and sequential fulfillment of Daniel's two time prophecies (covered in chapters six and seven) which also pinpointed 1st-century fulfillment, with no gaps, no interruptions, and no exegetic gimmicks.

These statements of Jesus concerning the imminence of his coming/return have proven especially perplexing for all postponement traditionalists. But why fight them? Why twist them? Why not just take Jesus' time-restricted words at face value, literally and naturally?

Every New Testament writer, the early Church believers, and even the unbelieving Jews did exactly that. They never imagined that Jesus might be referring to a distant event in 2,000 years. So why can't we just take Jesus at his word and leave this magnificent eschatological event in its proper time frame where it rightly belongs?

Thus, the 1st century should confirm when everything Jesus promised either did or didn't come to pass. If He was wrong, then He was neither inspired nor a Prophet of God (Dt. 18:21-22), nor the Messiah. There is no valid escape from this predicament. The texts demand it. Even appealing to the unknown time statement, "No one knows about that day or hour" (Mt. 24:36; 25:13) doesn't mean knowing the time was a futile task, nor does it override the nearness and time-restriction imposed by Jesus Himself. No one knows the day or hour of the birth of a baby following a nine-month gestation period either. And Jesus compared his return to just that (Mt. 24:8). But that's why He gave signs. By watching for these signs and obeying his instructions to flee, his disciples could know that the tough times of unequalled tribulation would not last forever and that his coming was very close.

Once more, we'd be well-advised to consider the words of the old hymn, *Tis So Sweet* (see chapter nine). Unfortunately, the over-whelming majority of Christians since Bible times have not been willing to just take Jesus at his word. They no more believe that Jesus' words of imminence applied to the time of his first disciples than did the scoffers of that day. So we've employed every means imaginable to side-step or distort their natural and time-restricted meaning. The fact is, these manipulations are necessitated by our preconceived notions about the nature of his coming. Since we haven't seen anything resembling what we've been told to look for, we've abandoned a literal hermeneutic and postponed the time of its occurrence to the future—now 19 centuries and counting.

Ironically, profound things can be simple. And apparently Jesus wanted to keep his statements simple. Otherwise, why say them? We know that "the common people heard Him gladly" (Mk. 12:37

KJV). But the traditions of men can make the word of God of little or no effect (Mk. 7:13; Mt. 15:6). It was true back then. It's still true today. Think about it, though. Why complicate Jesus' words? Why not keep them simple and just honor their plain meaning and adjust our notions of the nature of fulfillment. Maybe, just maybe, Jesus Christ knew in what generation He would return, and taught that very thing using words and meanings his hearers could easily grasp. And maybe, just maybe, it's the uninspired historic Church, its creeds, and our favorite theologians who have made the mistake. Jesus said it was the "evil servant" who says "My Lord delayeth his coming" (Mt. 24:48 KJV). The Church has been preaching "delay" for 19 centuries and counting.[5]

We should be able to stop here and rest our case. If you had heard Jesus' teachings first-hand, how would you have understood his words? Who would you have thought He was talking to? Then why should we believe any differently today? Why must we make excuses for Him? If Jesus said it, shouldn't we believe it and that settles it? This is our first evidence. Even if it isn't sufficient to "prove" our point, there's more—much more.

Evidence 2. Equally Inspired and Emphatic Imminency Statements and Expectations of Every New Testament Writer. In addition to taking Jesus at his word, we'd be well advised to take the New Testament writers at their word, too. Bible scholars generally agree that every New Testament writer, all the Apostles, and members of the 1st-century Church expected that Christ's coming again, his return (parousia), would occur within their lifetime. And why wouldn't they? 1) The Lord told them so. 2) Possessing the promised Holy Spirit, their expectations were evidently guided by the Spirit's disclosing work: "But when he, the Spirit of truth, comes, he will guide you into all truth. He will not speak on his own; he will speak only what he hears, and he will tell you what is to come" (Jn. 16:13; 14:25; also see 1 Jn. 2:20).

If Jesus' Apostles and first disciples were wrong or misguided in their Spirit-guided expectations of the Lord's return, what else might they have been mistaken about? How then could we trust them to convey other aspects of the faith along to us, such as the requirements for salvation? Whose expectations should we trust? Theirs? The historic Church's? The creeds'? Or ours today?

In the following examples, these New Testament writers were declaring inspired truth as emphatically as Jesus. Again, if their expectations failed to come to pass, as all postponement traditions are constrained to admit, they weren't inspired. There is no other valid option. If the Holy Spirit lied to them, misled them, or did an inadequate job, we would find it intolerable.

If Jesus' Apostles and first disciples were wrong or misguided in their Spirit-guided expectations of the Lord's return, what else might they have been mistaken about?

- **James.** Ten years before Jerusalem was destroyed, James declared that he was living "in the last days" (Jas. 5:3) and that "the Judge is standing at the door" (Jas. 5:9; also see Mt. 24:33). He admonished the 1st-century followers of Christ to be patient "until the coming of the Lord" (Js 5:7). Then he proclaimed "the Lord's coming is at hand" (Jas. 5:8 NAS). James' words are some of the strongest in the Bible indicating the nearness of the Lord's return just ten years later. James' sense of the closeness of "the time of the end" agrees with Jesus' teachings.

The same language was used to announce the arrival of the kingdom of God. John the Baptist proclaimed it "at hand" (Mt. 3:2 KJV, the Greek word *eggizo* from *engy*, meaning graspable). It was inaugurated within months. Jesus used the same idiomatic phrase when speaking of proximity ("behold, he is at hand that doth betray me" [Mt. 26:46 KJV]), and immediacy ("My time is at hand," [Mt. 26:18 KJV]). For Jesus' other uses of this "at hand" idiom, see: Mk. 1:15; Mt. 4:17; 10:7; 26:45; Jn. 2:13; 6:4; 7:2; 11:55 KJV.

James' readers did not, as we today do, interpret his "at hand" time terminology as a 2,000-years-or-longer period. Nor was James deceiving his audience with a different meaning of known words. He issued no disclaimers. His "at hand" demands the same "right there" or "almost right there" immediacy as other scriptures. "At hand" is the ultimate imminency idiom of Scripture. It means soon, not centuries later.

Some interpreters rationalize a long delay or elongation of the Bible's numerous imminency statements by ascribing to God a time scale different from our own, such as the oft-cited "a day equals a thousand years" (2 Pe. 3:8).[6] Not only does this tactic strip Scripture of a meaning we can grasp, it gives it a character of deception rather than revelation. It's the classic reason that so much confusion prevails. God's Word does *not* speak to man according to man's understanding of time, and then act according to a different scale. For God to inspire men to write words that meant nearness and imminence to humankind, but in reality meant a long time [many centuries], would be confusing and grossly inconsistent with God's character.

The good news is that we can trust God's time and imminency statements. We can be assured that God inspired the writers of Scripture to communicate time in a language that would be clearly understood in its plain literal sense by the common person. When God meant a long time, He used those words indicating just that. In Daniel 8:26, 10:14; and 12:2-9, a "distant future" was 400-600 years. In Jeremiah 29:10 and 28, a "long time" was 70 years. In Numbers 24:17, the Redeemer was "not near" (He was some 1,500 years away). On the other hand, when God meant a "short time," He inspired writers to use plain, ordinary words like "at hand," "near," "at the door," "soon," and "shortly." These are all well-understood, human terms that God inspired to communicate time truths to human beings. In the Bible, "near" never means "far" nor does "far" mean "near." Neither can words and phrases indicating imminency be stretched 2,000 years or so in order to protect a theological bias or postponement agenda. No principle of interpretation can justify twisting such plain statements of time.

- **The Writer of Hebrews.** In A.D. 64 the author of Hebrews stated, "In just a very little while, He who is coming will come and will not delay" (Heb. 10:37). He was quoting from Habakkuk's "appointed time...of the end" prophecy (Hab. 2:3). The entire book of Hebrews conveys this same sense of urgency and imminency. For example, "as you see the Day approaching" (Heb. 10:25), and other statements like it, cannot be ignored, twisted, or lightly brushed aside. They are indicative of the nearness and certainty of the Lord's return. When Hebrews was written, the early Church was undergoing intense persecution from the Jews and the Roman Emperor Nero. These believers were eagerly awaiting the Lord's promised return. How could they "see the Day approaching" if it was two millennia later? The popular notion that the Lord has delayed his coming directly contradicts these scriptures.

Let's recall that 2,000 years is over 400 years longer than the covenant nation of Israel even existed. That amount of time surely must be considered a "delay" by any one's vernacular. In essence, this "delay" would make the end longer than the period that it is ending! Further, what comfort would a distant-future fulfillment be to those suffering then and there? All of Jesus' parables about his coming again/return included an interval, but one that nevertheless concluded within the lifetime of its hearers, not long after their deaths. Remember that it was an evil servant who said "My Lord delayeth his coming" (Mt. 24:48 KJV).

- **Paul.** Paul also led his contemporaries to believe that some of them ("we" and "you," not "those" centuries removed from then) would still be alive on planet Earth when Jesus came

(1 Th. 4:15). Their "whole spirit, soul and body" [physical, *soma* bodies] would be "kept blameless at [until] the coming of the Lord (1 Th. 5:23-24). If they all died without receiving Paul's promise, and their bodies weren't kept but decayed in graves, hasn't his inspiration fail, too? Paul further told Timothy to "keep this commandment...until the appearing of our Lord Jesus Christ" (1 Ti. 6:14). He did *not* tell Timothy to keep it until he (Timothy) died. Around A.D. 57, Paul described the Corinthian believers as "eagerly" awaiting Christ's coming at "the end" (1 Cor. 1:7-8) and declared that "the time is short" (1 Cor. 7:29). In all his writings, Paul evidently had no need to clarify that he was referring to the nearness of any other coming, or end, different from that taught by Jesus in his Olivet Discourse. Paul anticipated the imminent return of Christ in his lifetime (had he not been killed) and in the lifetime of his hearers and first readers. The plain grammatical meaning of Paul's often-used pronoun "we" (1 Th. 4:15-17; 1 Cor. 15:51-52), and the saturation of his epistles with nearness expectations and exhortations allow no other conclusion than a contemporary one, if we're honest readers (Ro. 13:11-12; Php. 4:5; Gal. 4:4; 1 Cor. 7:29, 31; 2 Th. 1:7). Did Paul mislead God's 1st-century people? Of course not. They, not we, were to find rest and vindication from their persecutions when Christ came in vengeance upon his enemies. If these hopes failed to materialize and their expectations ended in disappointment, how can we believe anything Paul said?

- **Peter.** In his two epistles, Peter similarly admonished his hearers and first readers, exhorting them to live holy lives and hang in there for "a little while" (1 Pe. 1:6; 5:10; compare with Jn. 16:16-19). This was to be "until the coming of the salvation that is ready to be revealed in the last time" (1 Pe. 1:5) of "these last times" (1 Pe. 1:20). Peter is referring to the identical, 1st-century time frame for fulfillment, as do all the other New Testament passages. That's why, throughout his epistles, Peter employs the personal pronoun "you." Peter wasn't using this "you" editorially, as some argue (i.e., applying it to just anyone at anytime). It's bad hermeneutics to take personal pronouns in the New Testament letters—including Peter's letters—to refer to some other group who would experience these events. The imminency statements were addressed to people then present, and they meant what they said in that context. Peter also said that "the end of all things is at hand" (1 Pe. 4:7 KJV), Jesus was "ready to judge the living and the dead" (1 Pe. 4:5), and "it is time for judgment to begin with the family of God" (1 Pe. 4:17). What had once been seen as far off by the ancient prophets was now ready to be revealed to the "you" group in that "last time" (1 Pe. 1:5, 12; also Ac. 3:24).

- **Like a Thief.** Jesus' coming was often compared to the entrance of a "thief" (Mt. 24:43; 1 Th. 5:2; 2 Pe. 3:10; Rev. 3:3; 16:15), and therefore presumed by many to be a completely unpredictable event. But the reason for the thief metaphor was that, even though no one could know the precise time (day or hour), Jesus' followers were *not* to be caught off guard (1 Th. 5:4). His disciples could watch and see "the day" approaching by discerning the signs (Heb. 10:25; 1 Th. 5:5-6). A second reason for the thief metaphor is that no one concerns himself about a thief coming in the distant future, but anyone would be concerned about a thief coming in his lifetime, which the Bible sets at 70 to 80 years (Ps. 90:10). A 2,000-year delay violates both the imagery, sense of urgency, and contemporary significance of this descriptive phrase.

Paul and Peter both admonished 1st-century believers to not let the day overtake them as a thief (1Th. 5:4). Most of the people received these scriptures and believed them. Back then, they didn't have religious professionals explaining these inspired words away or telling them that these verses applied to some future generation 2,000 years down the road. They knew it applied to them.

Thusly, the New Testament writers were in one accord with Jesus as to his return. How many times, in how many ways, and with how many inspired words and phrases must these inspired writers express this 1st-century imminency before we moderns bow our knees in submission and cease persisting in our preconceived, postponement notions? The language of nearness forbids a protracted period of time.

But were the New Testament writers grossly mistaken or falsely led? Or did the Holy Spirit fail to do his job? These options pose an intolerable dilemma.

Without question, the Holy Spirit's guidance is the second strongest argument and demanding evidence that the 1st-century expectations of the early Church were correct and fulfilled (Jn. 16:13;

... the New Testament writers were in one accord with Jesus as to his return.

---

also 1 Jn. 2:20). If we deny this, aren't we denying the faith? If these severely persecuted people did not live to see the Lord's coming, weren't they victims of one of the cruelest hoaxes ever perpetrated on humankind?

No, the Spirit of truth did not become the Spirit of falsehood. Jesus' first followers were not kept in the dark. The specific time statements of Jesus and the imminency statements of the inspired New Testament writers confirm the time of his return as "at hand." Any attempts to mitigate the time element of Scripture must be condemned (2 Ti. 2:15).

Evidence 3. A Long Biblical Precedent. Jesus specified exactly *how* He would come again (i.e., the nature of his *parousia* coming). Twice He said He would come "on the clouds" (Mt. 24:30; 26:64). But what did He mean? If you were a 1st-century Jew raised in the synagogue, you would have known exactly what He meant.

This type of coming had a long biblical precedent. To appreciate the rich Jewish terminology for cloud-coming, we must enter the mind of a 1st-century Jew. If we look at these things only through 20th-century eyes, we'll become prisoners of what has become the traditional mindset of misunderstanding and confusion.

Christ's "coming on the clouds" is a common metaphor borrowed from Old Testament portrayals of God descending from heaven and coming in power and glory to execute judgment on a people or nation. In all the historic comings of God in judgment, He acted through human armies, or through nature, to bring destruction ("the Lord is a man of war" [Ex. 15:3 KJV]). Each was a direct act of God and each was termed "the day of the Lord." They were always described with figurative language, and empowered by supernatural support, and they brought historical calamity to Egypt, Edom, Assyria, Babylon, and even on Israel itself.

The Jews of Jesus' day had studied these "day of the Lord" occurrences and were familiar with "cloud-coming" phraseology, as well as the application of one with the other.[7] The Hebrew scriptures are rich in similes and figurative language that poetically portray this heavenly perspective of God coming among men in judgment:

- See, the Lord rides on a swift *cloud* and is coming to Egypt (Isa. 19:1). (For the earthly fulfillment, see Isaiah 20:1-6)

- Look! He advances like the *clouds,* his chariots come like a whirlwind (Jer. 4:13).

- For the day is near, the day of the Lord is near—a day of *clouds,* a time of doom for the nations (Eze. 30:3).

- Sing to God, sing praise to his name, extol him who rides on the *clouds*... (Ps. 68:4).

- ...He makes the *clouds* his chariots and rides on the wings of the wind. He makes winds his messengers, flames of fire his servants (Ps. 104:3-4).

- Also see Eze. 30:18; Ps. 18:9-12; 2 Sa. 22:10-12; Na. 1:3; Joel 2:1-2; Zep. 1:14-15).

With familiar cloud-coming imagery Daniel prophesied the coming of the Son of Man (Da. 7:13). Jesus, by deriving his "coming on the clouds" phrase directly from Daniel, was revealing Himself as God and the promised Messiah (Mt. 24:30; 26:64). The high priest Caiaphas immediately understood this claim of Jesus to be Deity and responded, "He has spoken blasphemy!" (Mt. 26:65). Jesus was also applying his coming in judgment and power of war in the *same* technical way as the Father had come down from Heaven many times before:

> Look! The Lord is coming from his dwelling place; he comes down and treads the high places of the earth (Mic. 1:3).

> See, the Lord is coming out of his dwelling to punish the people of the earth for their sins (Isa. 26:21).

> But your many enemies will become like fine dust, the ruthless hordes like blown chaff. Suddenly, in an instant the Lord Almighty will come with thunder and earthquake and great noise, with windstorm and tempest and flames of a devouring fire (Isa. 29:5-6).

Because of this background, Jesus' disciples would have understood what He was talking about in his Olivet Discourse (Mt. 24:30). The high priest understood it. That's why he was so offended by and accused Jesus of blasphemy (Mt. 26:64-65). Let's note that Jesus made no disclaimers to change the meaning or nature of this type of coming, and neither should we.

Another important factor is that in all these real biblical comings of God in the Old Testament, God was *never physically visible*; He was unseen by human eyes! Thus, cloud-coming is the language of divine imagery. It denotes divine action. In every instance, humans were fully aware of God's Presence and personal intervention in those events of history. Obviously, this Jewish perspective is quite different from the way we moderns have been conditioned to think of Christ's coming on the clouds. We imagine his coming to be spectacularly visible on the tops of literal fluffy cumulus clouds as they transport Him down to earth.[8] Yet every biblical instance of a cloud-coming was a real coming of God. Jesus employed the same figure of speech for his end-time prophecies. Thus for Jesus and a 1st-century Jew, coming "on the clouds" was not a claim to come visibly to the human eye.

Just as the cloud-coming Jehovah God came in Old Testament times, Jesus came "on the clouds."

With this understanding, we can see the Lord Jesus making his appearance, or coming again, in the events of the Roman-Jewish War and the final destruction of Jerusalem in A.D. 70. Just as the cloud-coming Jehovah God came in Old Testament times, Jesus came "on the clouds." He came utilizing the armies of Rome to deliver his people. And in keeping with the Old Testament pattern, He was not physically seen.

Another important fact to reflect in this judgment event is the change of covenant. Therefore, "the day of the Lord" (Jehovah) of the Old Testament became "the day of Christ" (*Christos* 2 Th. 2:2; *kurios* 2 Pe. 3:10) in the New Testament.

Look, he is coming with the clouds (Rev. 1:7).

Evidence 4. The Pattern of Other Apocalyptic Language. Jesus and the New Testament writers employed other common apocalyptic language (i.e., graphic images of astronomical upheavals which were frequently used by the Old Testament prophets to describe the many catastrophic comings of "the day of the Lord"):

- "Collapsing-universe" and signs-in-the-sky language: sun and moon darkened, fire, stars falling, sky rolling up, heavens rotting away.

- Or "earth-moving" language: mountains melting, shaking, etc.

They used the very same language to describe the great and glorious day of Christ's coming again.

In the history of the fulfillment of this cosmic catastrophic language, we look in vain to find these things literally occurring or visibly happening. The dramatic terminology is figuratively depicting the impending literal judgment, the utter devastation and eclipse of powerful political oppressors and sinful nations who opposed God, and even the punishment of his people (Isa. 13, 24, 34; Mic. 1; Zep. 1; Ob; Joel 1-2; Eze. 7-10; 2 Sa. 22). Sure, it sounds like the end of the world, but none of these acts of God was a universe-destroying or time-ending event. This apocalyptic language transcends its literalism. Its long history of fulfillment teaches us something very important about its nature. Dramatic figurative language was always used to describe the awful magnitude of impending judgment which would involve the direct intervention and unseen Presence of God—events so profound that they could not be described or comprehended in literal language.

We have a 1st-century "proof" that the New Testament Christians understood the use of apocalyptic language. The Thessalonians could only have believed that "the day of the Lord" had already come if they had understood the language in a figurative way (2 Th. 2:1-2). Had they been taught the traditional 20th-century concept you and I have been taught—featuring a visible cosmic cataclysm—no one could have confused them that the Day had already happened. The physical earth and heavens were unchanged during their time of confusion. Moreover, Paul did not correct their understanding of the nature of that event, nor did he use the existence of the physical creation as proof that this "day of the Lord" had not come. Rather, he only corrected the time issue (also see 1 Th. 5:1-4). Therefore, their concept of an invisible coming of the Lord must have been right. That would be consistent with the familiar use of this apocalyptic language by the prophets and its historic fulfillments. Further, neither Jesus nor any New Testament writer gave any hint that their use of this same language should be interpreted any differently. What, then, causes us to suddenly begin interpreting it differently?

A word of caution is in order. We have recommended a literal understanding of God's time and imminency statements. But literalism cannot be universally applied in interpreting the nature of fulfillments described in symbolic biblical language. Jesus was always correcting the physical literalism of some peoples' interpretations of his figurative teachings—for example: "the temple of his body," "born again," "a well of water springing up to eternal life," "cutting off hands and poking out eyes" just to mention a few. We would be wise to think like 1st-century Jewish believers. They were Old Testament-literate and apocalyptic-precedent thinkers. They knew that behind every descriptive symbol, image, or figure of speech was a literal reality. Consequently, whenever the literal reality of a "day of the Lord" came, they expected that it would be unmistakably evident but theophanic in nature, as it had been many times before, and as it was to be again.

Evidence 5. In the Same Way, For the Same Purpose. Jesus came in judgment against an apostate Judaism. James told his readers that "the judge is standing at the door!" (Jas. 5:9). Peter wrote plainly, "For it is time for judgment to begin with the family of God" (1 Pe. 4:17). Modern interpretations leave Judge Jesus standing at the door!

But Jesus' coming in A.D. 70 involved both visible and invisible aspects. Using the language of the Prophets, and comparing the biblical precedents of a coming "day of the Lord," we can document how Jesus' coming was accomplished. He came in exactly the same *way* ("on the clouds"), for exactly the same *purpose* (judgment), to accomplish exactly the same *thing* (destruction of a nation).

First, history records—quite literally—that Jerusalem and the Temple were destroyed by invading Roman armies in A.D. 70. "Not one stone [was] left upon another," just as Jesus had said (Mt. 24:2). Jesus had inseparably connected his coming with this dramatically visible, historical event (Mt. 24:1-34). This linkage of time, event, and place in his Olivet Discourse prophecy cannot be overstated. Even the 1st-century scoffers knew that the Temple's destruction was the corresponding physical event that signaled his coming (2 Pe. 3:3-4).

Second, the prophet Ezekiel said that in the latter days God would come up against Israel "as a cloud to cover the land" (Eze. 38:9, 16; see also Zec. 12-14). New Testament writers confirmed they were then living in those "last days" (Heb. 1:2; Ac. 2:17; 1 Ti. 4:1; 2 Ti. 3:1; Jas. 5:3; 2 Pe. 3:3; 1 Pe. 1:5, 20; Jude 18; 1 Jn. 2:18). At this time, Isaiah had prophesied, the Messiah would come robed "with the garments of vengeance for clothing" (Isa. 59:17f; see also Ro. 12:19), and He would proclaim not only salvation, but "the day of vengeance of our God" (Isa. 61:2). Jesus' statement in Luke's account of the Olivet Discourse contains this very wording: "When you [Jesus' audience] see Jerusalem surrounded by armies, you will know that its desolation is near...flee... For this is the time of punishment [*these be the days of vengeance*] in fulfillment of all that has been written" (Lk. 21:20-22 [in *KJV*]). The immediate historical setting and explicit framework for these happenings proved to be the Jewish-Roman War of A.D. 66 - 70. After A.D. 70, the "last days" were over.

Third, Isaiah foretold that during this time Israel would fill up the measure of her sin and she would be destroyed (Isa. 65:6-15) by the Lord, who would come with fire and judgment (Isa. 66:15f). Jesus said that this time of filling up would "come upon this generation" (Mt. 23:32-36). That 1st-century apostate Jewish nation, with its city and Temple, had become the great enemy of God's emerging new people, the Church.

Jesus, Ezekiel, Isaiah, and Daniel precisely pinpointed when everything promised would come to pass. If they were wrong, they weren't inspired. There is no valid way to escape it. As the time approached, James said, "The coming of the Lord is at hand" (Jas. 5:8 NAS). Paul reminded his first readers that "the time is short" (1 Cor. 7:29). Peter proclaimed, "The end of all things is at hand" (1 Pe. 4:7 KJV), and warned, "For the time has come for judgment to begin at the house of God" (1 Pe. 4:17). Urgency permeates Peter's sense of expectation. He is emphatic, "The time has come!" John wrote, "It is the last hour!" (1 Jn. 2:18b). How many "last hours" can there be? How long is short? How could these statements be more clear? How many declarations are required before we can believe this inspired imminency?

Fourth, the "sign" of his invisible coming would be:

Do you see all these things?' he asked. 'I tell you the truth not one stone here will be left on another; every one will be thrown down (Mt. 24:2)

As we've seen the destruction of Jerusalem and its Temple was the "sign" (Mt. 24:3). The "sign of the Son of Man ... in the sky [in heaven]" (Mt. 24:30) could have been the plumes of smoke arising from the burning fires above the mountain plateau on which Jerusalem sat (Mk. 10:33).[9] The destruction of the Judaic world followed the same pattern and nature of many Old Testament comings of God, or "days of the Lord." In every instance of God's intervention, his Presence was there, but He was never actually seen.

Let's also recall that God had set Jerusalem on a high place (Ps. 48:1-2; Isa. 2:2-3) at the crossroads of the world (three continents) and "in the center of the nations, with countries all around her" (Eze. 5:5-17). He had a definite purpose (see Eze. 5:8-17). After the fall of A.D. 70, transcontinental traders and travelers from near and far could readily see that something significant had happened. News of the devastation of God's chosen people, their Temple, and the

A sign isn't the reality; it points to the reality. It's something that is visible and points to something that is currently invisible.

entire nation thus spread rapidly throughout the Roman world.

Let's likewise note that Jesus did not appear "in person." His resurrected body did not appear in the sky to signal this special coming. Yet his bodily Presence was there, in keeping with the long-standing day-of-the-Lord motif. That's why a sign was needed. A sign isn't the reality; it points to the reality. It's something that is visible and points to something that is currently invisible. The fall of Jerusalem was the sign that announced the final "last days" of the Jewish age, not the Christian or Church age, to which there is no end. These days were still the *beginning days* of the Christian age.

Thus, Jesus' predictions were all fulfilled. This should be perfectly clear by now, unless you're looking through a futurist veil. There is no need to explain away anything or do a fancy dance around any scripture. Nor should we be surprised that God chose to send Christ in judgment to destroy Jerusalem in A.D. 70 in the same way He had come out of heaven many times before in Old Covenant times "with myriads of holy ones" (Dt. 33:2). Jesus, who had come, died, arose, and gone back to heaven, came out of heaven to judge the very people upon whom He had spoken seven woes (Mt. 23). The time of grace upon the Jewish nation had elapsed (Mt. 27:25; 2 Th. 1:7-8; Jude 14; Ro. 11:26; Isa. 59: 20-21; 27:9). It's a fact of biblical and redemptive history.

In all this, Jesus' prophetic words, the imminency statements of every New Testament writer, and the expectations of the early Church can be plainly understood, in our day, as true and inspired. Yet no one except God the Father knew the final day or hour (exact time) of this "time of the end" (Da. 12:7). Nor can we look back today and reconstruct or know for certain when the literal last day or final hour was. The exact day or hour is not important, but the destruction of biblical Judaism is highly important. It was prophesied; it was fulfilled.

Evidence 6. The Typology of the Jewish High Priest on the Day of Atonement and Jesus Both Appearing "a Second Time." The fall of Jerusalem and demise of the Old Covenant Temple system in A.D. 70 was no localized judgment event as some suggest, just as the cross was no localized execution event. Yet fewer people knew of Jesus' crucifixion than the destruction of the city. Jesus' coming in judgment in A.D. 70 was his appearing "a second time, not to bear sin, but to bring salvation to those who are waiting for him" (Heb. 9:28) and "the coming of the salvation that is ready to be revealed in the last time" (1 Pe. 1:5).[10] If He did not appear "a second time," we have a major problem on our hands.

Curiously, the Bible records that Jesus had already come and appeared *many times* following both his resurrection and ascension. Then what did this phrase appearing "a second time" mean? To understand this terminology, we must refer to the typology of the Jewish high priest, a figure central to Israel's existence. He was their connection to and mediator with God. Once each year on the Day of Atonement (the annual, sixth Jewish feast as prescribed by the Law), the high priest performed his most sacred duty (Lev. 16). He put on his finery, sacrificed a bull, put its blood in a bowl, tied a rope around his leg, entered into the Holy of Holies, sprinkled the blood on the Mercy Seat of the Ark of the Covenant, and made atonement for himself and his house. Then he came out and appeared before the crowd gathered in front of the Tabernacle (later the Temple), killed a goat, took its blood into the Holy of Holies, made atonement for the congregation of Israel, and reappeared a second time to bless the waiting congregation. Lastly, a second goat—the scapegoat—was released into the wilderness. Time spent by the high priest inside the Holy of Holies was a fearful time for the assembled crowd. But his second reappearance, alive, was the most-awaited and joyful part of this whole ritual. It completed the atonement process and revealed that both sacrifices had been accepted by God and that Israel's sins were forgiven for another year.

Jesus Christ, as our new and superior High Priest of the New Covenant (Heb. 4-10), had to perfectly follow and fulfill this typology (Heb 8:5; 10:1). The Bible tells us that the earthly Jewish Temple was only a copy of the heavenly one (Heb. 9, 10, especially 9:23 ff.). That's why Jesus had to depart and go *prepare* the heavenly place for his saints to occupy; He did this by going through these same atonement steps (Jn. 14:1-4). Therefore, after Jesus ascended to the Father, He entered the true Holy of Holies and offered up the perfect sacrifice of his spilled blood. But just as the atonement ritual of the Old Covenant was never considered complete with only the slaying of the sacrifice, neither was Jesus' atonement work finished at the cross, or even when He entered into the true Holy of Holies. Partway through is not the place to abandon this atonement typology, as most do. In order for Jesus to perfectly fulfill the high priest typology, He also needed to fulfill the final, inseparable, and essential act of atonement: to appear "a second time" to show that his sacrifice had been accepted, and to fulfill the role of both goats— one dead, one alive.[11]

If this final step has yet to occur, as all futurist schemes claim, we are faced with some big problems! If Jesus did not appear a second time, we must live with the following unpalatable facts:

1. 1st-century believers watched, waited and eagerly expected in vain (1 Pe. 1:5-9; 2:12; Heb. 9:28; 10:25; Lk. 21:28; Php. 3:20; Gal. 5:5; Ro. 13:11-13; 1 Cor. 1:7; Tit. 2:11-13).

2. Their salvation and ours is still incomplete. If no final sign or proof of atonement has been manifested from heaven, we cannot know if Jesus' sacrifice has yet been accepted by God.

3. We can't know for sure if our sins are fully forgiven, if we are

totally reconciled to God, if we are back in his Presence (where no one had been since Adam), or were we to die tonight, if we would immediately go to heaven (Jn. 3:13; 13:33, 36; 14:1-3).

Jesus appearing "a second time" is essential for complete salvation. This is the climax of the whole salvation event. It's where salvation and end-time prophecy (soteriology and eschatology) are inseparably intertwined. It's why eschatology is the story of our salvation in Christ. If this "salvation that is [was] ready to be revealed in the last time" (1 Pe. 1:5) hasn't occurred in almost 2,000 years, all we can be sure of is that we have the promise of salvation. But if that's all we have, how is the New Covenant any better than the Old in this important regard? If it doesn't supply what the Old could not provide, where are we? How much salvation do we presently have? How much of Christ's mission to "put away sin" is accomplished? Are we still in limbo (an intermediate state) and not yet in God's Presence?

Please note that any doctrine which says that Jesus has not returned and fulfilled salvation promises to Israel is actually saying that we don't have full redemption (1 Pe. 1:9-13; Ac. 3:24; 26:6-8; Eph. 4:4). There's no way around it. As our High Priest, Jesus had to carefully follow and fulfill all aspects of the sacrificial and atonement typology of the high priesthood pattern on the Day of Atonement. This is the crucial factor and meaning behind his appearing "a second time," and that is what was being "eagerly awaited" by the early Church (Gal. 5:5), as they saw "the Day approaching" (Heb. 10:25).

The good news is that postponement traditions are wrong. There was no 19-plus-centuries-and-counting delay. The atonement process was not interrupted. God's redemptive plan was fulfilled by Christ's appearing "a second time." As our High Priest, He did his atoning work during those "last days." He has been "revealed from heaven" (2 Th. 1:7; 1 Pe. 1:7; Lk. 17:30, 31). The sixth Jewish feast of the Day of Atonement is totally fulfilled. Jesus was and is "able to save completely" or "to the utmost" (Heb 7:25 [KJV]). The next question is, how did He appear?

He appeared by "coming on the clouds" in A.D. 70.[12] The invisible nature of that particular type of coming was why a "sign" was needed and was asked for by his disciples (Mt. 24:3, 30). As we've seen, Jesus clearly and inseparably designated the destruction of Jerusalem and its Temple as the sign of his coming. He said, "*Immediately*, after the distress [tribulation] of those days...the sign of the Son of Man will appear..." (Mt. 24:29-30). Immediately after the four sieges of A.D. 66 - 70, the sign appeared. In the final destructive event(s), his Presence was manifested and He was truly revealed as the Son of God. This sign also signaled God's acceptance of Christ's atonement (Heb. 7:25) and that the way into the Most Holy Place was now open (Heb. 9:8). By this sign we can be sure that Jesus completed everything for our salvation in the generation He named "this generation" (Mt. 24:34). Jesus said, "When you [his audience] see Jerusalem surrounded by armies, you will know that its desolation is near...When these things begin to take place, stand up and lift up your heads, because your redemption is drawing near" (Lk. 21:20, 28). No longer do we need to look for Jerusalem to be surrounded by armies. No longer are we living in that waiting period.

Confusion over this eschatological-soteriological issue only comes when we don't understand that the destruction of Jerusalem had redemptive/spiritual significance. If we lift the salvation process out of its "last-days" context at the end of the Jewish age and shift it to an alleged end of a Christian age, we have confused the very roots of our faith. No scriptural basis exists for removing Christ's appearing a second time from the end-time, last-days framework in history in which his sacrifice occurred—"once for all at the end of the ages to do away with sin" (Heb. 1:2; 9:26). God fully dealt with man's sin problem; it is not incomplete. It has been fully resolved.

When Jesus said "Not one jot or one tittle shall in no wise pass from the law until all be fulfilled," or "everything is accomplished" (Mt. 5:18 KJV-NIV), He meant exactly what He said. He came again to do just what He said He would (Mt. 5:17). Who among us would question that a large segment (not a mere jot or tittle!) was passing and did pass away from the Law back in the 1st century (Heb. 8:13; 12:26-28; 1 Cor. 7:31)? The Temple, rituals, genealogies, feasts, the sacrificial system, priesthood, and all they typified are totally fulfilled. They were necessary, but only temporarily. Nothing failed to come to pass. That's why "salvation is of the Jews" and their age (Jn. 4:22 KJV), not of the Gentiles or of an intervening Christian age.

Why then are we still waiting for Jesus to be revealed after almost 2,000 years? Whom should we believe, Jesus, or our postponing, futurist brethren? I believe Jesus. How could He be any clearer? Everything was accomplished. The typology is complete. The destruction of Jerusalem and its Temple was the sign of the final event in the consummation of God's plan of redemption. Let us recognize and loudly proclaim that we have received the goal/end/*telos* of our faith, the ultimate and consummated realization of the promise of the salvation of our souls (1 Pe. 1:9). The message is one of fulfilled redemption and completed salvation. What more could we ask for? Yet there is more!

Evidence 7. It Was Also the Lord's Return (His Parousia). Jesus' coming "on the clouds" in A.D. 70 was also his real, personal, bodily return. How can we know? It's as simple as answering the question, Where is Jesus now? Yet it's as complex as asking, Why don't we see Him with our physical eyes somewhere on this earth? Since we don't see him, we have decided that Jesus could not have returned. Yet Billy Graham most recently and confidently declared to a mass crusade audience, "This living Christ is in the world today."[13] Is He or isn't He?

The answer to our perplexity is simple. Authentic Christianity does not stand for an absent Christ, absent the entire length of the Christian age! It stands for a present and active Christ who is truly, wholly, totally here with us. Only at one point in history, after his ascension and during the closing period of the Jewish age ("the last days"), did He leave. His departure was required, and it was the

The bane and chief blind spot of Christianity for more than nineteen centuries has been its misunderstanding of Jesus' promised return.

decisive factor for the coming of the Holy Spirit (Jn. 14:2-3, 18-19, 28; 16:7; 2 Cor. 5:8; Ac. 2:16-17f). However, He didn't leave to send Himself back.[14] So if He's *now* present, and not off in some distant place waiting to come back, then at some point between his departure and his Presence with us today He *had to have returned*. The sequence therefore is: *presence, absence, presence*. It's *majorly inconsistent* to say that Jesus is with us today and then claim that He has not returned. Jesus cannot be here unless He has literally and bodily returned.

Make no mistake about it, A.D. 70 *was the Lord's promised and personal return!* He returned *as* and *when* He said He would! He also returned *as* and *when* He was expected to (Jn. 16:13; Jas. 5:7, 8). He doesn't need to return again from anywhere at the end of the Christian age or at the demise of the material universe, as is commonly asserted. He's back and He's here, in our midst. John, in the first chapter of the book of Revelation, saw Christ standing in the midst of the lampstands (his Church) clothed in his high priestly garments (Rev. 1:13, 20). This was one of the events that "must soon take place" (Rev. 1:1; 22:6).

The bane and chief blind spot of Christianity for more than nineteen centuries has been its misunderstanding of Jesus' promised return. Pragmatically, nonetheless, how can anyone say that He returned when no human eye physically "saw" Him do it? It's because we have grossly misunderstood the nature of his return.

The technical word most often used in the New Testament to speak of Jesus' coming/return is the Greek word *parousia*.[15] Although it's most often translated "coming," its primary meaning is the personal "arrival" or "presence" of one who comes. It's derived from two Greek words, *para* meaning "with," and *ousia* meaning "being." It conveys the idea of a visitation. And, as we've seen, Jesus inseparably linked and time-limited his *parousia* coming with the destruction of the Jewish Temple and the end of the Old Covenant Age (Mt. 24:3, 27, 33-34). All attempts to unlink these three events are indefensible. Moreover, these uncoupling devices are an affront to the veracity of Jesus Himself, the imminency expectations of his disciples and the New Testament writers, and the very soundness and inerrancy of Scripture.

No wonder his disciples asked, "What will be the sign of your coming [i.e., your *arrival*, or your continuing *presence*]?" (Mt. 24:3). They wanted to be sure! They wanted his real, literal, personal, bodily, living, tangible, and abiding but usually invisible Presence, and not anything less. That's exactly what happened at the destruction of Jerusalem and the end of the Jewish age. Jesus arrived in his fullness—not partially, and not in the form of the earnest or pledge of the Holy Spirit during his absence—but in his fully-returned and permanent Presence. If this didn't happen at the "appointed time," but He's nevertheless present with us today, when did He (in his Presence) return? All postponement belief systems must either deny or explain away the numerous time statements and imminency expectations concerning this event peppered throughout the New Testament. An impossible task!

Let's acknowledge that Jesus' return during the "last days" was just as much a part of his redemptive work as his death on the cross, resurrection, going away, sending of the Holy Spirit, coming in judgment, and completion of salvation. All of these redemptive acts were literal, "last days" events, and all were united in purpose—the consummation of God's kingdom and plan of redemption. Consequently, Christ's redemptive work is over, and He is now continually and fully present with us. Our better understanding of the fulfilled reality of his returned Presence will definitely affect the way we view the validity and viability of our faith.

What is most needed is for us to wean ourselves from the idea that the Presence of Christ must be visible, and to be reeducated on how to better worship, encounter, and enjoy Him. Unfortunately, for many believers, a 1st-century return of Christ is difficult, if not impossible, to fathom. One reason for this is due to the preconceived and widely accepted "second coming" idea that his return must be visible. But where does Scripture say that Jesus' return must be "visible?"[16] Just because it was invisibile does not mean that it was unreal, impersonal, non-bodily, or only symbolic or spiritual. Nor does its invisibility lessen its significance. Notably, it was not until the year 1560, in the First Scottish Confession of Faith, that an explicit declaration of a visible return was made in any of the historic creeds or confessions of the Church.

As we have said, the fact that a sign ("sign of your coming [*parousia*]" and "sign of the Son of Man in heaven" [Mt. 24:3, 30]) was necessary should tip us off that this coming would *not* be *visible to the naked-eye*, even though many of his other comings have been and are visible. The "sign" of his return was not a gigantic, multimedia display of his body up in the sky. It was *the fall of Jerusalem and destruction of the Judaic world.* This was and remains a sign for all ages.

Assumptions often blind us to realities. Let's take a closer look at the traditional visibility assumption. This is one area where biblical knowledge, not human speculation, must be applied. At Pentecost there was no visible or physical appearance of the Holy Spirit. Jesus said that God the Father is "unseen" (Mt. 6:6) and that the Holy Spirit is as well (Jn. 14:17). Regarding the nature of the coming of his kingdom, Jesus also said that it "does not come visibly" (Lk. 17:20b; 2 Cor. 4:18). Therefore, why must his "coming in his kingdom" (Mt. 16:28) be visible? Even the rapturists are (mistakenly) expecting an invisible coming of Christ to remove them from planet Earth.[17] What's more, doesn't faith in the Bible consist of being "certain of what we do not see" (Heb. 11:1), including being "surrounded by such a great cloud of witnesses" (Heb. 12:1)? But to top it all, Jesus declared that "the world would not see me anymore" (Jn. 14:19, also 14:22). Do we trust his words? Do we believe Him? Just how long is his "anymore"? How then can we turn and preach a universally visible coming? Even Revelation's claim that "every eye will see him" (Rev. 1:7) cannot be used. Let's recall that this "seeing" started in a 1st-century context with "those who pierced him" during his crucifixion. But it includes every eye of every person who has ever lived, lives now, or *will* live on planet Earth, not just the eyes of those people present on earth at some future time.[18]

We need to wean ourselves from the idea that the Presence of Jesus, who is God, must be visible or somehow material. To do so, we will need better to understand the nature of his resurrected body and the practical reality of the spirit realm in which He operates. "For where two or three come together in my name, there am I with them" (Mt. 18:20). Although unseen, Jesus is truly, fully, and personally present with them, isn't He?

Another example of the reality of the invisible is how Jesus Him-

---

But the Christian age is not an extension of Christ's absence. He has returned and received us unto Himself just as He promised ...

---

self interpreted the Old Testament prophecy of the coming of Elijah (Mal. 4:5-6). This fulfillment preceded the coming and anointing of the Messiah in the Jordan River. But it was not fulfilled by a literal reappearance of the Old Testament prophet Elijah, as the Jews were expecting. Instead, Jesus said that John the Baptist was the predicted Elijah. The invisible spirit and power of Elijah came into and operated through John the Baptist (Lk. 1:17; Mt. 11:14; 17:10-13). Also note that Jesus said, "And if you are willing to accept it..." (Mt. 11:14). Why did He use this disclaimer? Because He knew many would not accept the invisible nature of this fulfillment. Jesus also warned that a visible criterion was part of the deception of the elect (Mt. 24:23-36). This same unwillingness and same deception is paralleled today in failing to understand his return (see next chapter). Consequently, many have missed it.

But the Christian age is not an extension of Christ's absence. He has returned and received us unto Himself just as He promised, into the previously "off limits" Holy of Holies behind the veil (Heb. 6:19, 20; 9:11-12; 10:19-25, 37), and into the restored Presence of the living God (Jn. 14:1-4, 23). Father, Son, and Holy Spirit are One, and they tabernacle (dwell) in and among us forever (Jn. 14:18, 23; Rev. 21:3). This was never to happen in a rebuilt temple in the modern-day city of Jerusalem.

The Christian age is also the fulfillment of the seventh Jewish Feast of Booths or Tabernacles (Heb. 9:8; Rev. 21:3; Eze. 37:26-28), and it's the restoration of the fellowship that Adam lost (Ge. 3:24). If Christianity does not put us back into the Presence of God, then what does it attain? What good is it? It's that simple, and that profound. The tabernacle typology in the book of Hebrews is explicit. It reveals 1) man's salvation from sin, 2) Christ's preparation of a place (where He is) for his disciples, and 3) restoration into the Presence of God in the Holy of Holies, a place where the Old Covenant could never bring us. It's all complete (Heb. 9:8, 9; 10:19). We can now enter the Presence of God with all our sins forgiven. It's no less than the bottom line of our faith! This covenantal consummation is the meaning and fullness of Christianity. It's part of our heritage in Christ. It's the foundation of our faith (Eph. 2:20) on which we are to build. It is and was the goal of redemptive history. "And if I go and prepare a place for you, I will come again and receive you to myself; that where I am, there you may be also" (Jn. 14:3 KJV; see also Jn. 17:24).

What Christ outlined in John 14:1-3 was fulfilled in his end-of-the-age *parousia*. To extend this fulfillment to a yet future time frame is to leave a vacuum and do irreparable harm to God's redemptive plan. If Christ is still preparing that place and has not returned, no saint is yet in heaven! On the other hand, maintaining that if the Lord came in the fall of Jerusalem, we no longer have hope of the coming of Christ, is also a big mistake.

Be assured that Christ RETURNED ONCE, *as* and *when* He said He would. He doesn't need to return twice. We can now live and dwell in his abiding Presence, in both this life and the next. We also dwell in the Presence of God the Father, and no veil separates us. The Old Covenant could not achieve this consummated reality. Jesus foretold that "On that day you will realize that I am in my Father, and you are in me and I am in you...we will come to him and make our home with him" (Jn. 14:20, 23). After Christ's return, God the Father, God the Son, and God the Holy Spirit are "all in all" (1 Cor. 15:28; Eph. 4:6).

This goal and this prepared place is the reality of full redemption. All Christians should know about it, celebrate it, and experience it fully. Yet we do not. Much of the blame for the current ennui among Christians can be laid at the door of futurism, which robs the present of its vitality. *

If we wish to achieve a more responsible apocalypticism, we must take seriously the seven demanding evidences presented in this chapter. We must not diminish or rationalize away the Holy Spirit's 1st-century, disclosing work (Jn. 16:13), and his guiding into "all truth," not into nonoccurrence. We must also honor the time-statements and the imminency of Scripture, not insert gaps and manipulate words.

Believing that Jesus returned in the generation He named isn't heretical, it's biblical! The evidence is overwhelming—He's risen, He's returned, He's here!—wouldn't you now agree? But perhaps you have some lingering doubts. In our next chapter we'll address five classic questions (objections) that remain to be dispelled.

---

* *A discussion of the vital aspects of Christ's Presence and his many comings is a subject for a future book. However, before I leave this chapter, I feel I must mention that we cannot and should not dogmatically preclude a future coming that could be physically visible to the world at large and at the same time. Will it happen? God is sovereign, so it could. But, and here is the crucial and distin-*

guishing point that must be stressed, it doesn't have to happen to fulfill any unfulfilled biblical prophecy. Let's not forget Jesus' words, "Before long, the world will not see me anymore" (Jn. 14:19). If a universally-visible coming, which many expect, does occur someday, it will be as one of His many and countless comings in His everlasting kingdom. (See my paper, The Many Comings of Jesus, presented at the 49th Annual Meeting of the Evangelical Theological Society in November of 1997 in Santa Clara, California.)

13

Five Questions Answered

A re you shocked, flabbergasted, or perhaps even upset that Jesus might have kept his word and literally returned exactly *as* and *when* He said He would, and *as* and *when* every single New Testament reference promised and every early Church believer expected? Or are you afraid to admit that we might have missed the obvious truth for so many centuries?

In this chapter we will address five classic questions (objections) that have been raised by those struggling with the possibility and implications of our Lord's past return. They are: **1)** What about the "Second Coming"? **2)** What about Paul's "man of sin" who first had to be revealed? **3)** What about Church creeds and confessionals? **4)** Shouldn't Christians stop taking the Lord's Supper (communion) if Jesus has returned? **5)** Is it possible the elect have been deceived?

Question 1. What about the "Second Coming"?

No idea has gripped the human imagination more firmly, saturated the Church more completely, or been proclaimed as the hope of the world more frequently than the doctrine of a "Second Coming" of Jesus Christ. Its influence on the thinking of most Christians and non-church people alike has been a driving force in the world. Again, please be assured that we believe every word the Bible says about the coming again and return of Jesus. But do you know what the Bible actually says about a "second coming?" *Nothing*! Do you know what the historic creeds of the Church say about it? Again, *nothing*!

What's involved here is much more than semantics or a doctrinal dispute over some insignificant issue, like the ancient squabble over how many angels can dance on the head of a pin. What's at risk is plenty, and everything. We simply cannot afford to be misinformed or confused about this important element of biblical faith.

The Bible contains many references to many different comings of Jesus, but makes no references to a single "second coming." This post-biblical terminology is man-made. Unfortunately, it implies that there are only two comings of Jesus, one in the past and the other in

---

The many comings of Jesus run like a thread throughout the entire Bible.

---

the future. However, this limitation does not fit with Scripture. Even Jesus' birth, which is commonly called his "first coming," is never called that in Scripture, and for good reason. It wasn't. Documented throughout the Old Testament are many comings of Jesus. Theologians technically refer to them as "theophanies" (see Ex. 3:2-15; 17:1-7; Da. 3:24-27; Ge. 16:7ff; 21:17ff; 22:11ff; 31:11ff; Jdg. 6:11ff; 13:21ff; Mic. 5:2 in the Old Testament for example). Many more comings are recorded in Ac. 7:55-56; 9:1-8; Rev. 1; 1 Cor. 15:5-8 in the New Testament.

The many comings of Jesus run like a thread throughout the entire Bible. Some are visible. Some are not. He comes in many different ways, for many different purposes, and at many different times. All his comings, however, are personal, literal, and bodily. Many more comings are promised. But nowhere is the word "coming" ever preceded by the word "second." Nowhere are his comings ever limited, numbered, or terminated (i.e., a final coming after which there will be no more). The idea of limiting the comings of Jesus to two and calling the later one a "Second Coming," or limiting his comings at all, is simply a human notion, a phrase and a doctrine kept alive by tradition. Let's face it; we need to reform our ideas about a "second coming."

First, we should drop the use of this non-scriptural terminology and its unscriptural connotation of limiting his comings to only two. This man-made intrusion has led many astray and greatly nullified "the word of God for the sake of your tradition" (Mt. 15:6; Mk. 7:13). Second, we must reeducate God's people concerning the biblical reality—past, present and future—of one return, but many comings of Jesus.

Of course, a reformation of this magnitude, though desperately needed, is far easier outlined than accomplished. Blind allegiance to entrenched traditions stands in the way. However, the idea of a "second coming" has got to go. It simply won't stand up to a *sola scriptura* testing of Scripture (1 Th. 5:21). The only thing close is Hebrews 9:28: "...He will appear a second time not to bear sin, but to bring salvation." As we've seen, this was a particular coming for a particular reason; it followed the typology of the high priest on the Day of Atonement. And Jesus came in just this fashion. But this "second time" is neither equivalent to nor a synonym for a so-called "second coming." In no way does this verse limit his past or terminate his future comings.

The question then becomes, Are we willing to abandon tradition when its terminology and concept have been shown to be scripturally erroneous? For many, the answer will be Yes, absolutely. Others, we suspect, will dig in their heels and resist the truth of God's Word. But the return of Jesus and his many comings are two beautiful biblical truths and realities of his kingdom, so let's not be intimidated or brainwashed by the traditions of men. The plain, simple, yet precious truth of Christ's return and his many comings must be proclaimed in certain and Scripture-honoring terms. He is active in his creation. This is one of the ways. Let's stop limiting his comings! He comes! Come Lord Jesus!

Question 2. What about Paul's "Man of Sin" Who First Had to be Revealed?

The Apostle Paul wrote that the coming (*parousia*) of the Lord would not take place until the rebellion occurs and the "man of sin" (KJV) or "man of lawlessness" (NIV) was revealed. We suggest you read about it in 2 Thessalonians 2:1-12 before continuing on. This revealing was a definite prerequisite!

The most popular postponement tradition claims that this wicked one is some future "Antichrist" figure who has yet to be revealed. Over the centuries, he has been variously identified as Attila the Hun, Napoleon, the Pope, Martin Luther, Mohammed, Hilter, Mussolini, Stalin, Franklin Roosevelt, Henry Kissinger, and Mikhail Gorbachev. Virtually every unpopular public figure has qualified. Obviously, this tradition has proven totally inept at identifying Paul's "man of sin." Unfortunately, it's a tradition that has not died.

For a number of scriptural and historical reasons, the identity of Paul's "man of sin" should not be arbitrarily lifted out of its 1st-century context. So here's our pick: a contemporary of Paul's who fulfilled Paul's prophetic prediction and fit his destructive description to a tee. The following is a condensed version of an apologetic presented in *The Man of Sin of II Thessalonians 2*, by Evangelist John L. Bray:[1]

The Man of Sin. A study of 2 Thessalonians 2:1-12.
Verses 1-2. *"Concerning the coming (parousia) of our Lord Jesus Christ and our being gathered to him, we ask you, brothers, not to become easily unsettled or alarmed by some prophecy, report or letter supposed to have come from us, saying that the day of the Lord has already come."*

If the understanding of the nature of the coming (return) of the Lord by Paul's first readers was in keeping with most traditional, modern-day notions of a rapture-removing, visible, world-seeing, or world-ending coming, they could not have been led to believe that it had already come (see again our evidences 3 and 4 in the last chapter).

Verses 3-4. *"Don't let anyone deceive you in any way, for that day will not come until the rebellion occurs and the man lawlessness [man of sin] is revealed, the man doomed to destruction [son of perdition - KJV]. He opposes and exalts himself over everything that is called God or is worshipped, and even sets himself up in God's temple, proclaiming himself to be God."* Paul wrote during the time of a literal, standing, second Temple. He gave no hint that this event would occur centuries later in some other "rebuilt" temple. His first readers apparently expected this fulfillment in their lifetime. That's why some feared that that "day of the Lord" had already occurred. Also, let's note how Paul's prophetic words here match up with Jesus' Olivet Discourse (Mt. 24). Both speak of the same set of events, use similar language, and convey a strong sense of imminence.[2]

History records that the Jewish rebellion against Rome and apostasy from the faith was already underway in the early 60s, and reached its climax in the Jewish-Roman War of A.D. 66 - 70. We propose that Paul's "man of sin" was, most likely, a specific person who set himself up in the Temple that was standing when Paul was writing. He could have been (take your pick) Nero, Titus, a Zealot leader, the corrupt chief high priest, or a Christian Zealot. All except Nero physically entered the Temple. Although Paul never calls him "antichrist," the Apostle John tells us that there were many "antichrists" at work at that time (1 Jn. 2:18; 4:3). No doubt this "man of sin" was one of them. But he was also a special person who had to come on the scene prior to the Lord's return in A.D. 70 and before the Temple was destroyed.

Verses 5-7. *"Don't you remember that when I was with you I used to tell you these things? And now you know what is holding him back, so that he may be revealed at the proper*

time. For the secret power of lawlessness is already at work;
but the one who now holds it back will continue to do so till
he is taken out of the way."

Paul had mentioned this power of lawlessness on other oc-
casions (see 1 Th. 2:14-16; 1 Ti. 4:1). The Jews were revolting
against Rome and rejecting the sacred practice of biblical Judaism. Some followers of Christ who remained zealous for the
Temple system were departing from the new faith and falling
back into the old ways. But behind it all was "the secret power
of lawlessness." It was "already at work," there and then, but
something and/or someone was holding the "man of sin" back
at the time Paul wrote this letter (circa A.D. 51 - 52) . Whatever
that was, Paul reminded his first readers that they already knew
its/his identity. So Paul didn't have to tell them. And he didn't.
Since they knew who or what it was, it could not possibly have
been something or someone that would not exist for some nineteen or more centuries. But who or what was it?

Throughout Church history endless speculation has revolved
around the identity of this restrainer. However, we do know
that this restraint was in force when Paul wrote, and was actively holding back a "man of sin" alive at that time. This fact is a
time indicator and should answer the question of *when*. Some
have suggested that the "who" was Nero or the Roman government, which held back Jewish persecution of the early Jewish
Christians. Futurists say it's the gospel, the Church, the Holy
Spirit, or an angel. But if any of these is what was really meant,
why did the writer use such veiled language? None of these
things is ever portrayed in Scripture as restraining lawlessness
or being removed from the world.

The best answer—we believe—is that it was both an office
(the "what") and a person (the "one who" or "he"). More specifically, it was the institution of the Jewish priesthood led by
Ananus, the high priest. The priesthood opposed the Jewish,

Zealot-led rebellion. And Ananus wanted peace with Rome. As long as he and the priesthood stood in the way, the lawlessness of the Jewish Zealots was held back, the "work of Satan" couldn't reach its full realization, and the "man of sin" couldn't appear on the scene and cause the final destruction. In A.D. 68, however, Jewish Zealots, with the assistance of the Idumaeans, murdered Ananus and over 12,000 other priests and left their bodies unburied—a violation of the Jewish Law. Thus, the priesthood was "taken out of the way."[3] As Josephus wrote in his history of the fall of the city:

> I should not mistake if I said that the death of Ananus was the beginning of the destruction of the city, and that from this very day may be dated the overthrow of her walls, and the ruin of her affairs, whereon they saw their high-priest, and the procurer of their preservation; slain in the midst of their city...for he was thoroughly sensible that the Romans were not to be conquered. He also foresaw that of necessity a war would follow, and that unless the Jews made up matters with them very dexterously, they would be destroyed: to say all in a word, if Ananus had survived that would have certainly compounded matters... and I cannot but think that it was because God had doomed this city to destruction, as a polluted city, and was resolved to purge his sanctuary by fire, that he cut off these great defenders and wellwishers.[4]

Verses 8-10. *"And then the lawless one will be revealed whom the Lord Jesus will overthrow with the breath of his mouth and destroy by the splendor of his coming [parousia]. The coming [parousia] of the lawless one will be in accordance with the work of Satan displayed in all kinds of counterfeit miracles, signs and wonders, and in every sort of evil that deceives those who are perishing. They perish because they refused to love the truth and so be saved!"* All this happened in the very Temple that was standing until A.D. 70. As the war between the Jews and Rome developed, a strong leader of the Jewish Zealots emerged who would fulfill Paul's prophecy. He would soon become the key man in inciting the Jews against Rome, in bringing abominations into the Temple area, and in causing the final destruction of Jerusalem and the Temple. After Ananus' murder and the removal of the priesthood, Josephus records that a man named John, the son of Levi, fled to Jerusalem from the Roman-conquered area of Gischala in Galilee and became the treacherous leader of the Jewish Zealots in control of the Temple area. As Josephus wrote, "Now this was the work of God, who therefore preserved this John, that he might bring on the destruction of Jerusalem."[5]

Josephus also records that before this John of Gischala, the son of Levi, was established as the Zealot leader in control of the Temple area (there were three Zealot factions), the power of Satan was already doing his deceitful and treacherous work. This John physically entered the Temple, presented himself to the Zealots as a God-sent ambassador,[6] and persuaded them to defy the laws of Rome and go to war to gain independence. He also instigated the calling in the Idumaeans to keep the Jewish sympathizers from submitting to Rome.[7] He ordered the death of Ananus and the removal of the priesthood. After these atrocities, he became the official leader of the Zealot group in control of the Temple area—"John held the temple"[8]—and began disregarded the laws of Rome, God, and man, and promising deliverance from the Romans. Then he broke off from the Zealots and began "setting up a monarchial power."[9] He "set on fire those houses that were full of corn, and of all other provision...which would have been sufficient for a siege of many years."[10] He deceived the Jews about the power of the Roman armies.[11] In possession of the Temple and the adjoining parts,[12] he cut the throats of anyone suspected of going over to the Romans.[13] He performed many sacrileges, such as melting down the sacred utensils used in Temple service, and defiled the

Temple.[14] In short, this John established himself in the Temple, the one standing when Paul wrote, and put himself above Rome and above God, thereby taking the place of God in the Temple. All this happened, right then and there, and exactly as Paul had said the "man of sin" would do.

After the coming of the Lord and the destruction of Jerusalem and the Temple in A.D. 70, John of Gischala was "condemned to perpetual imprisonment" by the Roman authorities.[15] Thus was fulfilled Paul's prophetic and symbolic language that this man would be destroyed by "the spirit of his [Jesus'] mouth and brightness of his [*parousia*] coming" (see Isa. 11:4; 30:27-33; Hos. 6:5; also Da. 7:8, 19-28).

Verses 11-12. *"For this reason God sends them a powerful delusion so that they will believe the lie and so that all will be condemned who have not believed the truth but delighted in wickedness."*

Josephus records that the Roman General Titus had no intention of destroying the Temple. The Romans wanted to preserve it as a trophy and monument of their conquest. Even Josephus personally pleaded with John of Gischala to surrender. But such a "madness"[16] swept through him and his Jewish followers that they taunted the powers of Rome and refused to listen. This man, John, through the power of Satan and the delusion sent by God upon the Jewish people, forced the Roman armies to act. Instead of accepting Jesus as Messiah, King, and Deliverer, the unbelieving Jews placed their hopes in this false messiah, a man of deceit and wickedness. They looked to the "man of sin" to lead them to victory and independence. The priesthood, which stood in their way, had been removed. And by August or September of A.D. 70, Paul's entire "man of sin" prophecy of 2 Thessalonians 2:1-12 was fulfilled. The city and the Temple were burned and destroyed. The covenant nation of Israel and biblical Judaism were forever destroyed.

Only within this 1st-century context does the Apostle Paul's "man of sin" prophecy make sense and have its greatest significance. No justification exists for separating Paul's words from either the Temple standing at the time of his writing or the end of the Jewish age. John of Gischala, the son of Levi, was a contemporary of Paul. He was Paul's "man of sin." The eyewitness account of Josephus, a Jewish-Roman historian, truthfully and impartially documents his treachery and his critical role in Jerusalem's demise. No one else in history—Gaius Caesar, Nero, Titus, or Domitian—comes as close to fulfilling this prophecy as this most influential and deceiving Zealot leader. John of Gischala took over the forces of iniquity. He stood in the Temple itself and exalted himself above all that is called God. He put himself above both God and Caesar. He regarded neither the laws of God nor those of man (Rome). He therefore "set himself up" in the Temple, taking the place of God.

Judas betrayed Jesus. John of Gischala betrayed the Jews, **fulfilling Paul's "man of sin" prophecy to a tee.**

In dramatic parallel fashion, Scripture gives this "man of sin" — John of Gischala, the son of Levi—the name of "the one doomed to destruction" or "the son of perdition," the same name given to another infamous betrayer, Judas Iscariot (compare Jn. 17:12 with 2Th. 2:3 KJV). Both appeared in the same "last days" time frame of the Old Covenant age. *Judas betrayed Jesus. John of Gischala betrayed the Jews,* fulfilling Paul's "man of sin" prophecy to a tee. He was that 1st-century man who had to be revealed before the day of Christ in A.D. 70, and who was destroyed when it came. No future "man of sin" need come and fulfill this prophecy; it has already been fulfilled.

Question 3. What about Church Creeds and Confessions?

Don't the major creeds and the formal confessions of the historic Church, all held in high esteem and written several centuries after the fall of Jerusalem, speak of Christ's return in futuristic terms and therefore teach that He has not yet returned?

Yes, so it may initially appear. However, there are five important points to consider when using the creeds to determine the eschatological issue of the Lord's coming/return:

1) Scripture has authority, and final authority, over all creeds, confessions, traditions, and belief statements written by men. This is what *sola scriptura* is about. Scripture must be the final test of orthodoxy, not the creeds.

2) It's true that no Church council after A.D. 70 referred to a past fulfillment of Christ's coming or return *(parousia)*. They may have been too close and too involved in events to be able to see the big picture.

3) The framers of the creeds were primarily interested in setting down or reflecting the basics of the Christian faith *without interpretation*.

4) Two interpretative aspects were not addressed by the creedal framers—the issue of timing, and the nature of fulfillment. They did not devote any significant attention to eschatology. They only wanted to reflect the essence of Scripture and nothing more. That's why, for example, the phrase "second coming" is not found in any of the creeds.

5) Because the framers used a direct-lifting procedure to stay close to Scripture, the future tense is carried over. The Lord's coming/return was future at the time the New Testament was written. The framers thus repeated this language of im-

minency. As a result, Jesus' supposed "failure" to return *as* and *when* He said He would and was expected to has been embarrassing to the Church for centuries.

For these five reasons, the preterist view that Christ did return *as* and *when* He said He would and was expected to in A.D. 70, is not in conflict with, but *honors* the major creeds of the undivided Church.[17] This view is not heretical, it's biblical. It makes sense. It plainly explains and harmonizes difficult passages, and it makes the Bible come alive and become applicable in ways the Church has rarely before imagined. Thus, anyone holding a preterist view of the Lord's return can wholeheartedly subscribe to the eschatological portions of the major creeds. All preterists have done—and all we've done in this book—is put this climactic and redemptive event back into its proper biblical and historical context. This interpretative change is therefore only a matter of timing, and not of content.

Amazingly, no creed teaches or even recognizes that any kind of judgment or coming occurred in A.D. 70. But Eusebius, a 4th-century Christian leader and writer who is often called "the father of Church history," affirmed that Jesus "came" in the fall of Jerusalem and in fulfillment of Zechariah's end-time prophecy.[18]

Athanasius, also writing in the 4th century, declared that Christ came again and fulfilled all of Daniel's 70 weeks prophecy (Da. 9:24-27): "And Jerusalem is to stand till his coming, and thenceforth, prophet and vision cease in Israel...And this was why Jerusalem stood till then—namely that there they might be exercised in the types as a preparation for the reality...but from that time forth all prophecy is sealed and the city and temple taken, why are they so irreligious and so perverse as to see what has happened, and yet to deny Christ, Who has brought it all to pass? ...What then has not come to pass, that the Christ must do? What is left unfulfilled, that the Jews should now disbelieve with impunity?"[19]

These writings of Eusebius and Athanasius suggest some understanding among early-Church fathers of the fulfillment of Jesus' coming *(parousia)* in A.D. 70. R.C. Sproul, a renowned Reformed theologian of our day, adds: "...the destruction of Jerusalem...certainly spelled the end of a crucial redemptive-historical epoch. It must be viewed as the end of some age. It also represents a significant visitation of the Lord in judgment and a vitally important 'day of the Lord.' Whether this was the *only* day of the Lord about which Scripture speaks remains a major point of controversy among preterists."[20]

Whom should we believe? Jesus and the inspired writers of Scripture, or the uninspired framers of the creeds?

Whom should we believe? Jesus and the inspired writers of Scripture, or the uninspired framers of the creeds? Elevating these man-made documents to too lofty a position puts us in danger of committing the same sin for which Jesus condemned the Pharisees and scribes: "You have let go of the commands of God and are holding on to the traditions of men...You have a fine way of setting aside the commands of God in order to observe your own traditions!...Thus you nullify the word of God by your tradition that you have handed down. And you do many things like that" (Mk. 7:8-13).

Let's be blunt. If Jesus, the New Testament, or any of God's Word is in error on this matter, the position of the creeds (and confessions) is worthless. R.C. Sproul recently put it this way: "...skeptical criticism of the Bible has become almost universal in the world. And people have attacked the credibility of Jesus. Maybe some church fathers made a mistake. Maybe our favorite theologians have made mistakes. I can abide with that. I can't abide with Jesus being a false prophet, because if I am to understand that Jesus is a false prophet, my faith is in vain."[21]

Within our traditions, let's agree to support the view which best maintains the honor and integrity of Christ and confirms the inspired and inerrant Word of God. The creeds, confessions, and other "traditions of men" are secondary to the supremacy of inspired Scripture. They can be mistaken and must be tested by *sola scriptura* (1 Th. 5:21). After all, if the creeds had it all right, what was the Reformation about? And hasn't our understanding of Scripture been improving over the centuries as we've developed and refined our interpretive skills? John Calvin said, "The Church is reformed and always reforming." In this process of continuing reform, only Scripture can be trusted and used to determine true orthodoxy, not the creeds.

So what shall we do with the creeds? We recommend that their eschatological sections be revised—lest we be enslaved to an incorrect and uninspired interpretation of Scripture. Our rule of faith and practice should be as follows: *Jesus, in numerous places, clearly stated that his return would occur within the lifetime of his contemporaries. Every New Testament writer utilized urgent and imminent language confirming the immediacy of his return. We cannot overlook a biblical and time-restricted fulfillment in favor of man-made creeds and confessions.* As Edward E. Stevens, President of the International Preterist Association, said, "Which is the greater offense? To question the accuracy of *uninspired* creeds, or to declare that the *inspired* time statements of the Apostles were mistaken? Which would you rather throw out the window, the New Testament writings, or the creeds? And that is exactly the dilemma here."[22]

Question 4. Shouldn't Christians Stop Taking the Lord's Supper (Communion) If Jesus Has Returned?

The Apostle Paul's instructions for taking the Lord's Supper were that it be done "in remembrance of me [Jesus]" and included the verse, "For whenever you eat this bread and drink this cup, you proclaim the Lord's death until he comes" (1 Cor. 11: 23-26f). If Jesus has returned, the argument goes, doesn't it follow that we should no longer take communion?

Not so fast. First, Paul's "until" does not necessarily teach that communion observance would cease upon Christ's return. More importantly, his teaching was only an interim instruction that he had received from the Lord (1Cor. 11:23). Consequently, he was passing it on to the Corinthians during the transitionary period of A.D. 30 - 70. But Jesus also said concerning the taking of the Lord's Supper:

- *I tell you, I will not drink of this fruit of the vine from now on until that day when I drink it anew with you in my Father's kingdom (Mt. 26:29).*

- *...until it finds fulfillment in the kingdom of God (Lk. 22:16).*

- *...until the kingdom of God comes (Lk. 22:18).*

That day came. Jesus returned and the kingdom was taken away from the Old Covenant Jews and "given to a people who will produce its fruit" (Mt. 21:43). From then on, He's with us. No longer do we need to take communion in a somber, memorialized fashion, "in remembrance of" Him who had departed (Jn. 14:1-3). We take it "anew" with Him in celebration.

This word "anew" has great significance. We have a parallel event in history when new meaning was taken on by the Old Covenant, Jewish Passover supper. The Passover supper was instituted before Israel's deliverance from Egyptian bondage and was observed throughout the forty-year wilderness period. Likewise, the Lord's Supper was instituted before Jesus' death and observed during the interim forty-year period of A.D. 30 - 70 as a somber observance commemorative of his death, their deliverance from sin, and a longing for his return. But after entering the Promised Land, the Jews continued the Passover supper observance—no longer in anticipation of, but in *celebration* of entering. In a similar manner, after A.D. 70, the Lord's Supper was no longer to be a solemn, memorialized remembrance of Him, but a glorious and victorious feast with Him, anew in his full returned Presence, at his table, in our new inheritance, the new promised land, the consummated kingdom of God. Because Jesus kept his Word and returned *as* and *when* He said He would, the Lord's Supper has even more meaning and purpose. Like the Passover supper, it has changed from one of anticipation to one of celebration. What's more, the Lord's Supper is an eternal celebration because the kingdom in which it is taken is eternally established (Isa. 9:7; Lk. 1:33).

Question 5. Is It Possible the Elect Have Been Deceived?

Jesus warned his disciples of deception. He said that there would be "false prophets...to deceive even the elect—if that were possible" (Mt. 24:24). Insistence on a visible criterion (nature) for his end-time return/*parousia* was and still is part of this deception:

> At that time if anyone says to you, 'Look, here is the Christ!' or, 'There he is!' do not believe it...So if anyone tells you, 'There he is, out in the desert' do not go out; or, 'Here he is, in the inner rooms,' do not believe it (Mt. 24: 23, 26).

Some of "the elect" (the saints in the Church today, as well as back then) have succumbed to the visible criterion fallacy. Call it the "deception of the elect." Thus they, too, have been falsely prophesying. How so?

First, by their paralleled misunderstanding of the invisible nature for his promised and time-restricted return (Mt. 24:3, 30, 34; Jn. 14:19, 22). Many modern-day saints are waiting for a physically-visible sighting of Jesus in Person, in the sky, in the Israeli desert, in an inner room of a rebuilt temple in Jerusalem, or in some other geographic location to which they can definitely point and in like manner say, "There He is!"

Second, by their professing and proclaiming a half-truth faith in a world filled with competing religions and secular ideologies. The truthful half is that the promised Messiah (Jesus) came, lived, died, rose from the dead, and ascended to heaven exactly *as* and *when* prophesied. The untruthful part is that Jesus has not returned to finish the work He started, *as* and *when* He said He would and *as* and *when* He was expected to by his Spirit-guided, first followers and every New Testament writer (Jn. 16:13).

For 19 centuries and counting, the Church has been attempting to side-step and downplay this time-restricted, 1st-century "failure" or "nonoccurrence." As a result, it has been forced to settle for a faith that has *not* been "once for all delivered to the saints" (Jude 3) and whose "end of all things" was *not* "at hand" in that same 1st-century context in which these inspired words were penned (1 Pe. 4:7 KJV).

Thus the Church has, since the fall of Jerusalem, been falsely prophesying a half-truth faith. We must therefore ask, If this half-truth faith has been as effective as God has allowed it to be, how much more effective and God-empowered would the proclamation and practice of a whole-truth faith be—one that really "was [past tense] once for all delivered to the saints" (Jude 3)?

It's time for this reform, and for God's people to come out of this 19-centuries-and-counting "deception of the elect". In every generation except one, the Church has wrongly proclaimed the imminence of our Lord's return. No more. He has returned! Perhaps we should now expand our Easter proclamation to say:

> He is risen! He is arisen, indeed!
> He has returned! He has returned, indeed!
> He is here with us! He is here with us, indeed!

What We're Contending For

Jesus' words "anew in my Father's kingdom" imply a celebration communion, not a commemorative communion. What do we celebrate? Surely it's that He returned *as* and *when* He said He would, and is now with us. Many readers of this book may feel that we have been talking about something "new," but this should not be the case. We should have taken our Lord at his word long ago. Lest there be any misunderstanding, let us reiterate the positive, preterist view presented in this book. We are contending:

For... a world "without end" (Eph. 3:21 KJV) and a *terra firma* earth that "endures [remains] forever" (Ecc. 1:4).

For... "the faith that was once for all delivered to the saints" (Jude 3) in the 1st century—not one with any portion yet to be delivered—and just as Christ died "once for all" (1 Pe. 3:18; Heb. 10:10; see also Heb. 9:12, 26; Ro. 6:10).

For... an imminent "end of all things" which was "at hand," fulfilled in that same time-context (1 Pet 4:7 KJV), and not still future.

For... the Lord's anointing, crucifixion, resurrection, and "on-the-clouds" return, all of which were precisely foretold, time-specified, and time-restricted by Scripture, with no delays, gaps, nonoccurrences, failures, unmet expectations, excuses, or side-stepping-exegetic gimmicks. And He remains with us forever.

For... the Holy Spirit who did *not* obscure Christ's truth, and did *not* become the spirit of falsehood to 1st-century believers, but who guided their expectations correctly (Jn. 16:13).

For... the end of the age of Moses, the full atoning (salvation) work of Christ, and the consummated reality of our faith, which is finished and no longer our *hope* but our *heritage*. This is the *sure foundation* upon which Christians are to build (Eph. 2:20).

Lastly, we contend that a literal day in August or September of A.D. 70, was a third most important date in human history, along with Christmas and Easter. Call it Parousia, or Christ's Return, or

Consummation Day, or something else. Perhaps future Christians will someday celebrate its anniversary as well.[23] Dare we make less of it? And just wait until you see what else fully arrived on that day as well.

14

*The New Heaven and New Earth —Are They Really a Sequel?**

"**G**od has *not* created the new heaven and new earth yet," a pastor-friend of mine insisted. That was before he read the contents of this chapter.

With a wave out the window, he leaned back in his chair and sighed, "I believe the Bible says that there will be an end to all this someday." Will there?

The Frank & Earnest cartoon featured in the Introduction captures the heart of the issue. Is God really planning a sequel? If so, there are three sobering implications for us to ponder:

1) If the present universe (consisting of heaven and earth) is destroyed in a final cataclysmic disaster when God brings

---

Most of the material in this chapter was presented by the author at the Evangelical Theological Society's Midwestern Region Meeting in March 1997 in Chicago, Illinois at the Moody Bible Institute.

223

human history to a close (as many believe the Bible predicts), will God replace it with a new one?

2) If the current cosmos is purified through a fiery renovation (as others believe the Bible says), will those who have already gone on to heaven come back and spend eternity with Jesus on a recycled Earth? If so, does this mean that they will they no longer "dwell in the house of the Lord forever" (i.e., dwell in heaven) as the Psalmist claimed (Ps. 23:6)? Wouldn't this mean that our citizenship is not in heaven, as the Bible states (Php. 3:20, heaven being only a temporary resting place) and that man's destiny is ultimately an earthly one?

3) If either of these two popular and futuristic views is correct, shouldn't we just write off this present planet and start looking forward to the new one?

Once again we protest, Not so fast!

Both views—future destruction or cataclysmic renovation—of planet and cosmos are in conflict with Peter's 1st-century statement that "the end of all things is at hand" (1 Pe. 4:7 KJV); as well as with other consummatory scriptures (Lk. 21:20-22, 32; 1 Cor. 7:29, 31; 10:11; 1 Pe. 4:17; 1 Jn. 2:18). Did Peter mean what he said, or did he mean that only the end of *some* things was at hand? Taking such liberty with Scripture is unacceptable for those of us who believe in its Spirit-guided inspiration and inerrancy (Jn. 16:13). Something has to give.

In this chapter let's consider ten revelational insights which should help us gain a better understanding of Peter's prophetic words as they apply to the coming of the Bible's "new heaven and new earth." We believe you'll find these insights compelling. Please don't jump ahead; read them in sequence. They build upon each other and escalate in depth.

Ten Revelational Insights

One faithful day over nineteen centuries ago, on the small island of Patmos in the Mediterranean Sea, Jesus gave John a breathtaking vision of a new heaven and a new earth:

> Then I saw a new heaven and a new earth, for the first heaven and the first earth had passed away, and there was no longer any sea. I saw the Holy City, the new Jerusalem, coming down out of heaven from God, prepared as a bride beautifully dressed for her husband (Rev. 21:1-2).

What was John seeing? Did he see a sequel to our planet, a re-do of outer space, or something else? The meaning of this phrase "heaven and earth" cannot be found in a dictionary or casually assumed. If we are sincere in seeking a responsible apocalypticism (i.e., a view or expectation of the end), we must be willing to lay aside our preconceived ideas and carefully determine the identity and nature of this biblical reality, within its historical time constraints and contextual framework.

The following ten revelational insights may require many of you to rethink and readjust your traditional interpretation of the fulfillment of John's "a new heaven and a new earth." But surely God's truth is more precious than man's tradition. The primary hermeneutical question to keep in mind is this: Does time determine nature, or does nature determine time? This is a critical question, so pause a moment to think about your answer. Traditionalists assume the latter. Since they haven't seen what they expect to see (i.e, nature of fulfillment), they adjust the time factor to be yet future. It's their only option.

This book takes the view that *time determines nature*. Throughout, we've proposed that the *time* and *imminency* statements of Scripture be naturally and literally honored. Like a jigsaw puzzle, they provide the border (historical framework) in which all the other pieces properly fit. Therefore, it's our understanding of the *nature of fulfillment* which must be adjusted, not the time factor.

Let's begin with the first insight supporting the case for a past fulfillment of John's prophesied "a new heaven and a new earth":

Insight 1. Jesus Tied the Passing Away of Heaven and Earth to the Passing of the Law of Moses.

> Do not think that I have come to abolish the Law or the Prophets; I have not come to abolish them but to fulfill them. I tell you the

Truth, until heaven and earth disappear [pass away], not the smallest letter, not the least stroke of a pen [one jot or one tittle], will
by any means disappear [pass away] from the Law until everything is accomplished [all be fulfilled]. (Mt. 5:17-18 NIV [KJV])

For Jesus Christ, not the smallest component of the Law would
disappear or pass away until two events took place: 1) "heaven and
earth disappear" (pass away), and 2) "everything is accomplished"
(all be fulfilled). How could words be spoken more plainly?   All
three eschatological events are connected. They stand or fall together. The Law would disappear at the same time this "heaven and
earth" passed away, and both would happen when "everything is
accomplished."

Jesus began these prophetic words by saying that He came "to
fulfill the Law and the Prophets." His statement includes the entire
Mosaic, Old Covenant system (Ex. 19:3-8; 20:1-23:19). He did not
come to bring new prophecy, and neither did any of the writers of
the New Testament.[1]   Later He added, "When you see Jerusalem surrounded by armies...this is the time of punishment in fulfillment of
all that has been written" (Lk. 21:20, 22). "All that has been written"
refers to "everything... that is written about me [Jesus] in the Law of
Moses, the Prophets and the Psalms" (Lk. 24:44).   In other words, it
was the whole Old Testament. This would include Isaiah's promise
of a passing of "heaven and earth" (Isa. 51:6-16) and the creation of
"the new heavens and a new earth" (Isa. 65:17-18; 66:22).[2] The fact
is, neither the Law nor biblical Judaism has been practiced for over
1,900 years. They disappeared. If Jesus' words are to be trusted,
then the "heaven and earth" He had in mind must have disappeared
as well.

In perfect correlation with this passing, Jesus placed the destruction of the Jewish Temple and Jerusalem within the generation then
present—Jesus' "this generation" (Lk. 21:32; Mt. 24:34). The demise
of the Temple and its vital institutions of the Law was much more
than a "jot" or a "tittle, " or "the smallest letter" or "least stroke of a
pen." It was an entire system—all of biblical Judaism. If not even a

jot or tittle could pass away until *all* was fulfilled, we therefore have absolute confirmation that all was fulfilled in A.D. 70, for that is when the Law was finally and completely put out of business. The Law passed away at the end of the age (Mt. 24:3; 33-34). Whatever "heaven and earth" Jesus was referring to back then *cannot* now exist.

If Jesus was referring to the physical universe and the *terra firma* Earth, which has not passed away, then everything hasn't been accomplished and fulfilled yet, for they and the Law were supposed to pass away together. That would mean that the Law of Moses is still in effect, God's people are still under its authority, and we should be performing animal sacrifices, celebrating Jewish feasts and rituals, observing Jewish dietary laws, and honoring the Jewish priesthood. But neither the Christian Church nor the orthodox Jews have practiced these laws in almost 2,000 years. Such a literal interpretation simply doesn't make sense. As we saw in chapter three, the Bible declares that the earth and the whole material universe were eternally established. If Jesus was referring to the material heaven and earth in the passage above, He contradicted the Bible as well as Himself.

It's a case of all or nothing. Either *all* was fulfilled, or *nothing* was fulfilled.

But we cannot side-step the plain meaning of Jesus' words. He joined together the passing of the Law, the passing of the old heaven and earth, and the accomplishment and fulfillment of everything. What Jesus "has joined together, let not man separate" (Mt. 19:6). As we shall see, the heaven and earth that Jesus was talking about did indeed pass away and was superseded by a new heaven and a new earth. And it all came to pass precisely *as* and *when* He had said it would.

It's a case of all or nothing. Either *all* was fulfilled, or *nothing* was fulfilled. All passed away, or nothing passed away. If there is a single Old Testament promise or prophecy unfulfilled, and if the old heaven and earth did not disappear, then the Old Covenant and its Law system is still in effect. Ridiculous, you say? Exactly. But it's this simple: if the Old Covenant system passed away, then the "heaven and earth" that Jesus named has passed away. There is no legitimate escape from this conclusion. The problem disappears, however, when we understand that Jesus' "heaven and earth" is a figurative name for a spiritual reality, not for the material universe and earth. Let's see if there is a valid biblical basis for this type of understanding.

Insight 2.   *The Words Heaven and Earth Are Found in a Book that Abounds with Signs and Symbols.*

It is not unreasonable to deduce that the "a new heaven and a new earth" terminology contained in the apocalyptic book of Revelation may be a sign and symbol pointing to a reality beyond itself—something other than the physical creation (Rev. 21:1). If indeed it is, then its meaning, or clues to its meaning, will be provided in that book itself or elsewhere in the Bible. Using Scripture to interpret other Scripture in this manner is a valid method for determining the meaning of any apocalyptic sign or symbol used in the Bible, and works especially well with those found in the book of Revelation.

Whatever the "a new heaven and a new earth" symbol represents, it is part of the whole prophecy of the book of Revelation. That whole prophecy, from first to last, was affirmed by that book itself as being "at hand," "obeyable," "not to be sealed up," and certain to "shortly come to pass" (Rev. 1:1, 3; 22:6-10 KJV). These clear time statements are unequivocal and undeniable, and must be honored. They serve as hermeneutical guideposts or reference points. We cannot avoid them, stretch them like a rubber band, or change their natural meaning just because they may not fit our notions. They were given by the angel of Revelation as a guide for interpreting the rest of that book's content. Therefore, every sign and symbol in Revelation must be understood within this framework. We can be certain of this because of the angel's instructions to leave the book open.

If Jesus had meant for the prophecy of Revelation to become relevant 2,000 years later, He should have had John "reseal the book." He had told Daniel to seal up the prophetic sayings of his book "till the time of the end," which was six hundred years away from the time of his writing (Da. 12:4). But John was told to leave his book unsealed (Rev. 22:10). Why? Because its end-time events were to happen soon—soon enough to fulfill Jesus' prophecy within "this generation."[3] There is no room for a 1,900-year-and-counting gap before all that was "at hand" was fulfilled, established, and forever made available.

Even Jesus' first disciples did not always understand his allegorical messages and manner of speech. But Jesus gave an even greater sense of urgency and force to his apocalyptic message of "a new heaven and a new earth" by using the word "now." Let's emphasize Jesus' "nowness" from the ensuing verses of Revelation 21:3-7:

> Now...the dwelling of God is with men, and he will live with them. They will be his people, and God himself will be with them and be their God.

> [Now]...He will wipe every tear from their eyes.

> [Now]...There will be no more death or mourning or crying or pain, for the old order of things has passed away.

> [Now]...I am making everything new.

> [Now]...These words are trustworthy and true.

> [Now]...'It is done.'

> [Now]...To him who is thirsty I will give to drink without cost from the spring of the water of life.

> [Now]...He who overcomes will inherit all this."

What was to be inherited "now?" Everything He was describing, including "a new heaven and a new earth...and...the new Jerusalem"—then and there, not someday in the distant future.

The interpretative speculation that lifts these end-time events out of the period to which they belong does gross injustice to their imminent, 1st-century nature. A responsible interpretation—one using sound hermeneutic principles—will recognize the time context the book of Revelation imposes upon itself, and the normal meaning of words employed in establishing that context. Anything less does violence to the text.

If Jesus was not referring to the physical creation, what did He mean by "a new heaven and a new earth?"

Insight 3.   *Biblical Use of Both Literal and Figurative Meanings.*

The Bible, from beginning to end, contains not only literal language, but also symbolic or figurative language. Many things are described both ways. The term "heaven and earth" is a good example of this dualism. Throughout the Bible, it is used both literally and figuratively.

The first ten words in the Bible speak of a literal, physical heavens and earth. "In the beginning God created the heavens and the earth" (Ge. 1:1). God spoke his physical creation into existence (Ge. 1:3ff). Since He is sovereign, He could, no doubt, speak it out of existence, or into a different form, any time He so desired. But He hasn't. And, as we shall see, He doesn't have to in order to fulfill any unfulfilled promise or prophecy. Why? Because the "heaven and earth" terminology also has a figurative usage and meaning. For example:

- The Song of Moses in the book of Deuteronomy begins with the exhortation, "Listen, O heavens...Hear, O earth" (Dt. 32:1). Isaiah started his Old Testament book with the same words (Isa. 1:2a). To what or to whom were these two prophets directing their messages? Did they expect the actual physical stars and planets to hear, and the global Earth to listen and take note? Of course not. Isaiah tells us a little later that "O heavens" and "O earth" are simply other names for God's "children," or "my people" of Israel (see Isa. 1:2b-3). They were the ones who could hear and listen.

- God used this same symbolism in simile form in his promise to Abraham: "I will make your offspring like the dust of the earth" (Ge. 13:16). "Look at the heavens and count the stars... so shall your offspring be" (Ge. 15:5; also 22:17; Da. 12:3). The Apostle Paul stated that "we have this treasure in earthen vessels" (2 Cor. 4:7 KJV) and appealed to Genesis 2:7, where it is written, "And the Lord God formed man of the dust of the ground" (1 Cor. 15:45). Let's face it: we are earth! We "live in houses of clay whose foundations are in the dust" (Job 4:19).

- God spoke through Isaiah saying, "Turn to me and be saved, all you ends of the earth; for I am God, and there is no other" (Isa. 45:22). "Be silent before me, you islands" (Isa. 41:1). These "ends of the earth" and "islands" are people, not *terra firma*.

- "Lift up your heads, O you gates." Here the Psalmist calls us gates! "Be lifted up, you ancient doors" (Ps. 24:7, 9). We are those doors! "Tremble before him, all the earth" (Ps. 96:9). Here we are called earth again!

- Isaiah also refers to people as trees ("they will be called oaks of righteousness, a planting of the Lord for the display of his splendor" [Isa. 61:3]), and as grass ("the sons of men, who are but grass" [Is 51:12]). The Psalmist and Jeremiah use similar "tree" similes (Ps. 1:3; Jer. 17:8). Jude refers to people as "clouds without rain...autumn trees...wild waves of the sea...wandering stars" (Jude 12-13). The angel in Revelation interpreted, "The waters you saw... are people" (Rev. 17:15). And lastly, even God Himself is referred to as "the Rock" (Dt. 32:4, 15, 18, 30, 31), and Jesus as "that Rock" (1 Cor. 10:4).

- Jesus talked metaphorically of cutting off hands and feet and plucking out eyes (Mt. 5:29, 30), and spoke of "streams of living water" when referring to "the Spirit" (Jn. 7:38, 39). In the book of Revelation, Christ holds seven stars in his hand, explaining to John that they are the seven messengers (angels or leaders) of the seven churches (Rev. 1:16, 20; see also Da. 8:15-26). He's even the bright Morning Star (Rev. 22:16: see also Nu. 24:17). Many more scriptural examples could be cited to illustrate this point. It shouldn't be surprising, then, to realize that the fleeing of earth and sky from the Presence of the Lord in Revelation 20:11 f, which precedes the new heaven and new earth prophecy, most probably symbolizes the judgment of people and does not refer to the destruction of the physical/material earth and sky. After all, why would God judge the ground, the stars, the moon, or the planets? They can't sin. They can't choose to follow or not follow God or obey or disobey Him. How would God's judgment of inanimate objects serve any redemptive purpose?

Understanding the biblical pattern of figurative terminology, especially in the Old Testament, lets us see how 1st-century Jews would have taken these familiar symbols of "heaven and earth" to stand for humanity. But this scriptural phrase, in its apocalyptic, eschatological usage, symbolized more than just individual people.

Insight 4.   Heaven and Earth Symbolized the Israelites' World.

During the time of the Law and the Prophets, Israel and its people had no special meaning apart from their covenant-determined "world." In a similar fashion, we use the word "world" today, not just to refer to planet Earth, but figuratively when we speak of the sports world, sales world, religious world, workaday world, or society as a whole.

We find the word "heavens" used in the Bible in a figurative, corporate way to symbolize governments or people in authority.

Recall Joseph's prophetic dream. He saw the heavenly bodies of the sun, moon, and stars bowing down to him. They represented the leaders of the nation of Egypt, or perhaps the heads of the tribes of Israel (Ge. 37:9). "Earth," when used collectively, refers to a nation or nations and the people.

In the following short passage, Isaiah contrasts God's establishment of two different meanings for the Bible's "heaven and earth" terminology. He writes by inspiration: "And forgettest the Lord thy maker, that hath stretched forth the heavens, and laid the foundations of the earth..." (Isa. 51:13a KJV). Here God, through his prophet, uses the past perfect form of the verbs translated "stretched" (*natah*) and "laid" (*suwm*) in recounting his creation of the physical heavens and *terra firma* Earth. But notice what happens just a few verses later when the verb form switches to the infinitive: "But I am the Lord thy God, that divided the sea, whose waves roared: The Lord of Hosts is his name. And I have put my words in thy mouth; I have covered thee in the shadow of mine hand, that I may plant the heavens, and lay the foundations of the earth, and may say unto Zion, 'Thou art my people'" (Isa. 51:15-16 KJV).

What a difference. It's a totally different "world" in meaning. In this second portion of this same passage, God is still speaking to Israel. But here He says He gave them his Law ("words in thy mouth") and his covenant protection ("covered thee in the shadow of mine hand"). Next He uses the infinitive form of the verbs (to "plant" [*nata*] and to "lay" [*suwm*]) to speak of forming a "heavens and earth" different from the ones mentioned in verse 13. This latter "heavens and earth" He forms by the process of delivering his chosen people, the Jews, from Egyptian slavery by parting the Red Sea, giving them the Mosaic Covenant on Mt. Sinai, and protecting them from their enemies.

It's important to emphasize that this second portion of the passage could not be referring to the physical creation (it is improperly translated by the NIV translation[4]), because the material heavens and earth existed long before the first Jewish exodus out of Egypt and the giving of the Mosaic Law on Mt. Sinai. Neither is God saying through Isaiah that He created the *terra firma* Earth for Israel to occupy since Gentiles occupied it as well. What God is saying in these two infinitive purpose clauses is that He gave them the Law to establish a theocratic "heavens and earth." He gave his covenant to the Israelites to create their "world" of Judaism—the Jewish religious system. That's how the Jews became God's covenant people.

God later confirmed this establishment process through another prophet using the same infinitive verb forms: "And at what instant I shall speak concerning a nation, and concerning a kingdom, to build and to plant it" (Jer. 18:9 KJV; see also Jer. 1:10; Ecc. 3:2).

This historic background and apocalyptic framework lets us see more clearly the meaning of Jesus' teaching concerning the disappearing or passing away of the old "heaven and earth" and "the Law." Jesus' consistent usage of a figurative "heaven and earth" was focusing on that same theocratic entity of which Isaiah spoke. He was using those same covenantal terms to represent the people incorporated into the "world" of Judaism.

This interpretation harmonizes perfectly with Paul's statement that "this world in its present form is passing away" (1 Cor. 7:31), and that its "time is short" (1 Cor. 7:29). Again, the nature and time questions are crucial here. When Paul wrote these words, around A.D. 57, he was not deluded. Nor was he referring to an end of the material universe or the destiny of the physical planet. As we saw in chapter three, all the physical creation is established forever. What Paul envisioned did not fail to materialize. He was referring to the Old Testament Law system that was progressively disintegrating and disappearing as well as being transformed into a new order and reality in Christ before their very eyes (Heb. 8:13; 9:10). Very soon the Law would be fulfilled and its Old Covenant world annihilated. Its end did not require the end of humanity or the demise of the cosmic creation.

The Jewish historian Josephus corroborates this 1st-century Jewish understanding. In his book *The Antiquities of the Jews*,[5] he describes how the Jews of Jesus' time looked upon their Temple as "a Heaven and earth." They believed that their Temple was at the

the Jews of Jesus' time looked upon their Temple as "a Heaven and earth."

very center of the earth, and saw it as the place where heaven and earth came together, and where God met man. Josephus calls its outer tabernacle "an imitation of the system of the world" and "sea and land, on which men live." By contrast, the inner, Most Holy Place he terms "a Heaven peculiar to God." The veil that separated the two "was very ornamental, and embroidered with all sorts of flowers which the earth produces."

This veil was visible from outside the Temple area. It's not hard to imagine Jesus sitting on the Mount of Olives (just a short distance across a small valley from the Temple) gesturing toward this Jewish "heaven and earth," and speaking his prophetic words: "Heaven and earth will pass away, but My words will never pass away" (Mt. 24:35; Lk. 21:33).

His Jewish audience also might have recalled these other words of the prophet Isaiah and so understood that the "world" of heaven and earth which was to be destroyed was the Temple and the Jewish religious system:

> Lift up your eyes to the heavens, look at the earth beneath; the heavens will vanish like smoke, the earth will wear out like a garment and its inhabitants die like flies. But my salvation will last forever, my righteousness will never fail (Isa. 51:6).

The importance of this change of covenant worlds also can be seen in the inspired words of the writer of Hebrews:

> In the beginning, O Lord, you laid the foundations of the earth, and the heavens are the work of your hands. They will perish, but you remain; they will all wear out like a robe; like a garment they will be *changed*. But you remain the same and your years will never end (Heb. 1:10-12; quoting from Ps. 102:25-27—emphasis mine).

By calling this covenant 'new,' he [God] has made the first one obsolete; and what is obsolete and aging will soon disappear (Heb. 8:13).

If God destroyed the Old Covenant "heaven and earth"—the world of biblical Judaism—would He not establish a new one to replace the old? Or would He leave a multi-century void? As we shall see, the old "heaven and earth," which God had "planted," prefigured and linked directly into the new. The old indeed perished, and was "changed." But the transition and transformation from one covenant world to the other would occur through a "shaking" process.

Insight 5. Precedent and Type for "the Shaking."

..."In a little while I will once more shake the heavens and the earth, the sea and dry land. I will shake all nations, and the desire of all nations will come, and I will fill this house with glory," says the Lord Almighty (Hag. 2:6-7).

What did this Old Testament, *post*-exilic prophet Haggai mean by this second shaking? To find the answer we must discover the last time God shook the "heavens and earth," since this event will serve as the precedent and type for the next shaking.

As we've demonstrated, cosmic-collapsing, light-darkening, and earth-moving apocalyptic language is employed throughout the Old Testament. It was always used to vividly portray and prophesy an impending "day of the Lord," when God would pour out his judgment on a wicked nation or people, and there are a number of these occurrences. But God once warned through Isaiah, a *pre*-exilic prophet:

Therefore I will shake the heavens, and the earth shall remove out of her place, in the wrath of the LORD of hosts, and in the day of his fierce anger (Isa. 13:13 KJV).

This *pre*-exilic shaking and removing prophecy chronologically preceded Haggai's *post*-exilic, "once more" shaking prophecy. This

drastic language was employed to show the greatness and complete-
ness of these two judgments. The immediate historical setting for
the fulfillment of the Isaiah 13:13 prophecy was God's overthrow
and desolation of the Babylonians (see Isa. 13:19-22). Previously,
God had foretold through the prophet Habakkuk that He would use
the Babylonians to bring chastening upon Judah (the southern kingdom of Israel), to destroy Jerusalem and the Temple, and to deport
many Jews into captivity (Hab. 1:5-11). This occurred in the 6th
century B.C.

This first prophesied "shake" and "remove" judgment of Isaiah
13 was to come against those same Babylonians (Isa. 47:5-10; Jer.
51:6-10; Zep. 1-3; Hos. 11:5; Am. 6:14; 9:8-10). With God's divine
assistance, the Persian army was to be God's next instrument of
judgment. It defeated the Babylonians, laid waste to their country,
and took over the Babylonian empire. Afterwards Cyrus, the Persian
king, released the captive Jews to return to their land. The Jews
then rebuilt their capital city and the Temple and reinstituted the
practices of biblical Judaism.

As devastating as the 587 B.C. fall of Jerusalem and ensuing seventy years of Babylonian captivity were for the Jewish people, they
were only temporary and mild desolations compared to the greater,
cataclysmic judgment yet to come. Furthermore, God's shaking and
removal of Babylon was to serve as the *precedent* and *type* for that
future, "once more" shaking and age-ending judgment of Old Covenant Israel. This prior and divine judgment of Babylonian was well
ingrained in 1st-century Jewish thought and remembrance.

Early in Israel's history, God had promised that as long as his
chosen people kept the covenant, He would bless and protect this
nation more than any other. On the other hand, if they broke the
covenant He would withdraw his protective Presence, chasten and
scatter his people (Lev. 26:14-39; Dt. 28:15-68). Over the course of
Jewish history a cycle of apostasy, oppression, repentance, and deliverance was repeated numerous times, and as a result of this
perpetual, national disobedience, Israel's sin mounted. That's why
Jesus not only borrowed the same "shake" judgment language of the

Prophets (Mt. 24:29 from Isa. 13:10; 34:4), but confirmed another of Isaiah's prophecies by saying that Israel would "fill up, then, the measure of the sin of your forefathers" (Mt. 23:32; Isa. 65:6-19). This "filling up" would include the rejection of Jesus as the Messiah. When full, Haggai's prophesied "once more" shaking judgment would come—but this time that judgment would be upon the Jews.

The Jewish writer of the New Testament book of Hebrews readily made this connection. Writing in the decade of the A.D. 60s, he warned his readers that he and they were living in "the last days" of which Haggai had prophesied (Heb. 1:2). He quoted Haggai directly and referred to the last major judgment of God upon the Jewish people (Heb. 12:5-7, 25, 26 [i.e., the 587 B.C. destruction of Jerusalem and subsequent 70 years of Babylonian captivity]), but emphasized the imminency and permanency of that second, "once more" shaking prophecy and judgment. Here's how he put it:

> At that time his voice shook the earth, but now he has promised, 'Once more I will shake not only the earth but also the heavens' [from Haggai 2:6]. The words 'once more' indicated the removing of what can be shaken—that is, created things—so that what cannot be shaken may remain (Heb. 12:26-27).

Clearly, the writer tells us that to shake what can be shaken signifies removing it. As we've seen, the Apostle Paul taught the Jews the same thing—that their "world" in its present form was passing away (1 Cor. 7:31; also 1 Jn. 2:17). In Acts 13:40-41, Paul quoted directly from Habakkuk 1:5 and cited God's previous punishment of Israel through the Babylonians some six hundred years earlier. Then he warned that this type of judgment was about to come upon them. This is no doubt why the Jews in Asia later accused Paul, saying, "This is the man who teaches all men everywhere against our people and our law and this place" (Ac. 21:28).

Indeed, a massive judgment was forthcoming. Not only was God going to "shake" and "remove" the Judaic "heavens and earth" world; He was never going to bring them back. Instead, He promised to supersede them with that which "cannot be shaken." And what was that? The writer of Hebrews explains that it was to be the new kingdom of God, a kingdom that was already breaking into human history.

> Therefore, since we are receiving a kingdom (then and there) that cannot be shaken, let us be thankful, and so worship God acceptably with reverence and awe (Heb. 12:28).

Not one shred of evidence exists that these early Christians expected a destruction of the planet, an end to the cosmos, or the termination of human existence.

Obviously, this second, "once more" shaking was not a promise or prophecy to shake and remove the physical creation. Not one shred of evidence exists that these early Christians expected a destruction of the planet, an end to the cosmos, or the termination of human existence. Instead, God, in total consistency with the prophetic pattern of divine judgment upon nations in Old Testament times, and in line with the prefigured "shaking" and "removing" of the Babylonian "heavens and earth" via the Persian armies, was about to pour out this second judgment. But this time it was to be upon a rebellious and apostate Israel.

So it happened. God removed that Jewish world (heaven and earth) in A.D. 70. Its institutions were shaken to the ground and totally removed, never to rise again, just as Daniel had long ago prophesied would happen at "the time of the end" (Da. 12:4) "when the power of the holy people" would be "finally broken" and "all things will be completed" (Da. 12:7). All these prophecies and many others were fulfilled when the Roman armies, empowered by God, shook, removed, and left desolate the Temple, the city of Jerusalem, and the whole world of biblical Judaism. This was the historical setting for Christ's "coming on the clouds." The impressive parallelism, precedent, and typology of God's similar coming and "shaking" judgment upon the Babylonians must not be missed.

Insight 6. Isaiah's New Heavens and New Earth.

The book of Revelation's phrase "a new heaven and a new earth" is not new in scriptural terminology. Isaiah first foresaw a coming transformation from the old creation to the new in such radical terms that he twice speaks of "new heavens and a new earth:"

> "Behold, I will create new heavens and a new earth. The former things will not be remembered, nor will they come to mind. But be glad and rejoice forever in what I will create, for I will create Jerusalem to be a delight and its people a joy" (Isa. 65:17-18).

> "As the new heavens and the new earth that I make will endure [remain] before me," declares the Lord, "so shall your name and descendants [seed] endure [remain]" (Isa. 66:22 [KJV]).

Some interpreters think Isaiah's terminology refers to the return of Israel to her land from Babylonian captivity ("a second time" return [see Isa. 11:11], the first being from Egyptian exile), and the restoration of their "world" as an initial, but limited fulfillment of entering a "new heavens and new earth." This seems unlikely.

Isaiah's "new heavens and new earth" are absolutely Messianic and totally covenantal. They undoubtedly are tied into Haggai's "once more" shaking and go hand-in-hand with:

- Jeremiah's and Ezekiel's promises of a New Covenant for Israel (Jer. 31:31-32; 50:4-5; Eze. 34:25-30; 37:21-28; also Isa. 59:20-21).

- Jesus' conjoined passing of the Law and the old heaven and earth (Mt. 5:17-18; 24:34-35).

- Putting the Law in minds and writing it on hearts (Jer. 31:33).

- The making of a new people of God (Jer. 31:33bff; Isa. 65:13-16).

- The gift of a new name (Isa. 62:2; 65:15), a new heart, and a new spirit, and the placement of God's Spirit in his people (Eze. 11:19; 18:31; 36:26-27).

- Doing a new thing (Isa. 43:18-21); and making all things new (Rev. 21:5).

Daniel knew that the ultimate restoration of Israel was not its return to her land following Babylonian captivity. He prayed for divine insight into the greater and lasting restoration that would occur during the days of the Messiah and conclude at the "time of the end." That time would coincide with the fulfillment of Isaiah's vision of a "new heavens and a new earth," and with the arrival of the Holy City promised to Abraham and his seed through Christ, whose builder and maker is God (Heb. 11:16). In continuity with the old, this new heaven and new earth would also be determined by covenant (Gal. 4:21-31). In contrast, however, they would not be a heaven and earth that could be shaken (Heb. 12:18-29). It was the "world" that Abraham and his descendents (seed) would inherit (Ro. 4:13). Isaiah places this radical transformation in "the last days" (Isa. 2:2-4). The New Testament confirms that they were living in those very "last days," right then and there (Heb. 1:2; Ac. 2:17; 1 Ti. 4:1; 2 Ti. 3:1; Jas. 5:3; 2 Pe. 3:3; 1 Pe. 1:5, 20; Jude 18; 1 Jn. 2:18). This restoration and the fulfillment of Israel's hopes was consummated in A.D. 70 when Israel and its religious institutions and ordinances were destroyed by the armies of Rome. But this eschatological event had both a destructive and a restorative side.

Revelation's phrase "a new heaven and a new earth" was the restorative side. The destructive side was appropriately symbolized by Babylonian imagery (Rev. 18), the biblical precedent and type for this judgment. Such a figurative and symbolic approach neither diminishes its reality or importance, nor disguises its true identity. As we've seen, three times Babylon is called "the great city" (Rev. 18:10, 16, 19). And there is only one "great city" in Revelation. It's 1st-century Jerusalem. How do we know? Again, Revelation 11:8 tells us that "the great city" was "where also their Lord was crucified." No other city of any other time fits or will fit this description. The new creation was only fully realized and established when the Old Covenant "world" of Judaism was removed at the end of the age of Moses in that 1st century (Mt. 25:34).

A solemn warning: We must not make the mistake of interpreting the prophecy of "a new heaven(s) and new earth" independently from its established imagery, historical context, and scriptural roots. The facts of history and the pattern of terminology used in Scripture provide firm proof for the figurative, but nevertheless real, nature of the "heaven and earth" fulfillment as described in this chapter.

> For I tell you that Christ has become a servant of the Jews on behalf of God's truth, to confirm the promises made to the patriarchs (Ro. 15:8).

Jesus entered into the Old Covenant (heaven and earth) world of Judaism. He returned in A.D. 70 to complete the Old Covenant and bring the consummation of the promised "new heaven(s) and new earth" in the New Covenant world. The dual use of heaven and earth language indicates a continuity. Both were determined by covenant. And covenantal change is the key to understanding all Bible end-time prophecy (eschatology).

Peter's vivid description of the destruction of the earth and the universe in 2 Peter 3 uses the same figurative and symbolic language.

Insight 7. The Destruction of the World in 2 Peter 3.

> But the day of the Lord will come like a thief. The heavens will disappear with a roar; the elements will be destroyed by fire, and the earth and everything in it will be laid bare.
>
> Since everything will be destroyed in this way, what kind of people ought you to be? You ought to live holy and godly lives as you look

forward to the day of God and speed its coming. That day will bring about the destruction of the heavens by fire, and the elements will melt in the heat. But in keeping with his promise we are looking forward to a new heaven and a new earth, the home of righteousness (2 Pe. 3:10-13).

The Bible text most quoted to support a future and universal cataclysm is this passage from 2 Peter 3. The futurists see it as the end of time, the close of human history, and the final demise or fiery renovation of planet Earth and the solar system. Contemporary prophecy writers have had a field day applying Peter's language to the horrors of the atomic and nuclear bomb and terrorizing modern-day humanity with the supposed "hopelessness" of our present-day situation. But is a literal and materialistic reading of Peter's "heaven(s)" and "earth" terminology suddenly justified, as countless commentators have assumed? Or do Peter's words speak of the very same 1st-century consummatory event we've been addressing? To settle this question, let's investigate a trail of five clues. They should help us arrive at the true meaning of 2 Peter 3's supposed universe-destroying text.

Clue 1. Peter's Consistency. The same inspired Peter, in his first letter to these same people, writes, "The end of all things is at hand" (1 Pe. 4:7 KJV), and "the time is come that judgment must begin at the house of God" (1 Pe. 4:17 KJV). Now in his second letter, chapter three, he refers to his first epistle and reminds his readers that he is writing on the same theme (2 Pe. 3:1). Peter is consistent. He is not introducing a new topic. This chapter does not stand apart from his first epistle or the earlier part of his second. He uses the same apocalyptic language and style that is used over and over in the Old Testament. The meanings and historical fulfillments were well-known to the religiously educated people of his day.

Peter does admit that these things, about which Paul also wrote, are "hard to understand" (2 Pe. 3:15-16). In other words, they are not readily apparent. Why? If this chapter's text is "literal," it would not be hard to understand. If, however, it depends on biblical and historical precedent, then its terminology and fulfillment pattern require thought and spiritual understanding.

Peter's objective is for his readers to understand both the imminency and the nature of the end that's coming and not be carried away by error. He laments that some people living in those times only want to distort and complicate it (2 Pe. 3:16b-17), a problem in our times as well. If the many references to and fulfillments of the dissolving, shaking, and darkening of the heavens and earth in the Old Testament are to be taken literally, wouldn't it mean that our material planet and cosmos has been destroyed numerous times? Of course, this is ridiculous. And Peter's letter is no exception. He uses this same language without any qualification that he's using it differently. His language is consistent with figurative usage elsewhere.

Peter's objective is for his readers to understand both the imminency and the nature of the end that's coming and not be carried away by error.

Clue 2. What Are These "Elements" That Are Burned Up?
The Greek word translated "elements," which Peter said were to be "destroyed by fire" and "melt in the heat" [or "with fervent heat"- KJV], are assumed by most interpreters to be either the four physical substances that the ancients believed made up the material world (earth, water, air, and fire) or the modern chemical elements as they appear on a chemist's periodic table.

There are two problems with these interpretations. First, neither reading properly translates the Greek word in question. A quick glance into a Greek concordance—not into an English dictionary—

will dispel any doubt as to the primary meaning of this word for those who first received it. The Greek word for "elements" is *stoicheion*. It means something orderly in arrangement, a principle, or a rudiment. It's derived from the verb *stoicheo*, which means to arrange in regular line, to march in (military) rank (keep step), or, figuratively, to conform to virtue and piety or to walk orderly.

The second problem is that the word is *never* used to refer to the material creation in any other New Testament occurrence or context. As we compare Scripture with Scripture, we find its uses elsewhere in the New Testament will give us a clearer perspective of its intended meaning here. In Hebrews 5:12 and Colossians 2:8, 20, the same Greek word *stoicheion* is translated as "rudiments," "rudimentary and elemental teachings," "elementary principles" or "truths," and "first" or "basic principles" in various Bible translations (such as the KJV, AMP, NAS, and NIV). Paul uses the word twice in his letter to the Galatians (vv. 4:3, 9) to mean elementary teachings, elemental things, or basic principles. He says that under the Law people were held in bondage to these "elements of the world." Paul didn't mean that these Old Covenant Jews were under bondage to the physical substances of the material creation (earth, water, air, fire, or chemical matter). He meant that they were under bondage to the Law system, its institutions, its priesthood, and its sacrificial rituals. Paul then explains, in verses 4-5, that this was why "God sent his Son, born of a woman, born under the law, to redeem those under the law, that we might receive the full rights of sons." He wasn't saying that they would be freed from the physical world. Peter's meaning for "elements" is the same as Paul's. *It has nothing to do with the physical creation.*

This Greek word *stoicheion* could, of course, be used to speak of the four physical parts of which the ancients believed our universe was made. But such a usage would be an isolated exception to the way it is used everywhere else in Scripture. If Peter had intended a different meaning, he would have said so. But he didn't. For us to force a change of meaning from well-established usage is at best arbitrary and presumptuous. Should we presume to deter-

mine biblical truth by finding an exception to the normal and consistent meaning of often-used words, and to do so without some
overwhelming contextual reason?   Of course not. Any time we
have to create new or changed definitions for familiar words, something is wrong. We'd be much wiser to keep within this word's
primary definition and prevailing usage in Scripture. So what exactly are these "elements?"

The "elements" Peter is speaking of are the "elementary principles" or "rudiments" of Judaism, that Old Covenant "world" or system
which would soon be destroyed in the coming of "the day of the
Lord" in A.D. 70. These "elements" of the old Jewish religion—its
forms, institutions and mode of existence—were the types and shadows pointing to the new substance. They had served their purpose
and were in the process of passing away. Shortly, they would be
dissolved, melted, and destroyed by fire forever.

But what did Peter mean when he said that the elements would
be destroyed by "fire"? What was this fire? It was not a reference to
nuclear explosions, but, rather a reference to both the literal conflagration of A.D. 70, and, figuratively, to God Who is "a consuming fire"
(Heb. 12:29), and whose Messiah casts judgments with "fire."[6] Fire
is often used as a biblical symbol of judgment. This divine "fire"
destroyed the Temple, the city, the sacrifices, the priesthood, the
genealogies, the tribes, and the whole heart, soul, and physical components of the Jewish religious system and theocracy—forever. Truly,
Peter's "world" that was soon to perish was the world of biblical
Judaism: Old-Covenant Israel.

Not one shred of evidence exists that 1st-century Jews and Jewish Christians were anticipating a cosmic catastrophe that would
terminate time, burn up planet Earth, and end human history. Our
modern-day view would have shocked any biblically literate Old-
Testament Jew, and should give us a jolt, too. We must recognize
that the Holy Spirit is consistent with his use of words and
concepts in Scripture. The melting and dissolving of Peter's "elements" was a totally covenantal transformation, not a cosmic
conflagration. Dare we presume or teach otherwise? Unfortunately,

many do. They get away with it because their followers have little or no knowledge of the Greek, do not look in a concordance, or do not compare usages in other passages of Scripture. It's a sad commentary on modern biblical ignorance that many succumb to this erroneous, end-of-the-world sensationalism. God has promised not to "destroy" the world again (Ge. 8:21-22; 9:11). And nowhere in the Bible does God say that He'll destroy the entire universe. On the contrary, He states that it is eternal.[7] Peter's "elements" must be interpreted within their biblical, covenantal, and historical setting.

The melting and dissolving of Peter's "elements" was a totally covenantal transformation, not a cosmic conflagration.

Clue 3. Coattailing on the Prophets. In 2 Peter 3:2, Peter reminds his readers of what the prophets have said concerning the subject he is addressing. Peter's visual description of the coming "day of the Lord" is anchored in what the prophets had foretold. He speaks in their language, a language with which his audience was familiar.

Therefore, Peter prefaces his teaching by mentioning three different heavens and earths in verses 5, 7, and 13—the physical one "destroyed" in Noah's day,[8] the covenantal one ("the present heaven and earth") in Peter's day, and a new one to come. The contrast between the physical heaven and earth and the first covenantal one is exactly the same distinction and in complete harmony with the prophet Isaiah's dual usage detailed in our revelational insight 4 (Isa. 51:13, 16).

The Old Testament prophets never foretold an end of time, of planet Earth, or of human history. Those are *not* biblical subjects.

These prophets always used "heavens and earth" as a symbol associated with the downfall of nations or governmental systems by invading armies. Jesus utilized this same terminology (Mt. 5:17-18; 24:35). Paul affirmed that same thing saying, "this world in its present form is passing away" (1 Cor. 7:31). In an identical manner, Joel foretold the destruction of Jerusalem (Joel 2:30-31). Why then would Peter, a devout Jew, use this language any differently? He didn't. He simply drew on the long biblical tradition of the prophets as it applied to many past fulfillments of "the day of the Lord." This was Peter's theme, a "the day of the Lord" (2 Pe. 3:10), and its soon-coming to bring the demise of the Judaic system. Only those who are unaware of prophetic usage, or who try to interpret outside of context, will insist on a literal destruction of the universe, which—as we've seen—is eternally established.

Clue 4. The Promise of the Prophets. If we need further corroboration for a figurative interpretation, we will find it in the prophets. In 2 Peter 3:13, Peter says, "in keeping with his [God's] promise, we are looking forward to a new heaven and a new earth." As we've seen, Isaiah not only warned of the passing of the old (Isa. 24:1-6; 18-23; 51:6), he also foretold the promised coming of "new heavens and a new earth" in its place (Isa. 65:17-19; 66:22).

As far back as Moses, the Old Covenant people were trained to expect this passing if the Law was broken. They knew that national destruction was part and parcel of the consequences of breaking the Law (Lev. 26; Dt. 28-30). Moses foresaw what would befall Israel in its last days due to its repeated violation of covenant with God. The judgment of 2 Peter 3 is rooted in the fulfillment of the Law and the Prophets. It was a judgment appointed long ago, and, in Peter's day, it was very near. For us today, it is past.

After the cross, the Jews were allowed forty years to hear the remaining messengers sent by God and to accept or reject the atonement of Christ as the Passover Lamb and Messiah. God had given them plenty of warning, as far back as Moses. But their continual rebellion and blasphemy, foreknown by God, necessitated God bringing their system—that "heaven and earth" world—to an end. Jesus warned his disciples to be faithful to this "end"—the end of the Jewish age—not the end of the world, a topic He never addressed. Thus Jesus prophesied, "When you see Jerusalem surrounded by armies...this is in fulfillment of all that has been written" (Lk. 21:20, 22). Old Covenant Israel had failed to recognize the time of its visitation by the Messiah (Lk. 19:41-44), and the measure of its sin was filled up in that generation (Mt. 23:31-39; Isa. 65:6-19). Consequently, the Israeli covenant-determined world was dissolved.

Today we would be wise to interpret the Old Testament scriptures as Jesus did. This includes every Old Testament prophecy and promise relating to Israel and pertaining to the 1st-century destruction of Jerusalem. The whole of Peter's prophecy, as well as all of eschatology, is grounded in two covenants, two ages, two heavens, two earths, and, as we shall soon see, two Jerusalems. The Jewish writer of Hebrews quotes the promise of "a new covenant with the house of Israel" from the prophet Jeremiah (Heb. 8:7-12), then adds:

> By calling this covenant 'new,' he [God] has made the first one obsolete; and what is obsolete and aging will soon disappear" (Heb. 8:13).

The Old Covenant did disappear. Paradoxically, on one Sabbath day each and every year, modern-day Jews attending synagogue hear the song of Moses from Deuteronomy 32. It is read as their Torah portion for the week. They think it describes what's going to happen to them in the future if they don't obey the covenant. But this judgment is over. It's past. The ultimate Jewish rebellion against God was the Israelites' rejection of the Messiah. Their "world" was destroyed forevermore, and its "elements" melted in fervent heat. Recognition of this change in "heaven and earth" is the only redemptive-historical perspective through which a responsible apocalypticism can be achieved. It will enable us to biblically adjust our understanding of other "last things" as well.

Clue 5. Imminency Statements. Peter wrote his second letter in the mid 60's to the generation of his day. The text makes that clear. Peppered throughout his third chapter are imminency (immediacy) statements (2 Pe. 3:1, 12, 13, 14, 17, 18). Those who hold to a futuristic agenda reason that this passage has not been fulfilled. But these imminency verses cause them a great deal of difficulty. The clarity of the text cries out against the futurists and their position of nonoccurrence. Of course, their side-stepping efforts just provide skeptics and liberal theologians with ammunition to attack the inspiration of Scripture. Obviously, a future fulfillment cannot be harmonized with Peter's and Jesus' (and others) imminency statements without violating the integrity of the text. The common practice is to ignore them, but this is a colossal error. They will not go away. If Peter's 1st-century imminency failed, then Peter wasn't inspired. It's that simple.

The question then becomes, Was Peter right, wrong, or mistaken? For the honest believer in biblical inspiration there is but one answer. It all happened right on schedule, within the lifetime of the people he addressed. His use of imminency was accurate. His exhortations for holy living were also right on target, as they are for us today. But it was Peter's contemporaries who would soon be involved in this coming "day of the Lord."

Many more examples in the New Testament show that the original readers and hearers were led to believe these climactic "last things" would happen to them, in their lifetime. They weren't misled. That "end" came, the "elements" were burned up, and the old "heaven and earth" disappeared.

Peter likewise pinpointed his own contemporaries as the ones who would see imminent fulfillment in his first letter. In it he talks about how the Old Testament prophets "searched intently and with the greatest care, trying to find out the time and the circumstances to which the Spirit of Christ in them was pointing when he predicted the sufferings of Christ and the glories that would follow" (1 Pe. 1:10-11). Peter tells his readers that these prophets knew that the things they wrote about were not imminent in their day, but would be during his generation—for *you:* "It was revealed to them that they were not serving themselves but you ..." (1 Pe. 1:12a).

Peter wrote of covenant transition. His 1st-century generation was the group who would see it. The personal pronouns "you" and "we" in both of his letters referred to the saints of his day, not some distant and yet-unborn generation. Peter was admonishing 1st-century believers to be prepared for what was about to happen to them. Is there any more clear way we could express Peter's imminency?

Peter also said that scoffers would come in "the last days" (2 Pe. 3:3). Jude, writing just prior to A.D. 70, confirmed that the predicted sign was present, and that scoffers were dividing the faithful then and there (Jude 18-19). Without question, that 1st century time was the "last times" referenced in 1 Peter 1:20 and occurring in Jude 18.

The clarity of the imminency statements in 2 Peter 3 should force us to reexamine our beliefs about postponement and an end-of-the-world. How can we continue to trust Scripture if we insist that these verses do not really mean what they say? Many modern-day interpreters lean heavily on 2 Peter 3:8 ("With the Lord a day is like a thousand years, and a thousand years are like a day") to explain away the nearness of all New Testament time and imminency statements, including Peter's. They use this verse to affix a time scale to God different from what we humans understand. This side-stepping device enables them to evade imminency and provides an excuse for a long delay. But it also gives Scripture the character of deception rather than of revelation. God does not obscure truth with his Word.[9] The very next verse clarifies, "The Lord is not slow in keeping his promise, as some understand slowness" (2 Pe. 3:9). This verse confirms the trustworthiness of Peter's and all New Testament writer's time and imminency statements. Actually, 2 Peter 3:8 (from Ps. 90:4) is a statement portraying God's eternal character—period.

What do these five clues tell us? They tell us that Peter and the other New Testament writers were Jews steeped in Old Covenant history, thought, and language. They didn't suddenly develop a new vocabulary or a new style of expression. The Holy Spirit used their training and guided them to express New Covenant realities in a manner consistent with the prophets of old. Many modern-day Christians need to squarely face the consequences of deferment logic. But once done, we'll see Peter's text in a perfect harmony of convergence and chronological synchronization with all the other time and consummatory statements of the Scriptures. All pinpoint 1st-century fulfillment; such consistency is inescapable. And the context is covenantal, not cosmic.

Peter had still another significant thing to say about this new reality. It's the clincher. When we understand this attribute of the nature of the new heaven and earth, we will understand why the ancient prophet Isaiah saw it as the time when the hills would burst into song and the trees clap their hands (Isa. 55:12). We may want to dance and clap as well!

Insight 8.   Peter Clinches the New Reality by Defining It's Character.

Peter proclaimed that "righteousness" would dwell (find its home) in "the new heaven and new earth" (2 Pe. 3:13 KJV-NIV). Where this righteousness dwells, and where this home is, is where we will find "the new heaven and new earth." It's the defining characteristic that will enable us to get an unmistakable handle on its true identity, timing and location.

One thing is certain: this righteousness is not to be found in rocks and dirt—not even in new rocks and new dirt—and certainly not in a revived animal sacrifice system. The Old Covenant's animal sacrifice system could *not* take away sin (Heb. 10:4). It could not establish righteousness or make anyone righteous (Ro. 8:2-4). Paul states that "...for if righteousness come by the law, then Christ is dead in vain" (Gal. 2:21 KJV; see also 3:21). But righteousness came: "God made him [Jesus] who had no sin to be sin for us, so that in him we might become the righteousness of God" (2 Cor. 5:21; also 1 Cor. 1:30).

The same ancient prophet who saw hills dancing and trees clapping had this to say:

My righteousness draws near speedily, my salvation is on the way...

> Lift up your eyes to the heavens, look at the earth beneath; the heavens will vanish like smoke, the earth will wear out like a garment and its inhabitants die like flies. But my salvation will last forever, my righteousness will never fail...But my righteousness will last forever, my salvation through all generations (Isa. 51:5-6,8; also 56:1; Jer. 23:5-6).

Isaiah's prophecy connects God's righteousness to both salvation and the destruction of the Old Covenant "heavens and earth." It's most revealing. If this passage was referring to a cataclysmic end of the world (material cosmos) rather than a covenantal change, no future "generations" would have followed this event—at least on this earth.

Reading carefully, we see that "my salvation is on the way." That means that it was not available in Isaiah's time. It was the coming "everlasting righteousness" spoken of by the prophet Daniel (Da. 9:24). It was brought into human history (in-breaking) and being revealed in Peter's "last time" (1 Pe. 1:5, 20). It came through the cross. And once established, it would restore man back into the Presence of God. Moreover, God and his righteousness fully came to dwell inside his people—those who received the Messiah, Jesus Christ, as their Lord and Saviour. Before then, God's only earthly dwelling was inside the Tabernacle or in the Temple. This change of dwelling was part of the promised New Covenant:

> I [God] will give you a new heart and put a new spirit in you; I will remove from you your heart of stone and give you a heart of flesh. And I will put my Spirit in you and move you to follow my decrees and be careful to keep my laws (Eze. 36:26-27; also Jer. 31:33-34; 32:39-40).

In keeping with mistaken futuristic thinking, many people today think that we can only experience heaven after we physically die. They miss out on the heaven we can have right here and now. That's because heaven is not just "up there somewhere." It's wherever the omnipresent Spirit of God is. Individually, we become a "new heaven" when God comes to dwell inside us, in our spirit. That's probably why Isaiah prophesied of many new heavens (note the plural). They are the creation of new spirits in his people. The first, or former heaven, is a person's old natural spirit with which he is born. It is at enmity with God. The "new heaven" is the new spirit God gives a person at salvation (1 Cor. 3:16; Eph. 2:6). It is made new by God's Spirit and becomes the dwelling place or tabernacle of God inside the new believer (1 Cor. 3:17; 2 Cor. 6:16; Eph. 2:19-22). Thus the promise is fulfilled:

> Now the dwelling (tabernacle) of God is with men, and he will live with them. They will be his people, and God himself will be with them and be their God (Rev. 21:3).

This promise of a new dwelling place was now, at hand, and not to be sealed up in John's day because it was to take place very soon, according the first and last chapter of Revelation. "For the old order of things has passed away" (Rev. 21:4). A new way of relating to God is here! He and his righteousness dwell *with* us and *in* us! It's a done deal. But there's more.

There is to be a "new earth" as well. Isaiah used "earth" in the singular, probably because we are all made of the same physical stuff. We "have this treasure in earthen vessels" (2 Cor. 4:7 KJV).

This biblical new heaven and earth, where righteousness dwells, does not describe some future utopian existence, or redeemed cosmos, or even heaven itself, but refers instead to the radically contrasted life of people, individually and corporately, in the New Covenant world of righteousness in Christ.

That means that our former earth consists of our unregenerated physical bodies, and our minds and emotions. This is what the Bible calls our "flesh." As believers, our flesh is our biggest problem. It hampers righteous living. It's where we need to get the victory. After God (the Father, Son and Holy Ghost) comes to dwell within a believer (Jn. 14:23), a process begins wherein Christ is "formed" within that person (Gal. 4:19). Of course, this process requires one's cooperation. But once begun, Christ's redemptive work is enabled to go beyond our renewed spirit dimension to redeem our flesh. Our lives need no longer be dominated by our flesh. We can become wholly redirected by and benefit from the power of God (see Ro. 12:1-2; 13:14). This is how we can truly, fully, and individually become a "new heaven and new earth," "a new creation" or "a new creature," as the Bible says (2 Cor. 5:17; see also Eph. 4:22-24).

This biblical new heaven and earth, where righteousness dwells, does not describe some future utopian existence, or redeemed cosmos, or even heaven itself, but refers instead to the radically contrasted life of people, individually and corporately, in the New Covenant world of righteousness in Christ. This new "world" cannot be separated from, and has no meaning apart from, its people. No other salvation and no other dwelling place of righteousness remains to be fulfilled. In our day, this righteousness and freedom from sin's domination is available to "everyone (both Jew and Gentile) who calls on the name of the Lord will be saved" (Joel 2:32). Those who call on the name of the Lord are accounted righteous in God's eyes because of Jesus' righteousness. It's not something that is naturally in us; rather, it is in Christ, He who comes into us.

> For just as through the disobedience of the one man [Adam] the many were made sinners, so also through the obedience of the one man [Christ] the many will be made righteous (Ro. 5:19).

Putting away sin and bringing in everlasting righteousness were two of God's six ultimate purposes in history (Da. 9:24; Heb. 9:26). In this manner, "God was reconciling the world to himself in Christ"

(2 Cor. 5:19). He redeemed his people through a whole new reality of existence that fully came into being with the passing of the old heavens and earth, exactly as the prophets foretold. It's the central theme of the entire Bible. Such a central, ultimate purpose deserves the metaphorical magnitude of "heaven-and-earth-changing" terminology. All end-time Bible prophecy (eschatology) is anchored to, grounded in, and centered on this redemptive change of covenant and restoration back into the Presence of God.

Jesus said, "Behold, I make all things new" (Rev. 21:5 KJV). And so He has. So He does. The new substance has come. The old types and shadows have gone. The Old Covenant Mosaic age, which was not able to remove sin and death and was incapable of establishing righteousness, was equated with the heaven and earth which could be shaken and removed. This old order was removed and superseded by a "new order" (Heb. 9:10; also Gal. 5:5; Ro. 8:19-22), "the new heaven and earth" of the New Covenant kingdom age wherein righteousness dwells. Those who are Christ's are the places where this righteousness now dwells. We are this "home" and the defining characteristic of "the new heaven and new earth."

It's a done deal, and part of God's completed plan of redemption (1 Cor. 1:30; Ro. 1:17; 3:20-21; 5:17; 8:4; 10:4; Php. 3:9). In this new reality, God dwells with us and in us. This is not an interim plan that will be superseded by something better in the future! Those interpretive systems that attempt to compromise or postpone this theme are flawed. There is nothing better than the full redemption brought by Christ. It's far too beautiful to miss.

Yet current traditional views that anticipate the annihilation or massive renovation of the material heaven and earth persist, and rob God's people of a powerful reality. They cause many to miss the mark. We must conclude they have been led astray by a powerful deception.

Insight 9. The Satanic Deception of Cosmic Redemption.

Undoubtedly, God could create a new physical cosmos and/or *terra firma* Earth any time He wanted to. But He hasn't. And the point is, He doesn't have to produce a sequel or massively re-do the present one in order to fulfill any unfulfilled biblical promise or prophecy.

But think about this. Satan is smart enough to know that he cannot get Christians to abandon the idea of "a new heaven and a new earth," as promised in the Bible. He also knows that Christians long for a better day in a better world. And he knows that most are ignorant of Bible history and its precedent fulfillments. So what does that sly ole fox do? He takes God's truths and twists them just enough to make his distortions sound plausible.

He says, "Sure, there's going to be a new heaven and a new earth (and a New Jerusalem), and you can live and reign with God in it if that's what you want, and it will be a wonderful paradise, a golden age of peace and plenty... but that's all out in the future. In the meantime, it doesn't matter what happens, because God is going to destroy this world anyway someday soon."

Does his deception work? Just look around. Millions of Christians are deeply entrenched in this notion. They are looking for God to deliver more than He has promised. So they talk about the future dawning of a better day while they drag themselves out of bed each morning and go out to lead defeated lives. People who have a hard time controlling their own lives and who are not about to go out and attempt to expand God's kingdom or do the works of Jesus (Jn. 14:12) talk about reigning and ruling over the whole universe with Jesus someday. What these someday-glorified saints plan to reign and rule over isn't clear, since most or all of the opposition is supposed to be wiped out anyway.

Of course, Satan and his spirit-realm cohorts must be thrilled by this diversion. They have gone to elaborate lengths to keep as many of God's people as possible in the dark and grabbing onto these fantasies. Why? We can think of three very good reasons:

1) They know that human beings don't feel nearly the sense of urgency about future hopes and fantasies that they feel about the pressing concerns of their day-to-day lives.

2) They know that if they can keep us in the dark about what God has promised and delivered, they can keep us from reaching our potential in Christ here and now.

3) They know that once we grasp a hold of and enter into the present reality of the new heavens, new earth (and the Holy City, the New Jerusalem), they can never again use the weaknesses of this life to intimidate us, and they'll lose control. Such believers would pose a major threat to their strongholds in this world.

When Scripture is detached from its covenantal framework, it can be used to teach just about anything. We are convinced that a satanic deception lies behind the unbiblical practice of parceling out piecemeal the fulfillment of "all that has been written" (Lk. 21:22), giving some to the end of the Jewish age, some to the end of a Christian age, some to the end of a millennial age, etc.[10] It's a classic example of neglecting the context and reaching erroneous conclusions. This is precisely what Satan wants.

Thus, many Christians feel that their redemptive destiny is linked with an environmental renewal. Sure, God is capable of creating or re-creating a new universe to replace this one. That's not the issue here. But let's think a moment. What's wrong with our earth is not its plants, animals, rocks, dirt, atmosphere, or the cosmos surrounding it. The problem with this earth is the people who live on it. We are the corrupted; we are the ones in sin who need to be made new. The earth doesn't sin; it can't sin. There is nothing defiling about it. It's God's most beautiful and perfect planet in the universe. Yes, it has become polluted by people's sins and irresponsibility, and it's in need of a good cleansing, but it has proven resilient and can adequately recover on its own without a purging by fire. If we follow this logic, it stands to reason that the physical stars and other planets are not polluted or affected by human sin. So why would God need to destroy, rejuvenate, replace, or redeem them? To the contrary, "the heavens declare the glory of God" (Ps. 19:1a) and reveal his power and divine nature (Ro. 1:20). Remember, the two symbols go together. It's both "a new heaven(s)" and "a new earth" in which righteousness dwells.

In spite of all this, the postponement schools of end-time prophecy include the idea of inevitable cosmic destruction in their beliefs. But let's also remember what God promised after the flood which "destroyed" the earth in Noah's day:

> Never again will I curse the ground because of man, even though every inclination of his heart is evil from childhood. And never again will I destroy all living creatures [things], as I have done (Ge. 8:21).

As we discussed in chapter three, some assume that God disclaimed this verse a short time later in Genesis 9:11when He only promises not to destroy all living things by a flood, leaving Him free to destroy it by fire, bowling balls, or anything else. But is God more concerned with methodology than mercy? We think not. On the contrary, we, the inhabitants of this planet, can take this eternal promise of God quite literally.

Also noteworthy is Peter's comparison of the perishing of the world in Noah's day with his impending "day of the Lord" (2 Pe. 3:6-7). Since the physical earth and universe did not perish in Noah's day, why must it for Peter's? As we have seen, Peter wasn't introducing a new time-ending, universe-destroying event. Peter's event is now past. It was the same Jewish "passing of heaven and earth" that Christ addressed in his Olivet Discourse (Mt. 24:3, 34-35). Something better has come along, and look what's at its center.

Insight 10. The New Jerusalem Is Here.

If all we see in the events of A.D. 70 is the destruction, desolation, and abandonment of an earthly city, then we've only seen one side of a two-sided event. In addition to this being the setting and sign of the Lord's return, the passing of the earthly Jerusalem also signaled the consummated coming of the heavenly Jerusalem. Why? Because the New Jerusalem is at the center of "the new heaven and new earth."

It is unfortunate that so many people do not know what a landmark in human history we had in the breakup of the old Judaic system. They do not see that restoration is the immediate flip-side of desolation. So some think they will spend eternity in a space city which will someday come down from heaven and hover above the earth. They picture it as a visible cube (though perhaps a pyramid) "1,500 miles in length, and as wide and high as it is long" (Rev. 21:16).

But there's a huge problem with this idea: if it's true, then 1 Peter 4:7 is false, and so are all the other consummatory and time-restricted statements we've expounded upon throughout this book. The exact nature of God's Holy City, the New Jerusalem, must be understood within the time frame and spiritual relevancies of the text. Make no mistake about it, the destiny of the believer in Christ is a life in heaven, not on a new earth, and not in a space city hovering above the ground. Heaven is the eternal abode of redeemed people; it is no intermediate dwelling. If we are "in Christ" now, we already can enjoy a part of heaven here on earth: the covenant-determined New Jerusalem that came down from heaven (Rev. 21:2). It's here, it exists, and we can live in it now. Let's prove it using two simple syllogisms:

#1 Major premise: Most Christians believe they can now eat of the "tree of life" (Rev. 2:7; 22:14). On this we agree.

#1 Minor premise: The "tree of life" is located in the New Jerusalem (Rev. 22:2).

#1 Conclusion: The New Jerusalem is a present reality.

#2 Major premise: Most Christians believe they can drink freely of the "water of life" (Jn. 4:10, 14; 7:37-39; Rev. 21:6; 22:17). On this we also agree.

#2 Minor premise: The "water of life" is also located in the New
Jerusalem (Rev. 22:1).

#2 Conclusion: The New Jerusalem is a present reality.

It is simply not logical to think that these promises are fulfilled
spiritual realities in the New Covenant era, and then postpone the
arrival of the city in which they are located to sometime in the
future. Could God someday speak a physical space city into existence? Of course He could. But the idea that this is God's plan is
pure speculation, since no other Scripture in the Bible confirms this
interpretation. The key is that God doesn't have to do this in order
to fulfill any unfulfilled prophecy or promise of Scripture. The idea
of a "New Jerusalem" other than that which we already have in
Christ is pure fantasy Christianity.

The idea of a "New Jerusalem" other than that which we already have in Christ is pure fantasy Christianity.

The full descent of this Holy City, the New Jerusalem, "coming
down out of heaven from God" (Rev. 21:2) occurred immediately
upon the demise of the old Jerusalem (the one Jesus lamented over
in Luke 13:34-35). The Old Testament is filled with prophecies of
this coming, new, and different Jerusalem.[11] Daniel understood the
precise timing for this ultimate and true restoration of Israel. Remember also that Jesus said, "When you see Jerusalem surrounded
by armies...this is in fulfillment of *all* that has been written" (Lk.
21:20-22). The Apostle Paul, in his time, spoke of the old city as "in
bondage" (Gal. 4:25KJV) and the new city as a present, in-breaking
reality, "the Jerusalem that is above is free and is our mother" (Gal.
4:26). He contrasted it to the old Judaic system (Gal. 4:21-30).

This soon-coming reality was part of the unseen and eternal reality to which Paul directed the Corinthians:

> For our light and momentary troubles are achieving for us an eternal glory that far outweighs them all. So we fix our eyes not on what is seen, but on what is unseen. For what is seen is temporary, but what is unseen is eternal (2 Cor. 4:17-18).

Abraham looked for a "better country"—a heavenly one—and a heavenly city (Heb. 11:10, 13-16, 39-40) that would be enduring (Heb. 12:22-24; 13:14; Joel 3:14-17). He knew that the Promised Land of Canaan was "a foreign country" (Heb. 11:9). It was only earthly real estate and a type and shadow of the heavenly and true inheritance to come (Heb. 8:5). Abraham's hope for the future was based upon faith in the heavenly realm rather than upon sight in the earthly realm. That "better country" of Abraham's faith was rooted in the "better promises" of the "better covenant" (Heb. 8:6 KJV) where "in thy seed [offspring] shall all nations of the earth be blessed" (Ge. 22:18 KJV; 26:4; 28:14; Gal. 3:8). What Abraham was seeking was Isaiah's, Peter's, and Revelation's "new heaven(s) and new earth"— the true fulfillment of the real Promised Land. And located at its center is the New Jerusalem, the city from above.

Neither the Law nor a future reestablishment of any portion of it could ever fulfill God's promise to Abraham (Gal. 3:18). Nor could earthly things (Gal. 4:21-31). But the heavenly inheritance of "the new heaven and new earth" and "New Jerusalem" could and did (Heb. 9:23). The city is not heaven itself, as some believe (see Revelation, chapter 4 for that) because it comes down from God out of heaven to the earth (Rev. 21:2, 10). And it's not a literal city that comes visibly. Its invisibility, however, does not lessen its actuality or importance. This progressive nature follows perfectly the principle found in 1 Corinthians 15:46: "The spiritual did not come first, but the natural, and after that the spiritual." And the spiritual fulfillment is always the greater.

The coming of the New Jerusalem is and was the appropriate conclusion and capstone to the book of Revelation. It symbolizes the end-goal of the entire canon of Scripture and the grand climax of God's plan of redemption and "to bring all things in heaven and earth [back] together..." (Eph. 1:10). It stands in stark covenantal contrast to the old city and the Judaic system that passed away. As long as the theocratic, earthly form of Israel remained, the hope of Israel, the promise of God to Abraham, and Israel's restoration could not be fully realized by either Jew or Gentile (Gal. 3:26-29; Heb. 9:8). But in A.D. 70, all the old things were fully and finally redetermined and transformed anew "in Christ" (Rev. 21:5).

This fully available, transcendent reality of New Covenant life takes place in the New Jerusalem, where God and the Lamb are its light (Rev. 21:23; Ps. 43:3). Unlike the old Jerusalem, there is no temple in the city (Rev. 21:22), because God no longer dwells in temples made with hands (2 Ch. 6:18; Ac. 7:48-49; 17:24). Its people are its temple (Eph. 2:20-22; 1 Cor. 3:17; 2 Cor. 6:16). You can read a listing of who is in the city in Hebrews 11:22-24 and Revelation 21:7, 27. This heavenly city is the glorious dwelling place of those believers who overcome and keep God's commandments on this earth. According to the Bible, they are the ones who inherit all this (Rev. 21:7; Gal. 3:29). They are the city on a hill (Mt. 5:14), the bride (Rev. 21:9-10), and the new people of God (1 Pe. 2:9-10) born by a new birth (Jn. 3:3-7). They are the new priesthood (Rev. 1:5-6), they offer new sacrifices (Ro. 12:1-2; Heb. 8:23; 13:15-16; 1 Pe. 2:5f) in "the greater and more perfect tabernacle not man-made" (Heb. 9:11; Rev. 21:22; 1 Cor. 3:16; 6:19), and they operate in new powers (Heb. 6:5).

Although God never intended New Covenant life to be either the end of all human difficulties, or an escape from the frailties of the physical plane, the Holy City's symbolic description in Revelation 21 and 22 is given to encourage all saints of every generation. We can press on and overcome in the face of all opposition. We can win this inheritance and enter and live daily in the bliss and joy of this community of God. Jesus demonstrated its reality during his stay on earth. The New Jerusalem is the true climax of the Revelation, the goal of the New Covenant lifestyle, and the essence of community for its residents. What's more, "the leaves of ... [its] tree are for the healing of the nations" (Rev. 22:2). What a wonderful place to live! What a wonderful ministry to have!

Who wants to miss what we have now in favor of futuristic fantasies and postponement theologies? Naturally, there is a certain excitement in a science-fiction planetary destruction, but who could prefer it to the glories of the Christian age as the Bible describes them? Who would want a revival of the old Judaic system, when they have the hope and the promise of the something better that has replaced it? Let us lay aside all distraction and deception and enter the city.

Our inheritance is more glorious, more powerful, and far more joyful than most of us "sons and daughters of God" have been led to believe exists. It's an incomparable inheritance, and it's here and available in Christ. It's the New Jerusalem. It's located at the center of God's "new heaven and new earth." It's part of the "faith that was once for all delivered to the saints" (Jude 3). Please note that we are explicitly warned not to "add to" or "take away from" this prophecy or its established reality, for if we do, we'll be removed from this Holy City and miss its blessing and provisions (Rev. 22:18-19). It's the ultimate reality, the ultimate community, the ultimate joy for God's people here on this earth! Read about it, anew, in Revelation 21 and 22.

Are you inside or outside of the city? The New Jerusalem awaits!

Conclusion

Now You Know the Rest of the Story, What's Next?

Every Sunday in churches around the world people gather to hear a story. For almost two thousand years that story has been told and retold.[1] It's the greatest story ever told, and about a man called Jesus of Nazareth, his birth in 4 B.C., his life, and his death and resurrection in A.D. 30. But now (after centuries of confusion, thousands of failed predictions, and the recent bombardment of millennial madness) you know the rest of the story—from 30 A.D. through 70 A.D.

Never again should anyone fear the proverbial end of the world, or wonder, When will it all end? It won't ever end. The world is without end. Amen. And the only "end" proclaimed in the Bible was *for* the world, not of the world. That end, foreseen by the prophets, has come. For them it was future, but for us it's history. Its "last days" are behind us, not ahead. Today we are living beyond the end times.

There was only one correct time frame for the divinely appointed "time of the end." That time certainly came, was not delayed, and did not prove false (Hab. 2:3). It occurred exactly *as* and *when* Daniel and Jesus said it would, and exactly *as* and *when* expected (Jn. 16:13). It was right on schedule, "when the power of the holy people... [was] finally broken" (Da. 12:7). Such beautiful harmony of prophetic convergence is no accident. No other faith, religion, or philosophy is so well authenticated. Dare we make any less of it?

Jesus' first followers lived in expectation; we live in completion.

Jesus promised, "Then you will know the truth, and the truth will set you free" (Jn. 8:32). Only then can we walk confidently into the future. But Jesus also warned of the disastrous consequences of building a house upon a foundation of sand (Mt. 7:24-27). Futuristic endsaying is a house built on the sand of gaps, gimmicks, and twisted meanings. Let us build on the solid rock of Jesus as the "finisher of our faith" (Heb. 12:2), upon the firm ground of a "once for all delivered" faith (Jude 3), and upon the sure foundation of an "end of all things" (1 Pe. 4:7 KJV) that was "at hand" and harmoniously fulfilled in the same historical time-context in which these inspired words were penned. Jesus' first followers lived in expectation; we live in completion.

Covenantal, Not Cosmic, Transition

Covenantal transition, not cosmic cataclysm, is the central theme and unifying motif throughout the Bible. This is the point that is missed by interpreters who use 20th- or 21st-century, cosmic-

conflagration glasses. The Old Covenant world was the one burning up and changing, not the material cosmos. If we are sincere in
seeking a responsible apocalypticism, it's paramount that we ascer-
tain the original and divinely-intended time frame and nature of
fulfillment for end-time biblical prophecies, even if they don't
conform to the way we have been taught.

It was by covenant that the nation of Israel came into being. It
was by covenant that they produced the Messiah and the canon of
Scripture. The ending of that Old Covenant world was pertinent to
fulfilling the Law and the Prophets and ushering a new people and
a new reality fully into being. Although this new world was also
determined by covenant, it was to be a new and everlasting
covenant. Such is the identity and nature of the metaphoric and
apocalyptic phraseology of "new heavens and new earth."

We can now live confidently and abundantly in the fulfillment
of prophecy and the establishment of the kingdom. The passive
anticipation of a utopian existence on planet Earth someday pales
in comparison to this present-day, yet greatly unrealized, reality. As
fascinating as it may be, there is something dreadfully wrong with
what the postponing futurists keep telling us about this reality.

First, they tell us that, as wonderful as this glorious reality is, we
can't have it now. They want us to believe that God's most exciting
promises are all out in a yet-to-be-fulfilled future, somewhere, someday.

Second, they tell us that this reality consists of all literal, physical, and material objects. They want us to believe that God's highest
ideal for humankind is a physical, material paradise: a space city, a
new garden of Eden, and a re-Judaized Christianity which we do not
yet possess.

Third, they are looking for another or a yet-future end-times
"last days" period, separate and distinct from the one and only one
the Bible proclaims as existing in the 1st century. So they interrupt
time frames, insert gaps, and use other side-stepping devices to explain away clear Bible language and stretch out prophetic fulfillment
like a rubber band—now creating a "delay" over 400 years longer

than the length of time the covenant nation of Israel even existed. But how could the "last days" of an era last longer than the era itself?

The practical, everyday problem with pushing the fulfillment of this reality out into a protracted future is that it depreciates and devalues the Judeo-Christian faith. Furthermore, it dis-empowers people of faith. Those who should be reigning on this earth with Christ right now are not (Rev. 5:10; Ro. 5:17). They have been led astray by the popular misconception that God must solve our problems by destroying the planet and creating a new one before we can experience completed kingdom realities and victories.

As a consequence, most modern-day versions of Christianity have become pale shadows of the kingdom that Christ announced, modeled, and conferred. Nowhere is the disparity more obvious than in Revelation 21 and 22, where Jesus described the ultimate and normal state of those who live in the city of the kingdom. May God open our eyes to this ultimate, available, but greatly unrealized, reality. May we learn its lessons and live and thrive in its glory and grandeur. May we seek to understand what God wants us to accomplish in this world through it.

The Next Reformation

Today we stand poised on the doorstep of a new millennium, and on the threshold of a new awakening. Once again, the words of the 16th-century Reformer John Calvin couldn't ring more true: "The Church is reformed and always reforming."

We moderns have not reached the point where reform is no longer needed. And biblical, end-time prophecy (eschatology) is the next major area ripe for reform. But all reformations have their resisters. This next reformation will be no exception. For some, on the other hand, it will be a godsend and a breath of fresh air. Truth is what they are after. It must be the firm foundation upon which genuine, biblical faith is built and presented to the world.

As has been true of other reformations, this one will require a new way of thinking, a new perspective, and a paradigm shift away from some of the traditional positions. We will need to follow the scriptural admonition to "Test everything. Hold on to the good," (1 Th. 5:21). Our failure to do this has put us in our current eschatological dilemma of so many failed prophecies and conflicting positions. The world scoffs at our faith. Just how long can we continue stretching out the biblical "last days" and perpetuating biblical imminency before these biblical realities lose their meaning and value?

R.C. Sproul writes:

> The evangelical world cannot afford to turn a deaf ear to the railing voices of skepticism that gut Scripture of its divine authority, that assault the credibility...of Christ himself [with their] critique of the time-frame references of New Testament prophecy.[2]

Preterist author Authur Melanson predicts:

> There is coming a time when a future generation will be saying, "They used to believe what?" And Hal Lindsey's book will be in a museum.[3]

The good news is that the potential for reform is huge. And a responsible apocalypticism is within our grasp. But where do we begin?

First, we must be willing to admit that we were wrong and that we have misunderstood some very important, foundational aspects of Scripture. This is a necessary prerequisite. For far too long, far too many have been far too vocal and in far too great a frenzy to get the world destroyed. This fear-based, traditional, "orthodox" doctrine has been a fool's paradise. It is an outright misconception of God's redemptive plan of the ages. We have nothing to fear from the biblical end times—only positive things to gain, and much to celebrate because of them. Therefore, endsaying with its long record of negative impact upon the Church and the world, especially in this century, must be relegated to the ash heap of history.

Next, our current eschatological system needs a major overhaul. Minor tweaking within the structure of the various competing positions will not fix the problem. We propose the following four-step reformational process:

Four Steps to Prophecy Reform.

1. Acknowledge that the world is never going to end. By "world" we mean planet Earth, the cosmos, and humanity. *Terra firma* has been eternally established, and is sustained by our Creator God. He has charged us with the responsibility of keeping it, protecting it, and passing it along to future generations in better condition (spiritually, physically, and socially) than we found it.

2. Honor the plain, face-value meaning of all prophetic time statements, time frames, and imminency expectations—no gaps, no gimmicks, no twisted meanings. Our fundamental error has been the failure to understand the historical context of the 1st century for the fulfillment of all end-time biblical prophecies. Therefore, we've lifted end-time prophecy out of its appointed framework and exchanged our divinely determined heritage for a flawed human hope.

3. Contend "for the faith that was once for all delivered to the saints" (Jude 3). Biblical faith is a finished faith; its kingdom is a completed kingdom. This is the firm foundation that must be restored, better understood, and more fully realized. We need to take an honest look at history and see how all promised eschatological events happened and all redemptive realities were completely established and made everlastingly available when Jerusalem was destroyed and the Jewish age ended in A.D. 70. As our perspective changes, we will recognize this time as a third most important date in biblical and world history.

4. Expose the four false assumptions on which the current confusing and divisive system of eschatology is built and replace this system with a "solution of synthesis." These four false assumptions are: millennialism, adventism, 7-year tribulationism, and rapture-removal. Each is a contrived and unscriptural notion. All four need reformed. The four interpretative schools of end-time prophecy in the historic Church (preterist, historicist, idealist and futurist [which includes pre-mil, post-mil, amil]) are based on all or some of these four false assumptions. Each school has its strengths and weaknesses. A "solution of synthesis" would keep the strengths and dump the weaknesses of each school.

In this book we have begun this four-step reformational process. We've addressed steps one and two, and started on steps three and four. In the future, more will be addressed because the Prophecy Reformation has begun!

Our thesis has been grounded on the interpretative question, *does time determine nature, or does nature determine time?* That's the crucial question we must answer and the decision we must make. In this book, we've contended that time determines nature, since the scriptural time of Christ's generation determines the nature of fulfillment and the time now present. Without this sure foundation, we are open to speculations of every sort. Martin Luther said it well:

> No greater mischief can happen to a Christian people, than to have God's Word taken from them, or falsified, so that they no longer have it pure and clear. God grant we and our descendants be not witnesses of such a calamity.[4]

Let's grasp the courage of Luther and rise to the reformational task at hand. As word of this next reformation spreads, may it ignite a new age of world mission, and bring new and more effective ways of proclaiming God's grace, love, and salvation. This reformation could become as significant as the 16th-century Protestant Reformation because it proclaims the gospel of a finished faith and a completely restored relationship between God and humankind.

The time has arrived for each of us to rethink his approach to end-time Bible prophecy, commit to inspired truth, and rediscover the fullness of our historic faith. Upon this sure foundation the Prophecy Reformation will go forth—in sharp contrast to the glum predictions, repeated errors, and blatant scriptural manipulations of the endsayers. Sure there is much more to address, discuss, explain, and reform.

But listen—Do you not hear the cry ringing over the land? It's the Prophecy Reformation's cry of "once for all delivered!" Soon it may swell to a chorus, then to a roar. Listen! It's the sound of a faith coming together in a new harmony of perfection and power. It's a cry destined to revolutionize biblical faith in the new millennium, changing the way it's preached, practiced, and perceived. What a positive difference its discovery will make.

So will you join us as we sincerely and literally "contend for the faith that was once for all delivered to the saints" (Jude 3)? A world is waiting to be confronted with a precise, more powerful, more persuasive, more adept, and unflawed gospel. The days of escape and retreat are over. The time has come for the Church to enter into this next great scriptural and spiritual awakening.

In this book we have spoken plainly in order to educate and stir you to action. Of course, we've only scratched the surface. More books are needed, as is the involvement of many others. Will you join us? If enough will, it is possible for the Church to enter the next millennium with a bang, not a whimper, and once again be accused of turning "the world upside down" (Ac. 17:6 KJV). The choice is yours.

On with the Prophecy Reformation!

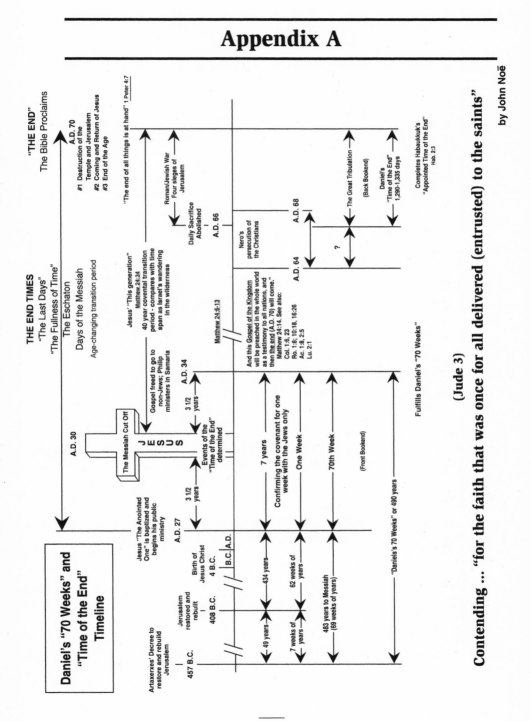

Daniel's "70 Weeks" and "Time of the End" Timeline

THE END TIMES
"The Last Days"
"The Fullness of Time"
The Eschaton
Days of the Messiah
Age-changing transition period

"THE END"
The Bible Proclaims

A.D. 70
#1 Destruction of the Temple and Jerusalem
#2 Coming and Return of Jesus
#3 End of the Age

Contending ... "for the faith that was once for all delivered (entrusted) to the saints"

(Jude 3)

by John Noē

273

The Olivet Discourse Cannot Be Divided

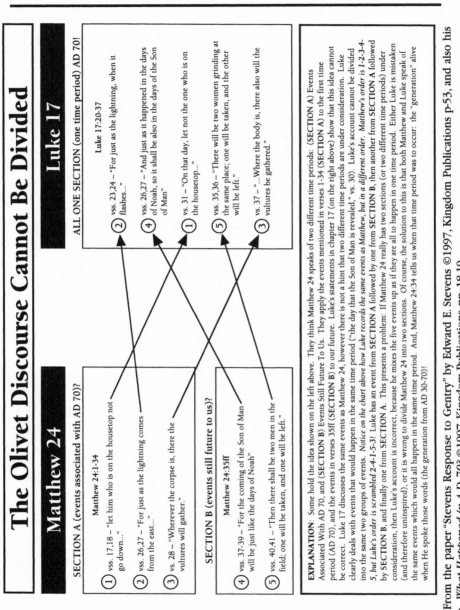

Matthew 24

SECTION A (events associated with AD 70)?

Matthew 24:1-34

(1) vss. 17,18 – "let him who is on the housetop not go down..."

(2) vss. 26,27 – "For just as the lightning comes from the east..."

(3) vs. 28 – "Wherever the corpse is, there the vultures will gather."

SECTION B (events still future to us)?

Matthew 24:35ff

(4) vss. 37-39 – "For the coming of the Son of Man will be just like the days of Noah"

(5) vss. 40,41 – "Then there shall be two men in the field; one will be taken, and one will be left."

Luke 17

ALL ONE SECTION (one time period) AD 70!

Luke 17:20-37

(2) vss. 23,24 – "For just as the lightning, when it flashes..."

(4) vss. 26,27 – "And just as it happened in the days of Noah, so it shall be also in the days of the Son of Man"

(1) vs. 31 – "On that day, let not the one who is on the housetop..."

(5) vss. 35,36 – "There will be two women grinding at the same place; one will be taken, and the other will be left."

(3) vs. 37 – "...Where the body is, there also will the vultures be gathered."

EXPLANATION: Some hold the idea shown on the left above. They think Matthew 24 speaks of two different time periods: (SECTION A) Events Associated With AD 70, and (SECTION B) Events Still Future To Us. They apply the events mentioned in verses 1-34 (SECTION A) to the first time period (AD 70), and the events in verses 35ff (SECTION B) to our future. Luke's statements in chapter 17 (on the right above) show that this idea cannot be correct. Luke 17 discusses the same events as Matthew 24, however there is not a hint that two different time periods are under consideration. Luke clearly deals with events that would happen in the same time period ("the day that the Son of Man is revealed," vs. 30). Luke's account cannot be divided into the same two groups of events. *Notice on the chart above how Luke records the same events as Matthew, but in a different order. Matthew's order is 1-2-3-4-5, but Luke's order is scrambled 2-4-1-5-3!* Luke has an event from SECTION A followed by one from SECTION B, then another from SECTION A followed by SECTION B, and finally one from SECTION A. This presents a problem: If Matthew 24 really has two sections (or two different time periods) under consideration, then Luke's account is incorrect, because he mixes the five events up as if they are all to happen in one time period. Either Luke is mistaken (and therefore uninspired), or it is wrong to divide Matthew 24 into two sections. Of course, the solution to this is that both Matthew and Luke speak of the same events which would all happen in the same time period. And, Matthew 24:34 tells us when that time period was to occur: the "generation" alive when He spoke those words (the generation from AD 30-70)!

From the paper "Stevens Response to Gentry" by Edward E. Stevens ©1997, Kingdom Publications p-53, and also his book, *What Happened in A.D. 70?* ©1997, Kingdom Publications, pp. 18-19.

Appendix C

Scriptural Foundations for the Prophecy Reformation

A Review List of Key End-time, Time, and Consummatory Statements.

Jesus' first followers were convinced He would return and fulfill all things within their lifetimes. And who can blame them? Put yourself in their shoes and ask yourself how you would have understood these words:

- ...the end of all things is at hand (1 Pe. 4:7 KJV)

- ...the fullness of time was come (Gal. 4:4 KJV)

- ...the time is fulfilled (Mk. 1:15 KJV)

- ...the fulfillment of the ages has come (1 Cor. 10:11)

- ...the ends of the world [ages] are come (1 Cor. 10:11 KJV)

- ...for these be the days of vengeance, that all things which are written may be fulfilled" (Lk. 21:22 KJV)

- I tell you the truth, this generation will certainly not pass away until all these things have happened (Mt. 24:34)

- ...the time is short (1 Cor. 7:29)

- ...for the world in its present form is passing away (1 Cor. 7:31)

- ...in these last days (Heb. 1:2)

- This how we know it is the last hour (1 Jn. 2:18)

- The coming of the Lord is at hand... the Judge is standing at the door (Jas. 5:8, 9 NAS)

- The day is at hand (Ro. 13:12 KJV)

- He who is coming will come and will not delay (Heb. 10:37)

- ...things which must shortly come to pass (Rev. 1:1, 22:6 KJV)

- Blessed is he that readeth, and they that hear the words of this prophecy [all of it], and keep those things which are written therein: for the time is at hand (Rev. 1:3; 22:7 KJV)

- Seal not the sayings of the prophecy of this book: for the time is at hand (Rev. 22:10 KJV)

These 1st-century pronouncements are some of the most profound time, imminency, and consummatory statements in the Bible. None is contradictory, vague, or ambiguous. Each emphatically and boldly speaks for itself. They were said and penned in plain, normal language to real people living then and there. In unison, they express an extreme sense of imminence and urgency. They make a lot of sense when left in their 1st-century context.

The popular misapplication of these prophetic scriptures by many of today's end-times proponents has fostered much confusion, and even deception. It's time for us to embrace biblical truth and dump the faulty exegesis, arbitrary eisegesis, and the man-made doctrines of postponement futurism.

Basic Truths for the Prophecy Reformation.

Jude 3 is the quintessential, consummatory statement of Scripture. It reads, "...contend for the faith that was once for all delivered to the saints." Note the use of the past tense. This verse also captures the essence of the classic preterist position in the historic Church. The preterist claim of past fulfillment is its major distinctive. It's the only view that's consistent with the literal, plain, face-value meaning of the Bible's time, imminency, and consummatory statements, and the Spirit-guided expectations of Jesus' first disciples and every New Testament writer. For this reason, the preterist position is the starting point for eschatological reform.

Likewise, the cry of the Prophecy Reformation is "Once for all delivered." It's a direct corollary to the cry of Martin Luther and the Protestant Reformation of the 16th century that "The just shall live by faith." Unfortunately, most Christians have been led to believe that their faith has *not* been once and for all delivered, but is in a state of partial delivery, with more yet to be delivered.

Let's take a closer look at what the words "once for all delivered" really mean in their literal, normal, and plain face value.[1] The use of this phrase at the time of the writing of Jude's book (mid to late 60s)[2] means:

1) The gospel had been "preached in the whole world as a testimony to all nations, and then the end will come" (Mt. 24:14). Other scriptures confirm this accomplishment (Ro. 1:8; 10:18; 16:26; Col. 1:6, 23; also Ac. 1:8; 2:5; Lk. 2:1).

2) The canon of Scripture was complete. A strong case can be made that all books later included in the Bible were written by that time.

3) Proleptically, Peter's "the end of all things is at hand" (1 Pe. 4:7 KJV) was so close (less than a handful of years away) that Jude speaks of it as prophetically present. Jesus spoke in a similar proleptic fashion in John 17:4 when He prayed, "I have brought you [God the Father] glory on earth by completing the work you gave me to do." This Jesus said even before He had gone to the cross.

4) Jude's "once for all" means the same thing it does in Romans 6:10; Hebrews 9:12, 26; 10:10; and 1 Peter 3:18. The faith, as well as Jesus' death, his entrance into the Most Holy Place, and his sacrifice, all of which are part of that faith, are all totally done deals. That means that nothing more remains to be done. Nor was anything only partially done. All are completed events, accomplished facts, and established realities.

Thus, "once for all delivered" means what it plainly and literally says—no more is to be delivered, even though much more is to be realized. Biblical faith is a *finished faith*. This is not some new idea we've concocted for this book. This reality is in perfect harmony and total consistency with the plain, face-value meaning of all the scriptures cited at the start of this appendix. Biblical faith, today, is not one with any portion postponed, delayed or yet to be delivered.

This past-fulfillment distinctive of the historic preterist position is its strength and the reason preterism is the starting point for eschatological reform. The respected Reformed theologian R.C. Sproul writes:

> The modern revival of preterism represents an interesting and important paradigm shift in eschatology. The advantage of preterism is that it 'saves the phenomena' of the New Testament time-frame references; it interprets biblical prophecy according to the images used in Scripture itself; and it offers a framework for consistent interpretation of the difficult apocalyptic literature of the Bible, such as that found in Daniel and Revelation... Serious study and dialogue are needed if we

are to reach agreement as to how far preterism is to go and what remains for the hope of the church's and the cosmos' future in the full plan of redemptive history.[3]

The issues of eschatology are not trivial pursuits of irrelevant matters. Once again, R.C. Sproul says it well, "It has been argued that no less than two thirds of the content of the New Testament is concerned directly or indirectly with eschatology."[4] Consequently, the very truth and nature of the gospel, the kingdom, the Church, and our salvation and resurrection are involved. Today we need teachers, pastors, and believers who will stick with Scripture no matter what traditions say or do, who will hold each other accountable for properly handling the word of truth (2 Ti. 2:15), who will honestly face the demands of the eschatological language, who will stand up for our fulfilled heritage, and who will help reform and restore the faith. In a word, we need Christians committed to the truth of Scripture and the Reformation principle of *sola scriptura*— only the scriptures.

God's Word speaks clearly, but doctrines of men bring confusion, deception, and divisiveness. Nowhere has this been more true than in the field of end-time Bible prophecy (eschatology). The good news is another reformation is here—the Prophecy Reformation. The choice is yours. Will you join us?

End Notes

Introduction

1 "The Rest of the Story" is the famous tag line from—and name of—radio news commentator Paul Harvey's syndicated show. *The Greatest Story Ever Told* is Fulton Oursler's 1949 timeless best-selling book and fictionalized narrative of the life of Jesus Christ, which covered the time between the betrothal of Mary and Joseph, around 4 B.C., through Jesus' death and rumors of his resurrection in A.D. 30. Later, this story was made into a movie with the same title.

2 "Preterist" means past in fulfillment, and is one of the four major schools of Bible prophecy interpretation in the historic Church. The other three are: historicist, idealist, and futurist. The futurist school includes the premillennial, postmillennial and amillennial views.

Chapter One

1 *Chicago Tribune*, Sunday, October 14, 1990, Section 1, p-1, 24.

2 *U.S. News & World Report*, December 19, 1994, p-1 of the Christmas Covenant article.

3 By the time you read this book, some of this material may be dated. But that just helps make the point.

4 See pages 121-136 and 157-179.

5 *Citizen* magazine, Focus on the Family, December 1998, p-6.

6 Some Bibles have this date printed at the top of the first page of Genesis.

7 Article by Barbara Demick, Knight Ridder Newspapers, in *The Indianapolis Star,* January 10, 1999, p-A18.

8 *Christianity Today* magazine, January 11, 1999, p-57.

Chapter 2

1 *Approaching Hoofbeats:The Four Horsemen of the Apocalypse*, 1983, p-221.
2 *U.S. News & World Report*, December 19, 1994.
3 *The Wall Street Journal*, front page, 8/11/92.
4 *The Wall Street Journal*, 8/5/91.
5 *History of the End*, by Rubinsky and Wiseman, 91.
6 History of the Church, Vol. 2, page 182.
7 (1/27/78, p.-22).
8 Line from the film, JFK, spoken by Jim Garrison as portrayed by actor Kevin Costner.
9 12/17/90, p-15.
10 *Christianity Today*, cartoon, 12/14/92, p-12.
11 *The Wall Street Journal*, 12/29/93.
12 Yet, "the fear of the Lord is the beginning of wisdom" (Pr. 9:10).

Chapter 3

1 Indianapolis Star, 6/17/98, 12/12/96 and 11/25/94, for example.
2 The King James Bible also mistranslates the Greek word *aion* as "world" rather than "age" in the phrase "the end of the world (age)" in Matthew 13:39 and 49. Most Modern Bible translations clear up this confusion and render it "age." Those who use fear to hold on to people hesitate to give up this translation weapon. What the Bible does say about "the end of the age" and "the time of the end" will be covered in subsequent chapters.
3 Compare with similar idiomatic uses in Heb. 1:8, Rev. 11:15, and Isa. 45:17. A few scholars feel that this double use in the idiom does not speak of eternity or endlessnes, but of aggregated or compounding periods of time—until all ages have run their course. Most, however, do agree with the explanation given here.
4 Washington Irving, one of the most popular American writers of his time, is credited by some historians with making up and popularizing the heroic saga of Columbus battling the flat-Earthers in his 1828 book about the explorer. Others claim that it was the Church which propagated this notion, along with the belief that the earth was the center of the universe.

5 From *Columbus' Book of Prophecies*, which is only available in Spanish and has never been published in this country—as quoted in *The Light and the Glory* by Peter Marshall and David Manuel, Fleming H. Revell, 1977, p-17, 360.

6 Some Bible scholars maintain that the book of Ecclesiastes cannot be relied on because the arguments it contains are man's, not God's. The New Testament book of 2 Timothy, however, asserts that "All Scripture [including Ecclesiastes] is useful for teaching, rebuking, correcting, and training in righteousness" (2 Ti. 3:16).

7 *Great Is Thy Faithfulness* by Thomas O. Chisholm (1866-1960) and William M. Rynyan (1870-1957).

8 For literature concerning the further use of apocalyptic language in the Bible, see:The Apocalyptic Imagination:An introduction to the Jewish Matrix of Christianity, by John Joseph Collins, Crossroad, 1984. The Old Testament Pseudepigrapha,Vol 1, Doubleday, 1983.

Chapter 4

1 ABC News reported on 4/20/98 that the United States has enough nuclear warheads to blow up the world four-times over.

2 *The World Book Encyclopedia*, 1982,T Volume 19, p-192, states that the laws of thermodynamics "are broad conclusions about the nature of energy, drawn from the results of many experiments."

3 New evidence presented at the annual winter meeting of the American Astronomical Society, as reported in the Indianapolis Star, 1/9/98.

4 *Jurassic Park* by Michael Crichton, Ballantine Books, 1990, p-367-369.

Chapter 6

1 See *Everyman's Talmud*, by Abraham Cohen, Schochen Books, p-356.

2 This term is used in theological circles and comes from the Greek *eschatos*, meaning "last" or "farthest." The eschaton is variously defined as: the days of the Messiah, the time of consummation of all last things in salvation history, the time of fulfillment of all God's promises, the end times, the "last days," the coming of the kingdom of God in power, and the "time of the end."

3 Traditionally and erroneously, Christians have transposed these words to mean that when Jesus returns it will be the end of time, and the end of this material world and universe.

4   Some liberal scholars have insisted that all or part of this book was
    written in the 2nd century B.C. in the time of Antiochus Epiphanes
    (175-163 B.C.). I, however, agree with the majority of biblical scholars
    who take Daniel at face value. Daniel states that it was written
    during the time of Babylonian exile, which was in the 6th century B.C.
    (Da. 1:1 f). The fact that 1st-century B.C. Qumran Jews viewed Daniel's
    book as inspired, and made more copies of it than any other Old
    Testament book is the best evidence for its stated date, and for a
    refutation of the "contemporary" forgery idea. But even if it was written
    in the 2nd century B.C., that still leaves an approximate two-century
    foretelling factor to explain. Many of these same scholars maintain that
    all of Daniel was fulfilled in the 2nd-century B.C. But they fail to explain
    how the six purpose clauses in Daniel 9:24 were fulfilled at that time.
5   It's difficult to fix the exact dates for the beginning and ending of the 70
    years of Babylonian captivity. Daniel was taken captive in 605 B.C.
    Another group was deported in 597 B.C., and the final destruction of
    Jerusalem did not occur until 586 B.C. Likewise, the return from exile
    was also staggered over a period of years. Contained within this time
    variance is the actual 70-year period prophesied by Jeremiah.
6   Although Ptolemy's chronology—developed in the 2nd century A.D. —is
    generally accepted by the majority of scholars, not everyone agrees it is
    correct. Philip Mauro, in his book, *The Wonders of Bible Chronology*
    (Reiner Publications, Swengel, PA, 1974) claims that "Ptolemy makes the
    duration of the Persian Empire more than eighty years too long." Mauro
    further claims that Ptolmey's chronological statements are "contradicted
    by the writings of Josephus...Persian traditions...and by the Jewish
    National traditions" (p-6). Mauro's chronology is derived from the Bible
    and recasts the chronology of the last 500 years of the Old Testament era.
    He, therefore, dates Cyrus' Decree at 457 B.C. Which ever way is correct,
    both Mauro and this author see 457 B.C. as the appropriate starting date
    for Daniel's 70 weeks. For readers interested in the details of Mauro's
    calculations and his proof, I refer you also to his book *The Seventy Weeks
    and the Great Tribulation* (ibid, 1975), and to John C. Whitcomb's book,
    Darius the Mede. All three are well worth one's time and careful
    consideration.
7   They actually did start rebuilding and inhabiting the city then, too.
    Also, I'm aware of the difference between the Jewish lunar year of

360 days versus our solar year of 365+ days. However, Israel made adjustments to its calendar on a regular, pre-determined basis to adhere to a solar year of 365$\frac{1}{4}$ days. Otherwise, the cycle of its seven feasts (related to the agricultural seasons) would have quickly gotten way out of synch. If such adjustments were not done, winter months would soon have occurred in the summer and vice versa. Therefore, the use of solar years for Daniel's 490-year time frame would be the one consistent with the Jews' method of tracking time.

8 The 444 B.C. date of Artaxerxes' letters is advocated as the starting point by some Bible scholars. But these "letters" are not accorded decree status in Scripture. Next, these scholars use what is termed "prophetic years" of 360 days each. This notion is taken from the use of the Jewish lunar year (see footnote 7) and from the idea that the 1,260 days of Revelation 12:6, the "time and times and half a time" of Revelation 12:14, and the 42 months of Revelation 13:5 as all representing a 3$\frac{1}{2}$ year period.

Calculation by this method brings scholars close to some of the same 1st-century time dates and events we present. But their explanations are not nearly as descriptive and precise as those presented here. Here's how they figure:

444 B.C.
+
$\underline{173,880}$ days (483 years of 360 days each or
A.D. 33   appoximately 476 solar years of 365$\frac{1}{4}$
                days to the Messiah)

Some Jewish scholars begin Daniel's 70 Weeks with God's decree announcement in Jeremiah 29:10, supposedly made in 587 B.C. They end it with the destruction of the Temple in A.D. 70. This raises even more problems, since the time span from 587 B.C. to A.D. 70 is 658 years, not 490.

9 Later books in the Old Testament give no information about how long this period of rebuilding took to complete.

"According to Barnes and several other trustworthy Bible commentators, the historian Prideaux declared that Nehemiah's last action in rebuilding the city occurred in the 15th year of the Persian ruler Darius Nothus (423-404 B.C.). His 15th year was the 49th year from the 457 B.C. (or 458) decree. Josephus seems to support this idea in his remarks about the death of Nehemiah. This can be viewed as an indication that the 457 B.C. date is correct. But it is possible that some rebuilding continued after that." (From, *The Daniel Papers Discovery Series* by Resources For Biblical Communication, Radio Bible Class, Grand Rapids, Michigan, 1994, pp. 15-16.)

In the absence of any better information, it is safe to assume that 49 years after the third decree was issued, the work was completed. Difficulty in reconstructing ancient chronology throughout these weeks means that we have to be satisfied with close, but approximate dating in confirming what most probably is absolutely accurate to the very year, if not very day.

10   "Anointed" is the Hebrew word *mashiyach* and means "Messiah."

11   Daniel uses the Hebrew word (*Karath*), translated as "cut off." This word was used for the death penalty (Lev. 7:20, 21, 25, 27), and often referred to violent death (1 Sa. 17:51; Ob. 9; Na. 3:15). In Isaiah 53:8, where it is prophesied of the death of Christ, "He was cut off out of the land of the living," the word is *ghzar* and has a nearly identical meaning.

12   Some scholars feel that Philip's journey to Samaria occurred five to ten years after Christ's crucifixion. The point remains the same, the time restriction had expired.

Chapter 7

1   Of course, Josephus' historical accounts are not as reliable as the accounts in the Bible. He is, nevertheless, considered a very reliable source, and the most accurate authority of the time for historical information. It is important to note that Josephus was not a Christian nor sympathetic to Christianity. He was a Jew and wrote under the auspices of, and to please, the Romans. There is therefore no hint of Christian bias in his works.

2   *Wars,* II. 17:2.

3   The word "temple" is not in the original language. "Wing" means "pinnacle," "height" or "top most" of the abominations.

4   *Wars.* V. 1:1-3.

5 I recommend these commentaries:

> *Josephus: The Essential Writings*, by Paul L. Maier, Kregel
>> Publications, 1988.
> *The Topical Josephus,* by Cleon L. Rogers, Jr., Zondervan, 1992.

Chapter 8

1 *Christianity Today*, February 6, 1987, p-1-I.

2 The prevailing view attempts to make five world kingdoms out of the four described in Daniel 2 and 7. It's done by spinning off some of the descriptive attributes of the fourth kingdom, inserting a time gap of indeterminable length, and making them into a futuristic, fifth earthly kingdom, which is then called the revived (or revised) Roman Empire. No sound reason exists for taking such latitude. It's totally arbitrary, and is only asserted in order to support a particular futuristic doctrine. Not only does it not fit the picture given in Daniel, Daniel emphatically stated that these visions represented four—not five— earthly kingdoms (Da. 2:40; 7:17). Their attributes were portrayed by *four* sections of a statue and *four* beasts, and not five. Furthermore, each of the two parallel descriptions of the fourth kingdom fully applies to the old Roman Empire, and was historically and precisely fulfilled. Several preterist and historicist scholars have documented the symbolically portrayed attributes of each kingdom, and I will not duplicate their work in this book. But Daniel assured both the king and us that his interpretation was "trustworthy" (Da. 2:45). All Daniel's prophesied events happened and were fulfilled within this time frame in history. There is no credible reason to repeat these events or to revive the political, social, and religious conventions of those times.

3 To date and in this author's opinion, no futurist has offered a valid justification for interrupting Daniel's 70 weeks time frame and inserting a time gap—except to assert that their interpretive system "necessitates" this methodology. Some justification attempts I've encountered are:

> 1) Using Old Testament prophecies that don't specify time frames as precedents for interrupting those that do—such as Isaiah 9:6 and Zechariah 9:9-10. But these are not analogous.

2) Citing conditional prophetic messages wherein God could change the outcome based upon the response of the people to whom they were given—such as Jonah 3:5 and Jeremiah 18:7-8. But Daniel's were unconditional, and therefore, not analogous.

3) Noting that the Church was a "mystery" in the Old Testament. But jumping from that to an interruption is—at best—a stretch.

4) Reasoning that other interruptions and gaps, also arbitrarily imposed, justify this one—for example, disjointing the book of Revelation, Jesus' Olivet Discourse, and Acts 2:17-21's description of the events of Pentecost. These other intrusions are just as erroneous and without scriptural justification. One cannot be used to justify another in an attempt to be "consistent." This logic is a case of circular error perpetuating itself.

What gap theorists need to prove their case is a clear statement or precedent in Scripture. This is exactly what they don't have. Mere assertion is insufficient justification upon which to hang such an abortive treatment of Scripture. The idea for interruption the time frame of Daniel's 70 weeks originated in A.D. 1585. A Jesuit priest named Francisco Ribera was the first to separate Daniel's 70th week from the other 69. This was done to deflect apocalyptic heat from the Pope and the Roman Catholic hierarchy, who were being attacked by the Reformers for being the Antichrist and beast of Revelation, respectively. Ribera said that the first 69 (483 years) concluded at the baptism of Jesus in A.D. 27 but that God had extended the 70th week into the future. Thus was born the popular "gap theory." In the early 1800s, J.N. Darby bought into this theory and added the rapture-removal idea. He and Scofield (1900s) popularized this teaching throughout America. For more on this, see my book, *Your Resurrection Body and Life*.

4 *Antiquities of the Jews*, XVII, 63.

5 Also, the idea that the beast of Revelation 13 is the Antichrist is purely assumptive. No such connection is ever made in Scripture. We must pay close attention to what the Bible actually says and does not say. But many haven't. Hence, for several centuries, Christianity has

appeared foolish as the popular endsayers of their day have continually attempted to name the latest global villain as the "biblical Antichrist."

Chapter 9

1 Mt. 11:16; 12:41, 42, 45; 23:36; Mk. 8:12, 12, 38; Lk. 7:31; 11:29, 30, 31, 32, 50, 51; 17:25: Ac. 2:40. Also see associated uses: Mt. 12:34, 39; 16:4; 17:17; Mk. 9:19; 13:30; Lk. 1:50; 9:41; 16:8; Ac. 8:33; 13:36; Heb. 3:10.
2 Not all Bibles do this. Some translators knew better.
3 Appendix B, "The Olivet Discourse Cannot Be Divided," from the paper, "Stevens Response To Gentry" by Edward E. Stevens 1997, Kingdom Publications, p-53, and also his book, *What Happened in A.D. 70?*, © 1997, Kingdom Publications, pp. 18-19.
4 This misconception is nurtured somewhat by the mistranslation of the Matthew 13: 39, 49; 24:3 phrase "the end of the world" in the King James Version of the Bible. The word "world" in the Greek is *aion* and is better translated as "age." Most later translations agree.

Chapter 10

1 *Ecclesiastical History*, Book 3, Ch. 7.
2 *Ecclesiastical History*, Book 3, Ch. 5.
3 *St Augustine*, vol. 6.
4 *The Festal Letters*, Letter IV, No. 3-4.
5 The prophecy does say "armies," not army. Why the plural use? Historical accounts reveal that Rome commonly conscripted soldiers from other nations into their fighting ranks. Titus's army below only contained 25,000 Roman soldiers out of approximately 54,000 in the combined armies that came against Jerusalem in A.D. 70.
6 *Wars* 5.451.
7 One can't know the precise day or hour for the birth of a baby, either. This limitation phrase cannot be extrapolated to mean that no one could/can know, as is commonly assumed. The only constraint is "day" and "hour," not week, month, season, year, or generation. The fact is, Jesus never identified a day or hour. Even He did not know (Mt. 24:36). But that was no excuse for not knowing when it was time to flee.
8 *Ecclesiastical History*, Book III, V. 86.

9 "The times of the Gentiles" does not refer to the 1967 Six Days War in which Israel recaptured the city of Jerusalem from Gentile control, as is claimed by some popular futurist interpreters. Either 1st-century Gentile (Roman) armies are meant here (see Mk. 10:33 and Rev. 11:2). Or "the times of the Gentiles" is a reference to the four Gentle world empires of Daniel 2 and 7 and their control over Palestine and the rebellious Jewish people until the coming of the Messiah and his kingdom. After the giving of the Law, four Gentile kingdoms occupied and ruled over Israel (starting with Babylon) until its desolation and the end of the Jewish age. Either way, this phrase has covenantal significance and limits. It cannot be extended for all time. After A.D. 70, God's new covenant people and the kingdom of God are not and cannot be subject to human rule. Dominion over the kingdom was taken away from these Gentile powers and given to the saints of the new Israel. Thus ended the "times of the Gentiles."

10 Eusebius, *Ecclesiastical History*, Book 3, chapter 5; from Edersheim, *Life and Times of Jesus the Messiah*, p. 448, Peabody, Mass.: Hendrickson; reprint of 1886 ed.

11 *Wars* 6, 289-300.

12 *The Histories* 1:5-7, 1. 2-3.

13 *Wars* 6, 420.

14 Only three towers and a portion of the wall that enclosed the city on the west was left. It was used for a Roman encampment (*Wars* 7. 1).

15 The immediate historical setting for this fulfillment was the destruction of Jerusalem by the Babylonnians in the 6th century B.C.

16 *Wars*, 7, 1, 1.

17 At Jewish weddings a crystal goblet is sometimes broken to commemorate the "breaking" of the Holy Place that occurred in A.D. 70.

18 *Wars*, 4, p. 528.

19 Ibid. p 536.

20 *Wars* 5. 24.

21 *Wars* 6. 205-219.

22 *Wars* 6. 259.

23 *Wars* 6. 6-7.

24 Some, citing the Jewish writing Yoma 21b as a source, think that God's Presence never entered or dwelled in this second Temple because no

manifestation of His Shekinah glory (the glory cloud) was ever witnessed, as it was with the Tabernacle and the Solomon's (the first) Temple.

25 *Wars*, 5. 9. 4.

26 *Wars* 6. 4. 5.

27 Others feel that Titus was the "ruler" or "prince" and the Romans the "people," since Rome carried out the actual destruction.

28 *Strong's Concordance*, #3625.

29 Eusebius, *Proof of the Gospel*, Bk. I, Ch. 6, p-34-35.

Chapter 11

1 Essay "*The World's Last Night*" (1960), found in *The Essential C. S. Lewis*, p-385.

Chapter 12

1 Some interpreters contend that this verse pertains to Jesus' ascension, and not his return to earth or the destruction of Jerusalem in A.D. 70. But if this is so, how could Caiaphas, et al. have seen the ascension? Others have postulated that this "seeing" of the coming of Christ is in the "hereafter" and therefore doesn't demand a 1st-century fulfillment.

2 Some contend that this verse has a more simple and obvious meaning (i.e. that Jesus is talking about rejoining them in their ministry trip). This contention is far too reductionistic in light of the eschatological wording used.

3 Some feel Matthew 16:28 was fulfilled on the Day of Pentecost (Acts 2). But Jesus did not come in his kingdom at Pentecost. Nor was that "the day the Son of Man is revealed" (Lk. 17:30). That day was still future and being waited upon thirty-some years after Pentecost (Heb. 10:25; 2 Th. 2:1-3; 2 Ti. 4:1). Jesus had just gone away and had sent the promised Holy Spirit in his absence. But the Holy Spirit is not a Being separate from the Father and the Son (2 Cor. 3:17; Gal. 4:6; Php. 1:19; 1 Pet. 1:11; Jn. 14:15-23). Only in this way and during this interim period was Jesus said to be with them until the end of the age (Mt. 28:20). Also, the outpouring of the Holy Spirit was a separately prophesied event in the Old Testament (Eze. 36:26-27).

Others claim that this verse was fulfilled at the transfiguration
(Mt. 17:1-3), or upon his triumphal entry (Mt. 21:5f), or at any of his
post-resurrection appearances, or at his ascension, or even during his
coming to John in the Book of Revelation. While the transfiguration
was a temporary and partial glimpse of Jesus' divine glory granted to
Peter, James, and John, the brother of James, it could not be the
fulfillment of this verse. How could judgment and Jesus' rewarding of
"every man," spoken of in the previous verse (Mt. 16:27), have taken
place then? And where were "his angels" at either of those events, as
stated in the previous verse? This same rejoinder is valid for all the
previously suggested fulfillment explanations. Also, only six days had
elapsed. That's not enough time for Jesus'"some… not taste death
before…" statement to make any sense. The fact is, all inspired New
Testament writers, some twenty and thirty years later, were still
looking for a future but imminent coming befitting this description, as
we'll see shortly. The fulfillment of this passage does not fit any of
these previously noted events, nor was Jesus speaking of two different
comings arbitrarily separated by eons of time. Verses 27 and 28 are
spoken by Jesus in the same breath and are indivisible! A forty-year
interval better suits Jesus' prophetic words.

The great preacher, Charles H. Spurgeon, said, "If a child were to read
this passage I know what he would think it meant: he would suppose
Jesus Christ was to come, and there are some standing there who
should not taste death until really and literally he did come. This,
I believe, is the plain meaning." Spurgeon later explained this
imminency away by claiming, "this tasting of death here may be
explained, and I believe it is to be explained, by a reference to the
second death, which men will not taste of till the Lord comes."
Spurgeon's view is an arbitrary and contrived way of looking at this
passage. Why not stick to how a child would understand it? That's
how Jesus' disciples understood his words. (Spurgeon's quotes are
taken from p-3-6 of *Twelve Sermons on the Second Coming of Christ*,
edition 1976, Baker Book House.)

4 While some interpreters agree that "this generation" is a reference to
  Jesus' contemporaries, they also contend that "all these things" only

cover verses 4-28, and that these events were the only ones which occurred at the destruction of Jerusalem. They point out that in verses 29-31 Jesus drops the use of the personal pronoun "you." Therefore, it's asserted, these events are for a different time, long after the destruction of Jerusalem. Obviously, this contention is an argument from silence. No textual justification exists for extracting verses 29-31 from the context.

5 The evil servant in this parable wasn't "evil" because he said, "My Lord delayeth his coming." He was evil because of what he did during his absence (Mt. 24:49 KJV). But he did declare "a delay." That is directly contrary to Scripture (Heb. 10:37; Hab. 2:3). Why shouldn't that statement be considered "evil?" The Church, post A.D. 70, has taken a short period of Jesus' departure and gradually developed it into a longer and longer "delay" idea rather than reexamine its notion of the nature of his return. Consequently, every generation except one has wrongly believed that Jesus would return in its time. The harm this has done must be "evil." Proverbs 13:12 tells us that "Hope deferred makes the heart sick, but a longing fulfilled is a tree of life." In this chapter, we are contending for the latter portion of this proverb, as it relates to the return of Jesus as and when He promised.

6 This quote from Psalm 90:4 has been used as a "scapegoat" text to void the New Testament's teaching of imminency (i.e., nearness or closeness of fulfillment). It actually describes the character and nature of God, his timelessness, everlastingness, eternalness, changelessness, etc. It's not an encoded time formula. Nor does it address how God thinks of time, as many have mistakenly taken it to mean. If it did, this would render meaningless all prophetic time and imminency statements.

7 Also, in the Old Testament, God dwelt in, or was present in, a physical and visible Shekhinah glory cloud. This is an entirely different matter and will not be addressed here. Our interest is how cloud phraseology is used in a symbolic manner in both prophetic and apocalyptic eschatology, namely that of swiftness and power of literal judgment.

Some interpreters contend that Acts 1:11's account of Jesus ascending into a cloud and two angels declaring that He would come back in "like manner" or "in the same way you have seen Him go into heaven" requires that He return visibly on a physical cloud(s). What's missed here is an equal argument that can be made from this same passage to support the *invisibility* of Christ at his return, since "a cloud hid him from their sight" (v. 9) before He entered heaven. This cloud was not an application in the same pattern of "cloud-coming" judgment. "Like manner" or "same way" refers to how He comes (i.e., the means of), which is in and out of the spirit realm, manifesting Himself in numerous forms and places for a wide variety of purposes. That has always been the way Jesus' many comings happened throughout both the Old and New Testament. The manner of Jesus' many comings is beyond the scope of this book. Those interested will find more on this topic in my paper, *The Many Comings of Jesus,* presented at the 49th Annual Meeting of the Evangelical Theological Society in November of 1997 in Santa Clara, California.

8 To be consistent, shouldn't we also think of Him coming on a white horse (Rev. 19:11), as riding on a literal four-legged steed?

9 Some suggest that these clouds of rising smoke compare with the cloud that hid Jesus from his disciples' sight upon his ascension (Ac. 1:9-11). In a similar manner, Jesus' coming here was hidden from sight. This is one possible way of interpreting the invisible nature of this coming. Interestingly, Josephus, Eusebius, and the *Talmud* record that angelic armies were visibly seen in the clouds just before Jerusalem's destruction. This also could be interpreted as "the sign of his coming," since Jesus is the commander of the heavenly hosts.

10 My thanks to Max King of Living Presence Ministries for introducing and explaining this fulfillment concept to me in his many writings and lectures.

11 Some suggest the typology of the sacrificed goat represents unbelieving Jews filling up their measure of sin. And the scapegoat typifies Christians escaping out of Judaism. These two goats may symbolize Jesus being dead and then alive. Also, all the high priest's work had to be performed while smoke filled the Temple. This may be a connection with the cloud at Christ's ascension and clouds of smoke in A.D. 70.

12 Some argue that this occurred on the day of Jesus' resurrection or at his ascension. His appearances after those events are viewed as

fulfilling the "second time" typology. One huge problem exists—
the inspired writer of Hebrews, as well as 1 Peter 1 and other New
Testament writers writing some 20 to 30 years later, never
acknowledged either as this fulfillment. To the contrary, they were
still anticipating this appearing as yet-future.

13 September 2, 1997.

14 Some postulate that He returned somehow in the sending of the Holy
Spirit at Pentecost. But this is scripturally impossible. Not only was
the outpouring of the Spirit a separate and distinctly-prophesied event
in the Old Testament, but no New Testament text acknowledges this
event as that fulfillment. To the contrary, all New Testament writers
were still anticipating Christ's coming again/return as yet-future.

15 Mt. 24:3, 27, 37, 39; 1 Cor. 15:23; 1 Th. 2:19; 3:13; 4:15; 5:23; 2 Th. 2:1, 8,
9; Jas. 5:7, 8; 2 Pe. 1:16; 3:4, 12; 1 Jn. 2:28. *Erchomai* is sometimes used:
Mt. 24:30, 48; 26:64; Mk. 13:26; 14:62; Lk. 21:27. *Erchomai* means
"comes and goes," and applies to and/or shares aspects with many
other and different types of comings. In these verses it refers to his
parousia coming as well. Its use, most likely, reflects this coming's
other aspect of a coming and going in judgment.

16 Many interpreters cite Jesus' comparison of his coming to "lightning
that comes from the east and flashes to the west" (Mt. 24:27) as proof
of visibility. But this does not prove visibility or his being "seen"
everywhere over the whole world for several reasons:

- Lightning is associated with a localized weather system and is
only seen in a specific locale.
- Lightning that flashes from east to west is the intra-cloud variety,
not cloud-to-ground type of which we normally think. 90% of
intra-cloud lightning is never seen or never directly seen. It's
usually veiled and/or muted by clouds, and what's seen is only
its reflections, results, or effects and not the lightning itself.
- This lightning is limited in visibility. Its use by Jesus does not
support a limitless or universal visibility. Quite the contrary.
Perhaps by referring to this type of lightning, Jesus meant to
symbolically illustrate the power and suddenness of his coming
upon a particular people, in a specific locale; Or to emphasize the
darkness of thunderclouds passing in judgment over Israel; Or to

underscore that his Presence would only be indirectly "seen" in the attending circumstances and results [sign] of the judgment that fell.

- We should understand that lightning imagery is a common theme and manifestation of God in power and judgment, and is used throughout Scripture (see Nahum 1:3-6, for example).

17 See author s book, *Your Resurrection Body and Life, Here, Now, and Forever:A Response to R.C. Sproul's Critique of Full Preterism*, PRI '99.

18 Again, those interested in how this occurred and is occurring should see my paper, *The Many Comings of Jesus,* presented at the 49th Annual Meeting of the Evangelical Theological Society in November of 1997 in Santa Clara, California., or my book *Top Ten Misconceptions about Jesus' Second Coming and the End Times*, PRI '98.

Chapter 13

1 For a copy of this booklet write: Evangelist John L. Bray
                                          John L. Bray Ministry, Inc.
                                          P.O. Box 90129
                                          Lakeland, FL 33804

2 Compare:

Matthew 24	to	2 Thessoloians 2
vv. 11-12		v. 3
v. 15		vv. 4-5
v. 24		v. 9
vv. 21-22		v. 2:8
v. 30		v. 8
v. 31		v. 1
v. 34		vv. 6-7

3 *Josephus*, 314-315, Bk. IV, Ch. 5 para. 2-3. Many modern-day futurists teach that this is still future, and that what must be removed is the Holy Spirit. But if Paul meant the "Holy Spirit" why didn't he say so? His words had specific, inspired, and relevant meaning for the hearers and readers of his day.

4 Ibid.   313-314, Bk. IV, Ch. 5, para. 2.

5 Ibid.   289, Bk. IV, Ch. 2, para. 3.

6 Ibid. 301-302, Bk. IV, Ch. 3, para. 14.

7 Ibid. 303-304, Bk. IV, Ch. 4, para. 1-2.

8 Ibid. 380, Bk. IV, Ch. 6, para. 3.

9 Ibid. 322, Bk. IV, Ch. 7, para. 1.

10 Ibid. 354, Bk. V, Ch. 1, para. 4.

11 Ibid. 291, Bk. IV, Ch. 3, para. 1.

12 Ibid. 380, Bk. IV, Ch. 6, para. 3.

13 Ibid. 401, Bk. 5, Ch. 10, para. 1.

14 Ibid. 448, Bk. VI, Ch. 4, para. 5.

15 Ibid. 471, Bk. VI, Ch. 9, para. 4.

16 Ibid. 418, Bk. V, Ch. 13, para. 6.

17 The confessions and catechisms of the divided Church (Catholic-Protestant) are another issue. Almost everyone in Reformed circles takes some exception to them. And strict conformity is not justifiable. So why must the preterist view conform? These will not be addressed. But one point should be mentioned. While the 16th-century Reformers didn't devote any significant attention to eschatology either, they did use it as a tool to demonize the Pope and the Roman Catholic hierarchy, thereby fueling reformation fervor.

18 Eusebius, *The Proof of the Gospel*, Book VIII, chapter 4 (Grand Rapids, Mi.: Baker Books, 1981): 144-6—his discussioin on Zechariah 14:1-5.

19 Athanasius' *On the Incarnation of the Word*, Section 39 Verse 3, Section 40 Verses 1-8.

20 *The Last Days According to Jesus*, by R.C. Sproul, Sr., Baker Book House, 1998, p-203.

21 R.C. Sproul, Sr., at the 1993 Covenant Eschatology Symposium in Mt. Dora, Florida. From *Steven's Response To Gentry* booklet, by Edward E. Stevens, Kingdom Publications, 1997, p-52.

22 9/23/98 fax to me.

23 Every August, some Jews remember the destruction of Jerusalem with a fast day, the Fast of Av. Also, at some Jewish weddings, drinking glasses are broken beneath the feet in remembrance of the shattering of Israel in A.D. 70 and "the end of biblical Judaism." According to Josephus, the Roman army burned the Temple on August 30, 70 "the very day on which the former temple had been destroyed by the king of Babylon" (*Wars* VI, 249). By September 26, the whole city was in

Titus' hands (*Wars* VI, 420). Over the next three years, the Temple stones were dismantled to the ground, after which the area was plowed over.

Chapter 14

1 Many believe that the New Testament ushered in a new set of promises and prophecies. It did not. The New Testament simply detailed the fulfillment of those in the Old Testament.

2 "Incredulous," one critic writes to this author's original paper and lecture presentation of this material, "that anyone could think that what happened in 70 A.D. was a fulfillment of 'all things that are written.' This is only in reference to the days of vengeance, i.e. the tribulation of Israel; not in reference to everything promised in the Bible... There is an indefinite period of time between verses 24 and 25 in Luke 21 and between verses 28 and 29 of Matthew 24, which has not ended yet." With all due respect to this critic, this is a classic example of allowing nature to determine time. This theologian's notion of the nature of fulfillment dictates a postponement of time out into the future.

3 The evidence for the early date for the writing of the book of Revelation (A.D. 65 to 68) is far superior to that for a late date (A.D. 95 to 98) in this author's opinion. This dating debate will not be addressed in this book, however.

4 KJV, AMP and NAS translate it properly. Perhaps the grammatically correct way didn't make sense to the NIV translators. But the more difficult and correct rendering does make sense when we understand what God is actually conveying here.

5 Book 3, chapter 6, paragraph 4, lines 122-126; also see Book 1, chapter 7, paragraph 7, lines 180-182.

6 Lk. 12:49; 3:9, 16; Heb. 10:26-31; 1Cor. 3:13-15; see also La. 2:3; Ps. 46:6; 50:3; 97:3; Isa. 4:4; 29:6; 30:27-28, 30, 33; 66:15-16, 24; Mal. 3:1-5; 4:1.

7 Ecc. 1:4; Ps. 78:69; 89:36-37; 93:1; 96:10; 104:5; 119:90; 148:4, 6; Eph. 3:21 KJV.

8 Some interpreters feel this first "world" that was "destroyed" or "perished" in the flood was the wicked system of things. Either way,

the physical real estate of our globe remained intact. See insight 9 for more on this.

9 If "one day" equals "a thousand years," and we're consistent, then did Jesus fast for 40,000 years? Was He in the grave 3,000 years before his resurrection? Or vice versa, is the thousand year reign in Revelation 20 only 24 hours long? How ridiculous is this kind of logic. It misses the intended application.

10 See author's book, *The Apocalypse Conspiracy,* 1991, Wolgemuth & Hyatt/Word.

11 Is. 4:2-6; 11; 12; 25; 26:1-4; 30:18-26; 35:3-10; 49; 52; 60; 61; 62; 65:17-25; 66:10-24; Jer. 3:12-18; Eze. 40-48; Joel 2:28-32; 3:1-21; Mic. 4:1-13; Zep. 3:8-20; Zec. 2:1-13; 8:1-8; 12:1-3; 14:1-21; Mal. 3:1-6. Jerusalem is often used as a metonym for Israel, the Jewish people, and/or the Judaic Old Covenant system. This is similar to how Washington, D.C. is used by extension to represent the national identity of the United States. The earthly city of Jerusalem in Bible times was the very heart and core of Israel's world.

Conclusion

1 Opening lines of PBS Special, *"From Jesus to Christ: The First Christmas,"* aired April 6, 1998.

2 *The Last Days According to Jesus,* by R.C. Sproul, 1998, Baker Book House, back flap.

3 His address at a preterist eschatology seminar in Bellmawr, New Jersey, September 26, 1998.

4 *Table Talk,* chapter one, section 12, translated by William Hazilitt, published in Philadelphia, PA, by the Lutheran Publication Society.

Appendix C

1 All futurists (premillennialists, postmillennialists, amillennialists and historicists) are forced to make a minimalist and non-literal interpretation of this verse to fit it into their postponement traditions. They explain that the intended meaning was "only the main body of truth" or only "all you need to know." But this is not what it says or meant to its original readers.

2 Compare vs. 17-19 with 2 Peter 3:3-4.

3 R.C. Sproul, Foreword, p-vii, *And It Came To Pass: The Third Annual C.E.F. Symposium: Preterism*, Cannon Press, Moscow, Idaho.
4 R.C. Sproul, "A Journey Back in Time," Tabletalk, January 1999, p-5. Others have estimated that 25 to 30 percent of the whole Bible is so concerned.

John Noē's book's—and other preterist books and resources are available from:

Preterist Resources
122 Seaward Avenue • Bradford, PA 16701-1515
1-888-257-7023 (orders only)

For More Preterist Information:

Contact: Preterist Resources

Ask for a FREE information packet (including):

- "What Is the Preterist View?" article

- Sample issue of the preterist newsletter —*The Preterist Link*

- Book List and Order Form (About 50 Books Available)

- Tape List (Audio and Video)

How to Contact Us:

- Phone: (814) 368-6578

- E-mail: preteristl@aol.com

- Browse Our Web Site:
  (Search for *Preterist Ministries,* formerly Kingdom Publications)
    - Read and Print Preterist Articles Online
    - Download Articles and Text Files
    - Buy Books / Tapes (MC and Visa accepted)
    - Ask Questions
    - Contact Other Preterists Online
    -Traditional Mail (see postal address above)

PRETERIST RESOURCES

FOR MORE PROPHECY REFORMATION MATERIALS
By JOHN NOĒ:
(USA Postage Included)

Books:

- TOP TEN MISCONCEPTIONS ABOUT JESUS'
  SECOND COMING AND THE END TIMES $6.00
- YOUR RESURRECTION BODY AND LIFE—HERE,
  NOW, AND FOREVER: A Response to R.C. Sproul's
  Critique of Full Preterism $7.00

Evangelical Theological Society Papers/Booklets:

- RESPONSIBLE APOCALYPICISM: What Is It
  and How Do We Achieve it? $3.75
- ISRAEL: Popular Misconceptions About
  this Modern-day Nation and Its Role
  in Bible Prophecy $3.75
- WHY WE MAY SOON SEE THE RETURN OF
  1ST-CENTURY CALIBER MIRACLES
  AND EFFECTIVENESS $3.75
- THE MANY COMINGS OF JESUS $3.75

Brochures:

- 12 MOST COMMON MISTAKES PEOPLE MAKE
  ABOUT BIBLE PROPHECY AND THE ENDTIMES $1.00
- THE SOLUTION TO THE PROBLEM OF
  THE END TIMES $1.00

To order, send check or money order. For more information about
John Noē's writing, speaking, and teaching ministry, contact:

PRI
PROPHECY
REFORMATION
INSTITUTE

John Noē
The Prophecy Reformation Institute
9715 Kincaid Drive • Suite 1100
Fishers, IN 46038
Ph.# 317/841-7777
Fax# 317/578-2110
E-mail: jnoe@prophecyrefi.org

NOTES

NOTES

NOTES

NOTES

NOTES

NOTES